WILLIAM GRAY

FAMILY WILDLIFE ADVENTURES

50 BREAKS IN SEARCH OF BRITAIN'S WILDLIFE

Bradt GUIDES

Bradt Guides Ltd, UK
Globe Pequot Press Inc, USA

"More than ever, we need to nurture and encourage our children's instinctive empathy and enthusiasm for nature – and what better way to inspire the next generation of conservationists than by filling their childhood with adventures in search of wildlife"

AUTHOR

Zoologist, conservationist and award-winning author and photographer, William Gray has been writing for newspapers, magazines, book publishers and environmental organisations for around 30 years. The author of several books on wildlife, family and adventure travel, his writing career began when he was 23, following the publication of *Coral Reefs & Islands: The Natural History of a Threatened Paradise*. Will has since won over 20 awards for journalism, including AITO Travel Writer of the Year and BGTW Travel Photographer of the Year. His travel, landscape and wildlife images are represented by AWL Images, and he runs photography workshops in Cornwall, the Cotswolds and beyond. Will's passion for wildlife has taken him from Alaska to Zambia, Svalbard to the Falklands. Islands teeming with seabirds are his particular passion – and he is also an Africa addict. After devoting countless weekends and school holidays over the past 20 years to travelling the length and breadth of Britain with his children in search of nature and wild places, *Family Wildlife Adventures* is the result. Will's message is simple: "More than ever, we need to nurture and encourage our children's instinctive empathy and enthusiasm for nature – and what better way to inspire the next generation of conservationists than by filling their childhood with adventures in search of wildlife." ⊘ **william-gray.co.uk**

ACKNOWLEDGEMENTS

This book wouldn't have been possible without my family. Lifelong partners in adventure, my wife, Sally, and children, Joe and Ellie, have joined me, field-testing each and every wildlife break in this book. I'm so grateful to them, not only for their support and encouragement, but also for the opportunity to have been able to share these special experiences with them. Too many to mention, I'd also like to thank the adventure operators, wildlife guides, accommodation providers and individuals who have helped with the research for *Family Wildlife Adventures* – I hope this book does justice to your wonderful tours and places to stay, and encourages many other families to follow in our footsteps. Finally, a big thank you to Adrian and his fantastic team at Bradt for making this book such a pleasure to work on – with particular thanks to my editor, Anna, for her enthusiasm, patience and attention to detail.

← Into the green unknown... (William Gray)

CONTENTS

Green circles indicate the location of each family wildlife adventure. *Chapters 17 and 21* each describe two locations and, therefore, have two circles.

INTRODUCTION

Can you remember your very first brush with wildlife? I wouldn't mind betting it was something as simple and fleeting as watching a ladybird trundle across the palm of your hand, reach the precipice of your outstretched finger before opening its scarlet wing cases and taking flight. A pretty astonishing sight for any child. But let's face it, for most youngsters, nature *is* astonishing. One of the first words our twins uttered was 'Wow!' and that was on a boat trip around the Farne Islands when they were 10 months old. I like to think that 'Dad' was added to their vocabulary shortly afterwards, but it seemed completely natural that the sight of thousands of swirling, screeching seabirds (and, no doubt, the encouraging noises of the twins' parents) should stimulate such a response.

In the months and years that followed, there have been many other 'Wow!' moments, from goggling at their first rockpool gobies to their first-ever close encounter with the swarming alien hordes of a wood ant nest.

When you're a child, everything about nature is a revelation. Every small wonder holds you rapt with curiosity. At about the age of ten, I kept water boatmen in an old Quality Street tin next to my bed, and I can clearly remember the *tick-tick-tick* sound they made as the aquatic bugs paddled around their metallic enclosure. The local pond was an endless source of hidden, twitching, squirming treasures. I scooped out my own miniature wetland in the corner of our garden. Scraps of wood were cajoled into odd-shaped nest boxes, while empty shoe boxes were requisitioned for shiny black ground beetles, worms, slugs, woodlice and all manner of other invertebrate escapologists.

As you'd expect, birdwatching became a natural obsession. I also searched for adders basking on the local heathland and grasshoppers ricocheting through the tickly long grass on the village common. My fascination with nature continued throughout my childhood – and beyond. Even when I met my future wife at university, one of our first dates was badger watching, huddled in swathes of wild garlic as twilight seeped through the beech copse.

It was perhaps inevitable that when we had children they would be exposed to as many natural wonders as possible – not that you have to be as fanatical about wildlife as I am to want your children to experience, appreciate and care for nature. Now more than ever, we desperately need to help young people nurture a love of wildlife and wild places – whether it's rekindling a waning passion in a teenager, or keeping that spark of innate enthusiasm burning brightly in the five-year-old with a ladybird on her fingertip. And that, in essence, is what this book is all about...

Opposite: common blenny; **right:** seven-spot ladybird (William Gray; Macronatura/S)

WAKING UP TO REALITY Set your alarm for a few minutes before sunrise tomorrow morning and bundle the kids outside, just as the first blackbird heralds the dawn chorus. His opening phrase – a stream of mellow, flute-like notes poured into the stillness – barely reaches its climax before a robin, and then perhaps a dunnock or wren, add their pitch-perfect descants. Collared doves chime in with a soft, purring percussion, jackdaws add their staccato, metallic chatter... then a song thrush – that most sought-after soloist – launches into a varied repertoire of chirps and whistles, uttering each one twice. The avian symphony builds and swells until it seems like every tree and bush around you is filled with songbirds. But just imagine what it must have sounded like 50 years ago, when there were 44 million more birds in the UK...

The world has changed profoundly in the five decades since I was a young boy. There are now half as many breeding farmland birds in Britain – some, like corn bunting, tree sparrow and turtle dove have declined by at least 80%. Our woodlands have a third fewer breeding birds since 1970, with lesser spotted woodpecker and willow tit down by more than 80%. Wetland species, like curlew, lapwing and redshank, also show downward trends, while populations of seabirds like kittiwake and great skua have crashed by 70% since 1986. One in four of the UK's birds is now on the Red List of Conservation Concern.

Compiled by 50 environmental organisations, the *State of Nature* report has been produced every three years since 2013, providing a health check on how the UK's wildlife is faring. The results are alarming. Since 1970, over 40% of the 8,431 species assessed have seen their populations decrease, with around 15% now threatened with extinction.

Of course, it's not just birds that are suffering. Hazel dormouse, hedgehog, red squirrel, Scottish wildcat and water vole are just some of the mammals under threat. Amphibians, lizards, fish, moths, butterflies, beetles, orchids, lichens... every animal and plant group has been affected. The natural world is reeling and it urgently needs our help.

A RALLYING CRY FOR WILDLIFE The causes of biodiversity loss are well known: climate change, urbanisation, intensive agriculture, habitat destruction, pollution, unsustainable fishing... the list goes on.

But there's positive news too. The success of Britain's red kite and white-tailed eagle reintroduction programmes, for example, has shown that we can bring back species from the brink. Britain's 15 national parks now cover over 10% of its land area, while our Wildlife Trusts look after 2,300 nature reserves, managing and restoring habitats for threatened species. The RSPB cares for land four times the area of the Isle of Wight; the National Trust protects over 1,250km of coastline. Butterfly Conservation, Plantlife, the Wildfowl & Wetlands Trust, the Woodland

Trust... there is no part of Britain's plant and animal kingdom that isn't championed by a passionate conservation charity.

Rallying to their causes, a growing army of conservation volunteers give up their time for nature, planting trees and hedgerows, organising beach clean-ups and monitoring everything from bats to bumblebees. Schoolchildren are creating miniature havens for wildlife in their playgrounds and campaigning against single-use plastics; gardeners are doing their bit for pollinating insects and garden birds – and we're all aware, as never before, of how we should reduce our carbon footprints to help fight the impact of climate change.

For many of us, the Covid-19 pandemic made us reconnect with nature and realise how wildlife can enrich our lives and benefit our health and wellbeing. Every parent can contribute to this groundswell of conservation action and caring for nature by instilling in their children a love of wildlife and wild places. My hope is that, in some small way, this book will help you towards achieving that.

A CHILDHOOD OF WILDLIFE ADVENTURES The research for this book has taken many years and includes well-established favourites, like seal watching in the Isles of Scilly and puffin spotting on Skomer Island in Pembrokeshire, as well as more recently discovered adventures, such as wild camping on the Hebridean Whale Trail and bike glamping in the Peak District. It's not only given us the opportunity to track down Britain's astonishing range of wildlife – from dolphins to dragonflies – but some of the adventures have rivalled anything we've experienced anywhere in the world. Seeing the reaction on the faces of my children has often been better than watching the wildlife spectacle itself.

As well as a practical guide to Britain's best family wildlife adventures, I hope this book transports you to the 50 wild places covered, giving you a real sense of what it's like to witness a seabird city, to walk in an ancient forest or paddle a canoe through a watery wilderness. The impact of these experiences can be profound on children – they can inspire lifelong hobbies, such as birdwatching and photography, or fuse an interest in nature with an exciting adventure sport, like sea kayaking, snorkelling or mountain biking.

↑ Back in Britain: the red kite (William Gray)

Most importantly of all, though, a childhood of wildlife adventures can foster a natural and instinctive ability to simply pause and stare – an underrated skill that will give you joy in watching the spiralling flight of a buzzard or studying the intricate mechanics of a beetle's exoskeleton. If we can instil in our children this simple appreciation of nature, lodging it in their psyche to carry forward into adulthood, then half the battle for nature conservation will have been won.

WHERE BRITAIN'S WILD THINGS ARE To be enchanted by nature, you need to experience it first-hand. Britain may not boast the biodiverse stew of the Amazon, the great herds of the Serengeti or the kaleidoscope of Indonesia's reef life, but for a relatively small, overcrowded island it does possess an impressive range of habitats. Delve into the pages of this book and you'll find rocky coasts, wild rivers and reed-cloaked wetlands. The summits of our tallest mountains bring a touch of the sub-Arctic to Britain, while the Gulf Stream enriches life along our western shores. Ancient woodland, chalk grassland and heather moorland teem with species, the cast of characters constantly changing with the seasons.

Britain's temperate climate ensures there is always something new and exciting to look forward to in the wildlife calendar. Even in the depths of winter, there are seal pups to seek out on remote islands and sandy beaches, or great flocks of migrant geese to track down on estuaries and floodplains. Lose yourself in a woodland during spring and you'll be surrounded by birdsong and bluebells. As daylight lengthens and temperatures rise, wildflowers and insects are stirred from slumber, transforming meadows, pastures and roadside verges into bright, buzzing habitats. Basking sharks, whales and dolphins arrive to feed along our coasts, accompanied by the clamour of nesting seabirds on the cliffs above them. And even as summer fades, we can look forward to autumn landfalls of migrant birds and butterflies, the bellowing of rutting deer and great clouds of starlings pulsing over wetlands in their mesmerising winter murmurations.

↑↗ Adventure calling: climb an oak tree, cycle or hike into the mountains, kayak through a reed-fringed wetland, snorkel over rocky reefs and kelp forests (William Gray)

The 50 wildlife adventures in this book have been chosen to show you as much of this rich variety as possible. Glance at the map on page 4 and you'll immediately notice that coasts, islands and highlands receive the greatest coverage, whereas more heavily populated and intensively farmed regions, such as central parts of England, are a less natural choice for a wildlife adventure. Having said that, however, there are also chapters on urban wildlife escapes and motorway stop safaris. Some chapters, such as *Sea Kayaking in Arisaig*, are adventure-biased, while others are more gentle pursuits in search of charismatic species, like *Seal Spotting in Norfolk*. The chapters also reflect a balancing act between the needs of a family holiday and a wildlife-watching adventure. But wherever you live and whatever the age of your children, I hope you find something that inspires you to get out and explore.

HOW TO PLAN A FAMILY WILDLIFE ADVENTURE Never work with children or animals. That phrase (coined by American actor and comedian W. C. Fields) certainly crossed my mind a few times while researching this book. Wildlife and kids are notoriously unpredictable – put them in the same equation and things can sometimes turn ugly. Add adventure to the mix, however, and it's a completely different story. That's why you won't find many instances in this book where you're expected to hunker down in a hide for hours, waiting silently for a rare bird to appear. Nor are there any cases where you're under pressure to tick off as many species as possible.

More often than not, it doesn't even matter if the main wildlife spectacle eludes you. It's the experience that counts. Wildlife sightings should always be viewed as a bonus and, while this book will guide you to many of Britain's nature-watching hotspots, its main aim is to transport you to wild places, enjoying exciting adventures along the way. From a practical point of view, there are several ways you can prepare for your family wildlife adventure:

1. Take stock. Assess your children's ages, their interests and how outgoing they are before picking appropriate adventures. Don't throw youngsters straight into a wild camping trip in the Northwest Highlands (page 286) before trying something less demanding, like a campervan safari on the Isle of Wight (page 70).

2. Get kitted out. For the vast majority of the adventures in this book, you won't need a lot of specialist gear. Essentials include good outdoor shoes or walking boots, waterproof jacket and trousers, sun protection for summer and warm fleece, hat and gloves for winter. Try and choose muted colours and non-rustling materials. If the wildlife adventure involves technical equipment, say for tree climbing or kayaking, you will be joining experts on a guided activity or tour. A few chapters include suggestions for launching your own kayak if you have one – but you should only undertake these on your own if you have adequate experience and take all necessary safety precautions.

3. Observe and record. Other items that will help you get the most from your wildlife adventures include binoculars, field guides and a notebook. A pair of 10x42 binoculars offers a good balance between magnification and brightness, but try before you buy to make sure they feel comfortable in your hands. Most young nature enthusiasts will start by focusing on birds, so get hold of a good identification guide, like the *RSPB Handbook of British Birds* (⊘ rspb.org.uk). To save you carting around an entire natural history library on your travels, the Field Studies Council (⊘ field-studies-council.org) produces over 80 wildlife guides on everything from seaweeds and shield bugs to flowers, fungi, bats and butterflies. The fold-out weatherproof leaflets are ideal for slipping in a pocket. Encouraging your children to record their observations in a notebook, meanwhile, is a great way of getting them to slow down and see nature in more detail. Once hooked, they may even start keeping a nature journal.

4. Capture it on camera. Photography is another immensely satisfying way of refining the art of nature observation. Keen amateurs should aim to start with a basic kit comprising a digital SLR or mirrorless camera and telephoto zoom lens – a 70–200mm or 70–300mm lens is ideal for photographing larger mammals (like deer and seals) or conspicuous birds, such as herons and red kites. Some zoom lenses have a decent macro range, allowing you to obtain close-ups of minibeasts, flowers and fungi. Serious wildlife photographers will often be using lenses in the focal range of 500mm or more, but wait to see if the photography bug bites before spending the children's inheritance on specialist gear, like fast telephoto lenses. A smartphone can be more than enough to photograph landscapes and habitats, or capture the detail at your feet.

RESPONSIBLE FAMILY WILDLIFE ADVENTURES

The Countryside Code (⊘ gov.uk/government/publications/the-countryside-code) offers guidance on how to enjoy the great outdoors safely, while minimising your impact on the environment. The bullet points below focus on specific activities:

BIRDWATCHING CODE
• Avoid going too close to birds or disturbing their habitats – if a bird flies away or makes repeated alarm calls, you're too close. If it leaves, you won't get a good view of it anyway.
• Stay on roads and paths where they exist, and avoid disturbing habitat used by birds.
• Think about your fieldcraft. You might disturb a bird even if you are not very close. For example, a flock of wading birds on the foreshore can be disturbed from a mile away if you stand on the seawall.
• Repeatedly playing a recording of bird song or calls to encourage a bird to respond can divert a territorial bird from other important duties, such as feeding its young. Never use playback to attract a species during its breeding season.
• Read the full *Birdwatchers' Code* at ⊘ rspb.org.uk

ROCKPOOLING AND SEASHORE CODE
• Check tide times to avoid being cut off.
• Take special care near cliffs and on slippery rocks, soft sand and mud.
• Keep to established paths and dune boardwalks to avoid trampling fragile plants.
• After looking under rocks, always replace them carefully as you found them.
• Put seawater in your bucket first and add no more than one creature at a time.
• Be gentle catching rockpool creatures – try to use your hands, not nets.
• Always return rockpool animals to where you found them.
• Take care not to damage anemones, molluscs or seaweed underfoot.
• Watch seals and seabirds quietly from a distance and keep dogs on leads.
• Take your rubbish home – don't bury it or burn it.

WILD CAMPING CODE
• Never light an open fire during dry periods or in sensitive places like forests or peaty ground. If you must have an open fire keep it small and under control, and remove all traces before leaving. Never cut down or damage trees. Use a stove if possible.
• If public toilets aren't available, carry a trowel and bury your own waste and urinate well away from open water, rivers and burns.
• Take away all your rubbish and consider picking up other litter as well.
• Avoid overcrowding by moving on to another location if it's already a busy spot.
• If in doubt about where to camp, ask the landowner.
• Read the full *Wild Camping Code* at ⊘ outdooraccess-scotland.com

5. Bites and stings. Britain is not a dangerous place when it comes to wildlife watching. You won't stumble across bears (they were persecuted to extinction over 1,000 years ago) or be stalked by wolves (killed off by 1760). Statistically, cows are now the deadliest large animal in Britain, claiming the lives of three or four people (mainly farm workers) each year. During the rutting season, deer stags become aggressive and should never be approached – just as you'd always observe Britain's only venomous snake (the adder) at a safe and respectful distance. There are only three common spiders capable of nipping you (the cellar, false widow and woodlouse spider), but although the bites can be painful, they usually only result in mild swelling for a few hours. Ticks, on the other hand, are potentially far more dangerous since they can transmit Lyme disease. Only a small number of ticks carry the bacteria that causes the disease, but you should always take precautions when entering high-risk areas by tucking your trousers into your socks, applying insect repellent, sticking to paths where possible and checking each other's skin for any unwanted hitchhikers when returning indoors. Your wildlife adventures might also lead to brushes with bees, wasps, hornets, horseflies and hairy caterpillars, but serious side-effects usually only result from an adverse reaction. None of them are out to harm you. The most sensible advice remains to treat any wild animal – large or small – with the respect it deserves.

6. Natural hazards. The chances of you being seriously injured or falling ill as a result of an animal encounter in Britain are extremely small. You are far more likely to endanger yourself by failing to respect natural hazards, such as cliff edges, incoming tides, rip currents and exposure to bad weather – particularly with children in tow. Most, if not all, of these dangers are avoidable if you take sensible precautions. Always ensure you have warm and waterproof clothing with you in case the weather suddenly changes for the worse, particularly in mountain areas or on any kind of boat trip. If it's hot and sunny, remember to take plenty of drinking water and don't forget sunhats and sun cream. If you have young children, caution should be exercised around any body of water, but the coast demands extra vigilance. Never stray too close to cliff edges for a better view of seabirds, or become so engrossed in rockpooling that you fail to notice the incoming tide and risk being cut off. Always check tide times and seek local advice before exploring on your own.

↑ Red deer stag in rut; adder, woodlouse spider and tick (William Gray; Taviphoto, K Hider, KPix Mining/S)

SCHOOL HOLIDAY PLANNER

Use the table below for an at-a-glance guide to the best holiday period for planning any of the wildlife adventures in this book – but check *Adventure essentials* at the end of each chapter for more detailed information on when to go, including seasonal variations.

Adventure	FEBRUARY HALF-TERM	EASTER HOLIDAYS	MAY HALF-TERM	SUMMER HOLIDAYS	OCTOBER HALF-TERM	CHRISTMAS HOLIDAYS	Adventure	FEBRUARY HALF-TERM	EASTER HOLIDAYS	MAY HALF-TERM	SUMMER HOLIDAYS	OCTOBER HALF-TERM	CHRISTMAS HOLIDAYS
1. Island-Hopping Adventure		■	■	■			26. Farne Islands Boat Trip		■	■	■		
2. Cornish Coast Wildlife Safari		■	■				27. Gower Coast Adventure		■	■	■		
3. River Fowey Adventure		■	■	■			28. On the Trail of the Puffin		■	■			
4. Foraging along the Devon Coast		■	■	■			29. Cardigan Bay Wildlife Safari		■	■	■		
5. Lundy Island Adventure		■	■				30. On the Trail of the Kite		■	■	■	■	
6. Exmoor Pony Trek		■	■	■			31. Tree House Adventure		■	■	■		
7. On the Night Watch		■	■	■			32. Snowdonia Wilderness Adventure		■	■	■		
8. Jurassic Coast Adventure	■			■			33. Journey to the Edge of Wales		■	■	■		
9. New Forest Reptile Ramble		■	■	■			34. Wild Winter Goose Chase	■					■
10. Island Campervan Safari		■	■				35. Seeing Red in Galloway	■				■	■
11. Rewilding Safari at Knepp		■	■	■			36. Tree Climbing Adventure		■	■	■	■	
12. Wildlife Tracking and Bushcraft		■	■	■			37. On the Trail of Leaping Salmon					■	■
13. A Day in the Urban Jungle		■	■	■			38. Bass Rock Boat Trip		■	■	■		
14. Wetland Wonders Adventure		■	■	■			39. Loch Lomond Farm Adventure		■	■	■		
15. Cotswold Water Park Safari		■	■	■			40. Hebridean Island Escape		■	■	■		
16. A Paddle Along the River Wye		■	■	■			41. Isle of Islay Adventure	■				■	■
17. Witness a Murmuration	■					■	42. Eagle Island Adventure		■	■	■		
18. Canoeing on the Broads		■	■	■			43. On the Trail of the Otter		■	■	■		
19. Seal Spotting in Norfolk	■					■	44. Sea Kayaking in Arisaig		■	■	■		
20. Bike Glamping the Peak District		■	■	■			45. Hike and Kayak on Skye		■	■	■		
21. Motorway Stop Safari	■	■	■	■	■	■	46. Cairngorms Wilderness Adventure		■	■	■		
22. On the Trail of the Red Squirrel	■	■	■	■	■	■	47. Dolphin Beach Watch		■	■	■		
23. Yorkshire Moors by Rail and Bike		■	■	■			48. Wild Camping on the Whale Trail				■	■	
24. Farm and Fell Safari		■	■	■			49. Western Isles Wildlife Safari		■	■	■		
25. Dark Sky Adventure	■				■	■	50. Journey to the End of Britain		■	■	■		

HOW TO USE THIS GUIDE Each chapter starts with a summary of key information, including a **Wildlife wishlist** of target species and the **Adventure potential** of each break, highlighting the range of activities available. You will also find at-a-glance information on the best time of year for the adventure, how long you'll need and whether there's a minimum age requirement. At the end of each chapter, an **Action plan** provides more detailed information on practicalities. The nuts and bolts of your adventure are covered in **Adventure essentials** – this is where you will find out how to get there, where to stay and details of wildlife tours and other activities relevant to the chapter. One or two additional suggestions in the area are provided in **More adventure**, while **Also consider** offers a quick reference to related breaks in this book that you might like to try.

Every adventure has been field-tested by the author and his family, but it is up to parents to assess whether they are suitable for their own children – and we'd welcome your feedback (see below). Although this book doesn't attempt to be a wildlife identification guide or a comprehensive site guide, you can find a list of useful websites in *Further Information*, page 308.

FINDING YOUR WAY

Throughout the book, locations have either been given a postcode (♀) suitable for satnav, or a What3Words identifier (▦) when more accuracy is required, or where a postcode doesn't quite get you there. Download the app at ⊘ what3words.com.

FEEDBACK REQUEST

Have you been inspired to try one of Will's family wildlife adventures? Or want to suggest one that you feel should have been included? Perhaps you would like to tell us about a particularly good adventure or wildlife encounter you enjoyed while using this book? You can send your feedback to us on ℐ 01753 893444 or **e** info@bradtguides. com. We will forward emails to Will who may post updates on the Bradt website at ⊘ bradtguides.com/updates. Alternatively, you can add a review of the book to ⊘ bradtguides.com or Amazon. Please also communicate your adventures on Twitter, Instagram, Facebook and YouTube using the hashtag #FamilyWildlifeAdventures and we'll share it for you.

- **f** Bradt Guides & willgrayphotography
- **y** @BradtGuides & @William_D_Gray
- **⊙** @bradtguides & @willgrayphotography

← Budding birdwatcher (William Gray)

1 ISLAND-HOPPING ADVENTURE

DISCOVER WHAT LIES ABOVE AND BELOW THE SEAS OF ENGLAND'S REMOTE ISLAND OUTPOST

WHERE	Isles of Scilly, Cornwall
WHEN	Anytime from Easter to Oct half-term, but book early if you want to visit in the summer holidays
HOW LONG	A day-trip is possible, but a week or two is ideal
WHO FOR	Any age, but you must be eight to snorkel with seals
ADVENTURE POTENTIAL	Island hopping, boat trips, camping, snorkelling, rockpooling, beachcombing, birdwatching
WILDLIFE WISHLIST	Grey seal, seabirds (including puffin, common tern, Manx shearwater, guillemot, shag & storm petrel), waders (such as ringed plover & oystercatcher), island rarities (like the lesser white-toothed shrew & moss carder bee), plus the chance of dolphins & basking sharks on the ferry trip from Penzance

The adventure begins the moment the *Scillonian III* leaves the harbour at Penzance. Cornwall's wild west coast slips past in a rocky procession of granite cliffs and boulder-strewn coves – Lamorna, Logan Rock, Pednvounder, Porthcurno, Porthgwarra, Land's End… And then Wolf Rock appears, the

↑ Pitch perfect: Troytown Farm Campsite, St Agnes (William Gray)

lighthouse rising from the Atlantic like a wave-gnawed exclamation mark; the mainland falls astern and 40km of open ocean lies ahead.

You can fly to the Isles of Scilly – a mere 15 minutes compared to the 2½-hour voyage – but nothing can match the excitement or anticipation of sailing there. If you're lucky, you might glimpse the twin, black triangles of a plankton-hoovering basking shark – its dorsal fin and tail scything back and forth at the surface. Or you could be joined by a pod of common dolphins, bow-riding alongside the ferry, their slender, cream-streaked bodies coursing through the waves at speeds of up to 50km per hour. Gannets, shearwaters and petrels skim the Atlantic swells; a minke whale surfaces – blink and you'll miss it – and that strange, pale circular 'blob' you glimpsed drifting in the waves… well, that could have been a giant, jellyfish-eating ocean sunfish.

Pelagic wildlife aside, travelling to the Isles of Scilly by boat also makes it easier to transport your camping gear. There are plenty of hotels, B&Bs and cottages on the islands, but pitching your tent is the most liberating option for playing castaways on a family holiday. Arriving at St Mary's, the largest of five inhabited islands, the *Scillonian III* nuzzles into the jetty at Hugh Town and,

almost immediately, smaller boats begin fussing around her, like worker bees attending their queen. Operated by the St Mary's Boatmen's Association, this colourful fleet of ten water taxis ply the archipelago, creating an intriguing web of opportunities for your island-hopping adventure.

Whether you make camp in the old fortifications of the Garrison on St Mary's, pitch up next to a sandy beach on St Martin's or hunker down at the ocean's edge on St Agnes, island hopping quickly becomes part of everyday life. Each morning, there are boats waiting to take you to a neighbouring island for the day, or a cruise to some of the Scilly's 130-odd uninhabited isles to spot seals and seabirds. You can even hire a private boat for a free-spirited voyage of discovery – simply land on an island, then wander off to find your own secluded beach.

TIDAL TREASURES On a fine summer's day, Great Bay on St Martin's can feel like the Caribbean – sugar-fine sand gently lapped by turquoise water. Bookended by granite boulders and backed by dunes and heather-blushed slopes, the beach is utterly unspoilt. Wade into the shallows and the water is so clear you'll be mesmerised by gently swaying forests of kelp – even before you slip on a mask and snorkel, dip your face beneath the surface and glimpse green-and-blue-speckled ballan wrasse flickering like sparks through the amber fronds. Comb the strandline for periwinkle shells and don't forget to bring a picnic – Great Bay is blissfully bereft of facilities.

Another beach beauty to add to your island-hopping schedule, the Cove is located on the south side of a sandy bar linking St Agnes to the small isle of Gugh. At low tide,

↑ **Top:** the 90-seater *Osprey* water taxi; **above:** ballan wrasse (William Gray; ABS Natural History/S)

long whip-like strands of seaweed coat the rocks like drizzled honey – carefully pick your way through it and you'll discover rockpools studded with strawberry anemones. Look closely and you might spot the common grey sea slug, a woolly-looking species of nudibranch (known locally as the 'sheep slug') covered in tiny plumes called cerata, and reaching lengths of up to 12cm.

Rockpooling in the Isles of Scilly is a real treat – never leave basecamp without a bucket, a tide chart and an identification guide to the wealth of seaweeds, molluscs and crustaceans (see the rockpooling code on page 13). Managing nearly 700 hectares of the islands, the Isles of Scilly Wildlife Trust (*℘* 01720 422153 *✇* ios-wildlifetrust.org.uk) organises rockpool rambles and beach clean-ups. You can also support their work by becoming a Friend of Scilly Wildlife.

SEABIRDS ON THE EDGE Nurtured by the Gulf Stream and basking in one of Britain's mildest climates, the seas around the islands are protected by a mosaic of Marine Conservation Zones, home to vulnerable habitats such as seagrass beds, and providing a refuge to rare species like the pink sea-fan and stalked jellyfish.

The Isles of Scilly also support over 8,000 pairs of breeding seabirds from 13 different species. As well as internationally important colonies of lesser black-backed gull and storm petrel, the islands have nesting colonies of common tern, cormorant, fulmar, great black-backed gull, guillemot, herring gull, kittiwake, Manx shearwater, puffin, razorbill and shag.

Keep an eye out for some of these on your daily island-hopping excursions, but to boost your ticklist join a dedicated wildlife-watching boat trip. St Mary's Boatmen's Association offers two or three a day during summer, visiting seabird strongholds in the Eastern Isles, Annet bird sanctuary and Norrard Rocks. If you have your heart set on puffins (and who doesn't?) remember that they only breed on the islands from April until late July.

For a land-based alternative, Samson (the largest of the Scilly's uninhabited islands) is a nesting site for terns, gulls and oystercatchers. Abandoned in the mid-1800s, it has no slipway – you have to wade the last few metres ashore. Terns skip overhead, terrorising small fry in the shallows, while gulls pepper the skies above the island's twin hills. Push through swathes of chest-high marram grass, daubed with purple bursts of agapanthus, and you reach the island's interior to find the ruins of cottages belonging to Samson's last two families – the Webbers and the Woodcocks. Scale the hills to find ancient burial chambers and take a

↑ High seas drifter: Manx shearwater (Tony Mills/S)

moment to study the shallow channel between Samson and neighbouring Tresco. If it's low tide, you might be able to make out the remains of field walls – now submerged and covered in seaweed – that suggest the entire area between the main islands was fertile farmland some 2,000 years ago.

DOLMEN TRAILS AND DAISY CHAINS You can time-travel all over the Isles of Scilly. Catch a water taxi to St Mary's, hire bikes in Hugh Town and it's an easy cycle to Bronze Age burial chambers, stone-capped dolmens and the Iron Age village of Halangy Down.

Hop to Tresco and you can travel to other parts of the world. The island's famous Abbey Garden (℘ 01720 424108 ⊘ tresco.co.uk) is a sheltered oasis where New Zealand tree ferns and Asian bamboo run riot with Namaqua daisies from South Africa, spiky succulents from the Canary Islands and bright-red banksias from Australia.

SNORKELLING WITH SEALS Perhaps the biggest eye-opener of all, however, can be found in the Scilly's Eastern Isles. Atlantic grey seals are often spotted on rocky shores throughout the islands, but the ones that haul out on this cluster of 12 uninhabited skerries are likely to give you more than a passing glance. Operating a fast RIB out of St Martin's, Scilly Seal Snorkelling (℘ 01720 422848 ⊘ scillysealsnorkelling.com) immerse you in the underwater world of these inquisitive pinnipeds. The minimum age is eight and you need to be confident swimming in open water.

Squirming into thick wetsuits (the sea temperature in the Isles of Scilly rarely creeps above 15°C), you are given a mask, snorkel and fins before flopping overboard. Snug in blubber, the seals are already in the water, waiting for you. Take a peek beneath the surface and you may well find a round, whiskered face with puppy-dog eyes staring back at you. The encounter is entirely on the seals' terms. If they're feeling particularly curious, they might swim right up to you and nibble your fins. Don't be alarmed – it's just their way of investigating unknown objects.

Peering through flickering columns of sunlight, you begin to make out other seals – silver-grey bodies embraced in swirling fronds of golden kelp or twisting and turning effortlessly in the gentle current. It's utterly captivating. These graceful, sinuous creatures are the very same ones you're used to seeing lounging on rocks like bloated maggots.

Snorkelling with the Scilly's seals not only offers a privileged view of their aquatic prowess, it also gets you close enough to realise that each one has distinctive markings – something the Cornwall Seal Group uses to identify and monitor individuals in this nationally important colony.

ACTION PLAN

ADVENTURE ESSENTIALS To reach the Isles of Scilly you can fly from Land's End, Newquay or Exeter airports, or take the *Scillonian III* ferry from Penzance. For details, contact Isles of Scilly Travel (✆ 01736 334220 ✆ islesofscilly-travel.co.uk). Once you arrive in the islands, the St Mary's Boatmen's Association (✆ 01720 423999 ✆ scillyboating.co.uk) offers water taxi services between St Mary's and the other four inhabited Scilly Isles: Tresco, Bryher, St Martin's and St Agnes, as well as multi-island trips and wildlife cruises. Book tours and events at the Isles of Scilly Tourist Information Centre (✆ 01720 620600 ✆ visitislesofscilly.com) at Porthcressa Beach on St Mary's. You can also buy boat tickets here, or on the quayside.

Garrison Holidays (✆ 01720 422670 ✆ garrisonholidaysscilly.co.uk) has a campsite tucked into the old fortified walls above Hugh Town, St Mary's. Close to the harbour, Bryher Campsite (✆ 01720 422068 ✆ bryhercampsite.co.uk) has ready-pitched bell tents to rent. Sheltered by pittosporum hedges in a natural suntrap, St Martin's Campsite (✆ 01720 422888 ✆ www.stmartinscampsite.co.uk) is scant metres from a sandy beach, while Troytown Farm Campsite (✆ 01720 422360 ✆ troytown.co.uk) enjoys a spectacular location on St Agnes, right on the shore, with bracing views of the Atlantic and Bishop Rock Lighthouse. As well as grass pitches, you can rent bell tents. The only dairy farm in the islands, it keeps campers happy with delicious ice cream.

The Isles of Scilly Wildlife Trust (page 23) links up with St Agnes Boating (✆ 01720 422704 ✆ stagnesboating.co.uk) to run weekly cruises in search of seals and seabirds. As well as snorkelling with seals (see opposite), St Martin's is the base for glass-bottom boat trips with Sea Quest (✆ 07884 055122 ✆ seaquestscilly.com). For birdwatching tours, join local naturalist Will Wagstaff from Island Wildlife Tours (✆ 01720 422212 ✆ scilly-birding.co.uk).

MORE ADVENTURE If your voyage out to the Isles of Scilly has stirred an interest in ocean wildlife, Scilly Pelagics (✆ scillypelagics.com) heads into the blue yonder in search of shearwaters, storm petrels, blue sharks and even humpback whales.

ALSO CONSIDER Outer **Hebrides** See *Western Isles Wildlife Safari*, page 294; **Shetland Islands** See *Journey to the End of Britain*, page 300.

"Peering through flickering columns of sunlight, you begin to make out other seals – silver-grey bodies embraced in swirling fronds of golden kelp or twisting and turning effortlessly in the gentle current"

2 CORNISH COAST WILDLIFE SAFARI

SET SAIL ACROSS MOUNT'S BAY ON THE LOOKOUT FOR CETACEANS AND OTHER OCEANIC WILDLIFE

WHERE	Mount's Bay, West Cornwall
WHEN	May–Sep for best chances of cetacean sightings
HOW LONG	At least a weekend; boat trips last 2–4hrs
WHO FOR	Children aged four & above
ADVENTURE POTENTIAL	Boat trips, birdwatching, rockpooling, sea kayaking
WILDLIFE WISHLIST	Harbour porpoise; bottlenose, common & Risso's dolphin; minke & occasionally humpback whale; grey seal (harbour seal is rare); numerous seabirds, including fulmar, gannet, guillemot & Manx shearwater; basking shark, bluefin tuna & sunfish; barrel, blue, compass & moon jellyfish

The sea was smooth and velvet-blue, like a royal sash, as we sailed out of Penzance harbour. Etched by morning sunshine, the tidal island and medieval castle of St Michael's Mount loomed across the bay, its cobbled causeway

↑ Out of the blue: a young common dolphin surfaces in Mount's Bay (William Gray)

submerged by the high tide. Beyond, stretching in a broad arc towards the southeast, the serpentine cliffs of the Lizard Peninsula formed a thin silhouette between the cloudless sky and flawless sea. From Lizard Point at its tip to Gwennap Head, near Land's End, Mount's Bay spread before us. Around 35km wide as the gull flies, Cornwall's largest bay faces the open Atlantic. Over 150 shipwrecks bear testament to its wild shores – but this is also a treasure chest for oceanic wildlife.

Our catamaran, *Shearwater II*, had barely passed the fishing village of Mousehole before we sighted black dorsal fins ahead. Seconds later, dozens of common dolphins were racing towards us – an exuberant cetacean cavalry, the sea erupting with golden splashes beneath their leaping bodies. Some were swimming in close pairs, and it soon became clear that there were several mothers with calves. The pod began to swirl around our boat. Unruffled by even the slightest breeze, the sea was like glass and we could look straight into its cobalt-blue depths to watch the dolphins twisting and turning beneath us.

Smaller than bottlenose dolphins, common dolphins grow to around 2.5m in length and have a more exotic appearance than their gunmetal-grey cousins, their cream-streaked flanks forming a distinctive hourglass pattern. Renowned for their speed and curiosity, they often bow-ride with boats, so we clambered on to the rope netting strung between the twin hulls of the catamaran, lying face-down an arm's length above them. Every few seconds, two or three dolphins would surface, their smooth, domed heads glinting in the sunlight, droplets of water sparkling from their blows. We felt the fine mist of each breath on our faces and heard the high-pitched squeaks and whistles of 'dolphin talk'.

This was an encounter entirely on the dolphins' terms. Our skipper maintained a constant speed and course. There was no question of following the pod or 're-engaging' with the dolphins when they decided that the fun was over and it was time to return to the more serious business of mackerel hunting.

Once the dolphins had gone, we continued cruising across Mount's Bay, a steady breeze now swelling the catamaran's white sails. Marine Discovery Penzance (☏ 07749 277110 ☍ marinediscovery.co.uk) have operated wildlife-watching boat trips out of Penzance since 2005. They switched from using a RIB to a sailing boat, not only to cut their carbon footprint, but also to reduce acoustic pollution and the impact it has on the echolocation used by cetaceans to navigate and detect prey.

WHALES AND DOLPHINS OF MOUNT'S BAY As well as common and bottlenose dolphins, Mount's Bay is often visited by Risso's dolphins – easily identified by their stocky, pale-grey bodies and bulbous, blunt heads. Pods of up to 30 individuals of these squid-hunting cetaceans are sometimes sighted.

Occasionally, minke whales are also spotted, particularly during late summer and early autumn when you might witness them 'lunge feeding', scooping up entire shoals of fish at the surface. The smallest of the rorqual family, minkes

grow up to 9m in length – barely a third the size of the mighty blue whale. You won't see the world's largest animal in Mount's Bay – the closest they get to the Cornish coast are the deepwater canyons off the southwest coast of Ireland. Very occasionally, though, humpback whales enter the bay. The 17m-long leviathans are making a slow comeback to British waters – you never know when you might spot their 3m-high blows, or witness one of these acrobatic whales breaching, launching their 40-tonne bodies clear of the water.

Humpbacks are big show-offs, unlike their diminutive relative, the harbour porpoise. Blink and you'll miss this shy, largely solitary, cetacean. Measuring around 1.8m in length, they surface only briefly and rarely approach boats. It's thought that they have an extremely high forage rate, feeding up to 90% of the day and night, with little time left over for playful nonsense like breaching or bow-riding. In contrast, common dolphins work in teams to round up 'baitballs' of herring or mackerel, driving them to the surface before stunning them with tail-slaps and picking off the dazed fish. A good tip is to look out for a seabird feeding frenzy – gannets plunge-diving, or gulls swarming near the surface – it could well be a sign that dolphins or whales are pursuing fish from below.

CORNISH BIG FISH STORIES When it comes to feeding techniques, there is one particularly big mouth in Mount's Bay. Basking sharks often arrive during late spring – sometimes hundreds can be seen in a single day in late May or June. Typically growing to around 9m in length, the world's second largest fish (after the whale shark) is a gentle giant, straining up to 2,000 tonnes of water through its gaping mouth every hour. Microscopic zooplankton – copepods, fish eggs and the larvae of crustaceans – become snagged on its long, comb-like gill rakers. All the shark has to do is swim through a patch of plankton-rich water with its mouth open, and occasionally swallow. No large, ferocious teeth required!

↑ Basking shark (Simon Burt/S)

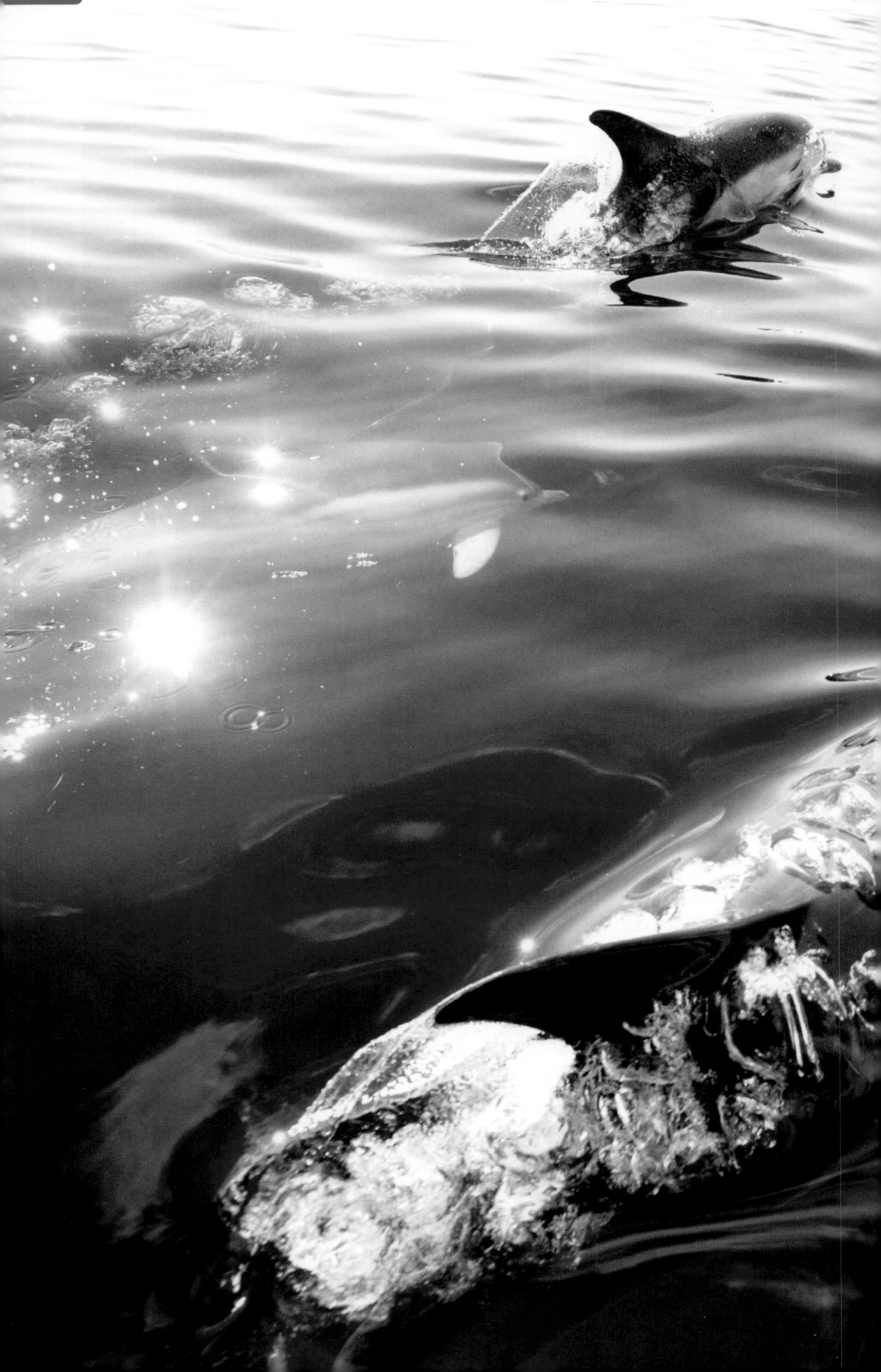

"Every few seconds, two or three dolphins would surface, their smooth, domed heads glinting in the sunlight, droplets of water sparkling from their blows. We felt the fine mist of each breath and heard the high-pitched squeaks and whistles of dolphin talk"

▲ Common dolphins bow-riding the *Shearwater II* catamaran in Mount's Bay (William Gray)

Look for a broad, triangular dorsal fin breaking the surface. If you're lucky enough to encounter large congregations of sharks, you might see one breaching – no-one knows quite why they do this, but it might be an act of courtship.

Another heavyweight fish encountered in Mount's Bay during summer, the bluefin tuna is also a big jumper. Reaching 2m in length, weighing up to 250kg and swimming at speeds of 60km per hour, these agile predators can leap clear of the surface, often several times in quick succession. Ocean sunfish, meanwhile, are the complete antithesis. Odd creatures, resembling a 'head with fins', they get their name from languishing at the surface on their sides, basking in the sun. They might flap their elongated dorsal and anal fins a bit – but that's about the extent of their exertions. Almost circular in shape, large specimens can grow to 3m in diameter and weigh over 2,000kg – which is all the more remarkable considering their diet consists almost entirely of jellyfish. Several species of the latter drift into Mount's Bay during summer, ranging from common moon jellies to sporadic swarms of enormous barrel jellyfish, which can grow to the size of dustbin lids.

SEALS AND SEABIRDS Large, oceanic visitors tend to steal the show on a boat trip in Mount's Bay, but don't overlook coastal residents like grey seals – they can often be seen dozing on rocks at low tide, especially around St Clement's Isle, just off Mousehole. This is also a good spot to look for birds. Great black-backed gulls nest among grassy tufts on top of the island, while oystercatcher, whimbrel, turnstone and other waders forage in the tidal zone. Further offshore, look for rafts of guillemot – they may be small, but these resilient seabirds are superbly adapted to life in the ocean, diving to depths of 180m using their stubby wings as paddles.

Above: Land's End **right:** barrel jellyfish (William Gray; G Dibenedetto/S)

ACTION PLAN

ADVENTURE ESSENTIALS The most direct way to reach Penzance by road is via the M5 and A30, or by train with GWR (⌀ gwr.com). Visit Cornwall (⌀ visitcornwall.com) has details of places to stay and eat. Operating from Albert Pier (♥ TR18 2LL), Marine Discovery Penzance offer daily trips (March–November) on their sailing catamaran *Shearwater II*. The two-hour Bay Discovery (minimum age three) explores the inner parts of Mount's Bay where you're likely to see seals and possibly porpoises, dolphins and basking sharks. The three-hour Ocean Discovery (minimum age six) takes you along the coast towards Land's End and ventures further offshore to spot pelagic species, while the four-hour Discovery Voyage (minimum age 12) aims to locate offshore feeding grounds and is more suitable for wildlife enthusiasts. All voyages operate under a strict environmental code established by the Sea Watch Foundation (⌀ seawatchfoundation.org.uk) to minimise disturbance to marine life.

MORE ADVENTURE Based in Marazion, Ocean High (♥ TR20 9TT ☎ 07801 438320 ⌀ oceanhigh.co.uk) offers kayak hire, allowing you to paddle in the bay and out to St Michael's Mount – but not out of sight on the far side of the island. Stand-up paddleboarding and kitesurfing lessons are also available. Head south to the Lizard National Nature Reserve for a walk on the coast path at Mullion Cove or Kynance Cove, renowned for their clifftop flowers in early summer, as well as choughs and peregrines.

CONSERVATION HEROES Caring for sick and injured birds since 1928, Mousehole Wild Bird Hospital (♥ TR19 6SR ⌀ mouseholebirdhospital.org.uk) is open daily.

ALSO CONSIDER Northumberland See *Farne Islands Boat Trip*, page 156; **Ceredigion** See *Cardigan Bay Wildlife Safari*, page 176; **Moray Firth** See *Dolphin Beach Watch*, page 282; **Northwest Highlands** See *Wild Camping on the Whale Trail*, page 286.

↑ *Shearwater II* sailing past Tater Du Lighthouse near Mousehole (Marine Discovery Penzance)

3 RIVER FOWEY ADVENTURE

EXPLORE ONE OF CORNWALL'S WILDEST RIVERS FROM MOORLAND RAPIDS TO ESTUARY CREEKS

WHERE	South Cornwall
WHEN	Golitha Falls is perfect for walks year-round, but kayaking on the Fowey Estuary is best Apr–Oct
HOW LONG	Allow 1–2 days; plan kayaking to coincide with high tide if paddling the upper reaches of the estuary
WHO FOR	Even young children can join adults on larger kayaks
ADVENTURE POTENTIAL	Hiking, kayaking, paddleboarding, birdwatching
WILDLIFE WISHLIST	Otter on quiet stretches of the river; harbour porpoise near estuary mouth; buzzard, dipper, grey wagtail & kingfisher; wading birds such as common sandpiper, curlew, grey heron, little egret & whimbrel in tidal areas

A river's journey is one of the most compelling stories in the natural world. At some stage in their lives, schoolchildren will hear their geography teachers gushing over meanders, floodplains and ox-bow lakes, but it's only when you get your feet wet and actually experience the different moods of a river that you

↑ The River Fowey at Golitha Falls National Nature Reserve (William Gray)

truly appreciate just how diverse their landscapes and wildlife really are. This adventure comes in two parts: the first walking among jumbled mossy boulders beside chaotic rapids; the second paddling a kayak through calm, tidal creeks. Many of Britain's beautiful rivers fit the bill, but I've chosen the Fowey because in just a single day you can witness both the river's exuberant youth as it sluices through woodland on the southern flanks of Bodmin Moor, and its old age, as it nuzzles into quiet backwaters on the Fowey Estuary.

Before you rush off, check the tide times. Kayaking on the Fowey is best on a rising tide, aiming to reach creekside settlements like Lerryn and St Winnow at high tide, rather than low water when large mudflats emerge. You can either launch your own kayak, hire one or join a guided tour (see *Action plan*, page 39). Once that's arranged, you can plan the Bodmin part of your adventure...

THE VERDANT WOODS OF GOLITHA FALLS The River Fowey's 43km journey to the sea begins in a remote, saturated patch of Bodmin Moor. It's barely a trickle as it passes Brown Willy, the moor's high point at 420m. But by the time it reaches Golitha Falls National Nature Reserve (📍 PL14 6RX 📞 01726 891096 🌐 naturalengland.org.uk) it's not only swollen by countless other streams, but also squeezed into a long gorge. Walking from the car park into a dense woodland of oak and beech, it doesn't take long to reach the first set of rapids and waterfalls. Otter are occasionally glimpsed slinking along the fern-strewn riverbanks or writhing in pools, hunting salmon and sea trout. Sit quietly and your patience may also be rewarded with sightings of dipper or grey wagtail – their names neatly capturing their fidgety movements as they search for insects in or around the river.

Golitha Falls is vibrantly green – and that's largely due to its bryophytes: the 120-odd species of mosses and liverworts that seem to cloak every rock, root and tree stump at the water's edge. Visit in late spring and this emerald canvas is daubed with the purple and white splashes of bluebells and wood anemones. Nearly 50 species of lichen festoon the ancient woodland, providing the perfect foil for some of its 83 varieties of moth. Noctule, long-eared and lesser horseshoe bats roost in hollow stumps, while dormice doze in patches of old hazel coppice.

SECRET BACKWATERS OF THE FOWEY Whereas Golitha Falls requires little more than a gentle stroll, a riverside picnic and a game of 'stick racing' through the rapids, kayaking on the Fowey further downstream demands a bit more effort.

Kenneth Grahame's classic, *The Wind in the Willows*, was partly inspired by his holidays at Fowey, and now it's a simple matter to follow in the wake of Mole and Ratty by launching a kayak on the estuary.

Although harbour porpoises and seals can sometimes be seen in the deeper waters off Fowey itself, your best chances of spotting wildlife are further upstream in the narrow creeks, away from all the boat traffic. Paddling north from Golant, the estuary channel narrows as you approach the hamlet of Lerryn. Oak and beech tower overhead and all you can hear is the trickle of water beneath your kayak's hull and the gentle percussion of woodland birds – churring blue tits, fluting blackbirds, mewing buzzards. Having lost their grip on the riverbank, skeletons of fallen trees provide ideal perches for kingfishers. You check every seaweed-snagged limb. Then, skimming over shallow water, you enter a small inlet to find a trio of common sandpipers probing the last remaining slicks of mud before they're inundated by the rising tide. A flash of white catches your eye: a little egret, its exotic head plumes tusselled by the breeze. As you watch it take flight, it feels like you could almost be paddling through the Everglades...

↑ Little egrets first bred in the UK (in Dorset) in 1996 and they've been slowly spreading ever since (William Gray)

ACTION PLAN

ADVENTURE ESSENTIALS Golitha Falls NNR can be accessed from minor roads off the A30, A38 and B3254. Woodland trails are clearly signed from the car park which has a café and toilets. The river is fast-flowing, especially after heavy rainfall, so take care with young children on slippery boulders near the water's edge. The two main sites for launching kayaks on the Fowey Estuary are Caffa Mill, adjacent to the Bodinnick car ferry slipway (♀ PL23 1DF), and Penmarlam Boat Park (♀ PL23 1LZ) – both of which fall under the jurisdiction of Fowey Harbour (☏ 01726 832471 ⌂ foweyharbour.co.uk). Smaller public slipways are dotted around the harbour. Alternatively, get afloat at villages like Golant and Lerryn, checking that your paddle coincides with high tide. You must wear buoyancy aids and be confident on the water. Kayak hire and guided tours (including SUP) are available from Encounter Cornwall (☏ 01726 832451 ⌂ encountercornwall.com) and Fowey River Hire (☏ 01726 833627 ⌂ foweyriverhire.co.uk).

MORE ADVENTURE On Cornwall's north coast, the Camel Estuary is the setting for a cycling adventure along an 8km stretch of the Camel Trail between Padstow and Wadebridge. The flat, traffic-free route takes around 45 minutes each way – longer if you stop to scan the sandbanks and saltmarsh for birds such as curlew, heron, little egret, oystercatcher, peregrine and shelduck. Rent bikes on the quay at Padstow from Trail Bike Hire (☏ 01841 532594 ⌂ trailbikehire.co.uk).

ALSO CONSIDER **Herefordshire** See *A Paddle along the River Wye*, page 102; **Norfolk** See *Canoeing on the Broads*, page 110; **Gwynedd** See *Journey to the Edge of Wales*, page 198; **Scottish Borders** See *On the Trail of Leaping Salmon*, page 224.

↑ Going with the flow at Lerryn (William Gray)

4 FORAGING ALONG THE DEVON COAST

LEARN HOW TO HARVEST WILD FOOD FROM THE HEDGEROWS AND ROCKPOOLS OF SOUTH DEVON

WHERE	Wembury Point, South Devon
WHEN	Each season has its foraging potential, but spring & autumn are two of the best times
HOW LONG	A full day will give you time for foraging along the coast, as well as rockpooling
WHO FOR	All ages, but children must be accompanied by parents or guardians on wild foraging courses
ADVENTURE POTENTIAL	Foraging, rockpooling, birdwatching, insect spotting
WILDLIFE WISHLIST	As well as edible plants, look for birds such as cirl bunting, skylark & whitethroat, reptiles (adder & common lizard), beetles, butterflies, bush-crickets & rockpool critters

I f you've ever been blackberry picking, you'll understand the simple pleasures of foraging – the thrill of discovering something edible growing in a hedgerow; plucking the sweet, juicy fruits and popping one or two straight into your mouth. To harvest food, fresh and free of charge, directly from the wild is immensely satisfying. For many of us, however, blackberries, sloes and elderflower are about as far as we dare go. There are simply too many strange, unknown and potentially dangerous plants out there to slip into full hunter-gatherer mode. Add fungi to the menu and you really need to know what you're looking for.

Children, in particular, should be taught that some things growing in the wild are not only inedible, but potentially lethal if eaten. Inevitably, this harsh truth has given most of us a strong mistrust of wild food gathering. But as long you follow the first rule of foraging – never eat anything you cannot positively identify and deem completely safe – then there's no reason why you should keep the countryside at arm's length. An expert-led foraging course is not only the safest way to learn about wild food gathering, but the very act of foraging – slowly perusing hedgerows, meadows and seashores – slows you down, opening your eyes to insects, birds and other wildlife all too easily missed on a 'normal' walk.

FIRST TASTE OF THE WILD Foraging courses are available throughout Britain, but Wembury Point (park at ⌘ blip.tactical.aviators) in South Devon is a great family option, combining a headland smothered in wildflowers with a coastline renowned for its rockpools. After introducing the rules and ethics of the foraging code (see *Action plan*, page 43), your guide will take you on a slow safari through the undergrowth. The 'green wall' of a hedgerow starts dissolving as individual plants are pointed out to you. Hogweed is one of the most conspicuous, its tall, branching stems topped with dainty umbrellas of tiny white flowers – often flecked with red soldier beetles. The young buds are tasty when cooked like broccoli, while the seeds can be dried and used as a spice. With

← Harvesting seaweed at Wembury (William Gray)

an expert guide on hand, you may also spot other members of the umbellifer family with frothy mops of white flowers, and this is where you need to hone your detective skills. Common hogweed stems are celery-shaped and furry, but the plant is not to be mistaken for giant hogweed, which grows to 3m in height and produces sap that can cause severe skin burns. Poison hemlock, meanwhile, has smooth, round stems blotched with red as if they've been bled on – all parts of the plant are highly toxic and can be fatal even in small amounts. Growing nearby, however, you might find wild carrot – easily distinguished from its dangerous relatives by the presence of forked bracts beneath the flowerheads.

In just a few metres of foraging, you could also add black mustard leaves to your wild larder (for spicing up salads), dock seeds (ground up for cakes and bread), nettle (for cordial, soup, tea or even a pizza topping) and wild garlic (for flavouring yoghurt dips). Other plants growing in the area have medicinal properties: the leaves of mullein can be crushed, simmered and infused with oil to treat earache, while agrimony – another plant with yellow flowering spikes – is traditionally used as a remedy for sore throats and upset stomachs.

Wembury's rich tapestry of plants attracts an equally fascinating fauna. As you slowly forage, keep your eyes and ears open for great green bush-crickets which, at 7cm in length, produce a rapid, persistent, high-pitched chirping. Marbled white, grayling and dark green fritillary are just some of the butterflies found here, while other insects include the bloody-nosed beetle – aptly named for its defensive trick of squirting an unpleasant red liquid from its mouth. Stealthy foragers might spot common lizards or adders basking in the sun, or glimpse a whitethroat skulking to its nest deep in the undergrowth. Far less common, the cirl bunting is a relative of the yellowhammer, the males smartly turned out with black bibs and eye-stripes. Wembury is one of the few places in Britain where you can find this gorgeous little bird with its trilling song.

ROCKPOOLING FOR DINNER Sooner or later, your foraging amble will lead you to the beach where, at low tide, a salty smorgasbord of rockpool delicacies awaits. Check the low, sandy cliffs for clumps of pungent, zingy-tasting rock samphire, then venture across the seaweed-covered rocks. Green weeds, like sea lettuce and gutweed, can be dried and crumbled over stews and salads, while the tender tips of horned and serrated wrack can be eaten raw or diced into sauces. A prized find, however, is pepper dulse – a red seaweed that's delicious fried or as a stock flavouring. As you turn over mounds of seaweed, looking for choice pieces to collect, you'll uncover countless molluscs and crustaceans – from blue-rayed limpets and sulphur-yellow periwinkles to shore crabs and common starfish. Just remember to gently push the seaweed back again after you've had a chance to study them.

ACTION PLAN

ADVENTURE ESSENTIALS Led by professional foragers and wild food experts, Totally Wild (☎ 07423 753212 ⌕ totallywilduk.co.uk) offers a wide range of foraging courses in Britain, with an opportunity to collect and cook wild edibles. Children are welcome, but must be accompanied by an adult. Your guide will introduce you to the foraging code, which includes the following key points: Never consume a wild plant or fungus unless you're certain of its identity – it could be rare and protected, inedible or even deadly poisonous; seek permission to enter land that does not have public right of way; and only take what you need, taking care not to trample areas or uproot plants.

MORE ADVENTURE Located 14km east of Plymouth, Wembury Marine Centre (📍 PL9 0HP ☎ 01752 862538 ⌕ wemburymarinecentre.org) runs regular rockpool rambles and snorkel safaris (minimum age eight), as well as other marine-themed events, such as beach clean-ups and dolphin watches. Open from Easter to the end of September, the centre is perfectly placed for exploring Wembury's rocky shore, slate reefs and wave-cut platforms – home to prolific marine life, ranging from porpoises, seals, basking sharks and thornback rays to cuttlefish, sea slugs, sunstars and snakelocks anemones. The Wembury coastline is owned and managed by the National Trust (☎ 01752 346585 ⌕ nationaltrust.org.uk).

ALSO CONSIDER **West Sussex** See *Rewilding Safari at Knepp*, page 76; **Kent** See *Wildlife Tracking and Bushcraft*, page 80; **Moidart** See *On the Trail of the Otter*, page 256.

↑ Look for the distinctive forked bracts under the flowerheads of wild carrot (William Gray)

5 LUNDY ISLAND ADVENTURE

SAIL AWAY TO 'TREASURE ISLAND' IN SEARCH OF WILD RICHES IN THE BRISTOL CHANNEL

WHERE	Lundy Island, Bristol Channel
WHEN	You can reach Lundy by ship Apr–Oct; visit late Apr–Jul to see puffins, & book well in advance to secure accommodation in the summer holidays
HOW LONG	You can visit for a day trip, but try to stay for a short break or even a week for a proper adventure
WHO FOR	Any age, but minimum of 10 for snorkel safaris
ADVENTURE POTENTIAL	Birdwatching, letterboxing, snorkelling, rockpooling
WILDLIFE WISHLIST	Grey seal, bottlenose & common dolphin, harbour porpoise, seabirds (including puffin, Manx shearwater, guillemot, razorbill, kittiwake & fulmar), basking shark, sunfish, ballan wrasse, spider crab & five species of cup coral

↑ Lundy landfall: the *MS Oldenburg* docked in the island's sheltered southeast (Diana Mower/S)

When Julian, Dick, Anne, George and their dog Timmy arrive on Kirrin Island in Enid Blyton's *Five on a Treasure Island* (her first book in the Famous Five series), they quickly get caught up in a tale of shipwrecks, ancient castles and hidden gold. Their 'treasure island' wasn't based on Lundy, but you can't help but feel a prickle of excitement as you contemplate landfall on this intriguing lump of granite looming from the Bristol Channel – 19km from the Devon coast as the gull flies. It has treasure island stamped all over it. Shipwrecks? Yes, around 200 of them. Castle? Check. Smugglers? Plenty. Piracy? Of course.

By the 8th century, Vikings were thought to be using the island as a base for raiding Britain ('Lund-ey' is Norse for 'Puffin Island'). It then became a lair for Barbary corsairs, kidnapping fishermen along the Devon and Cornwall coast for Arab slave markets in North Africa. Lundy itself was pillaged by Spaniards.

Even the French invaded, hurling livestock over the cliffs – Dead Cow Point is on Lundy's west coast, chewed over by the Atlantic.

From this murky maelstrom of fact and fable, one name emerges: Marisco. The notorious family ruled Lundy from around 1150 to 1321, terrorising passing ships. The island then passed through various owners – one tried quarrying; another farming. Augustus Christie encouraged day trippers, while Martin Harman sought independence by introducing puffin stamps and currency.

But what about the treasure I hear you cry?! It's unlikely you'll uncover a stash of gold ingots during your adventure, but you will discover plenty in the way of natural gems. When Lundy's colourful history culminated in its purchase by the National Trust in 1969, the charity began nurturing the island's wild riches.

Leased to the Landmark Trust, which manages Lundy's day-to-day running, the island now supports over 20,000 breeding seabirds. Standing on the deck of the *MS Oldenburg* as she makes the two-hour crossing from Ilfracombe or Bideford, you approach the island's east coast. Nutrient-rich waters from the Bristol Channel bathe this more sheltered side of Lundy, in contrast to the Atlantic-scoured western shore. The result: a heady cocktail of habitats squirming with fish, kelp, sea fans, cup corals and some 200 grey seals. It's small wonder that, in 1971, the seas around Lundy were declared the UK's first Voluntary Marine Nature Reserve. A pioneer of marine conservation, the island and its surrounding waters have become a magnet to wildlife lovers.

LETTERBOX CHALLENGE Lundy's granite cliffs rise to a gently undulating plateau about 140m above sea level. From the landing jetty at the southeast tip of the island, follow the cliff track to reach Lundy's tiny community: a castle and church, a small working farm, a shop, pub and campsite. Built around 1250 and paid for by the sale of rabbits when Lundy was a royal warren, the castle contains three self-catering cottages – just some of the options for short breaks and holiday lets. The Landmark Trust offers accommodation in 23 properties across the island, including one of Lundy's three lighthouses, an isolated coastguard watchhouse, a fisherman's cabin, a former Sunday school and even a late Georgian villa. Try to stay for at least a few nights. If you're a day tripper, you will have just 4–6 hours to explore the island.

One of the best ways for families to discover the island and its wildlife is by setting off on the Lundy Letterbox trail, solving clues to find 27 hidden boxes and collect the rubber stamps from each one. They're widely scattered and often take visitors several days to find them all. If you're only on Lundy for the day, pop into the shop to pick up a sheet of letterbox clues focusing on the south of the island. Remember to take care when following the trail, especially near clifftops.

← Thrift flowering on the clifftops (Jill Tate/Landmark Trust)

Hiking along the heather-lined footpath that straddles the 5km-long island, look out for the huge stones that were originally positioned to guide lighthouse keepers in fog – but now serve as welcome seats from which to listen for the wind-dashed songs of nesting skylarks and meadow pipits. If you're visiting in spring or autumn, you may see flocks of migrant finches and thrushes or glimpse a rarity, such as a hoopoe or golden oriole.

Letterboxing on Lundy can lead to all kinds of unexpected discoveries: an abandoned battery, built into a rocky headland in 1863 to fire blank warning shots at fog-bound ships; a chasm caused by the Lisbon earthquake of 1755; the rusty remains of a German bomber that crash-landed in 1941. From the Devil's Slide (a 117m-long slab of granite revered by climbers) to the remains of a Victorian quarry with its own railway track, Lundy is full of surprises.

PUFFINS, PEREGRINES AND PECULIAR PLANTS Stake out a safe vantage point on the clifftops during late spring or early summer – especially along Lundy's west coast at spots like Jenny's Cove – and you should be rewarded with views of puffins. Dapper in their black-and-white plumage, clownish eye-shadow and flamboyant bills, these charismatic seabirds return to Lundy in April. To begin with, they congregate offshore in large rafts. But the urge to raise 'pufflings' is overwhelming. Furiously flapping their stubby wings to get airborne, they skitter across the surface like overwound bath toys. As the nesting seasons gets underway, puffins can be seen buzzing the island, their bills stuffed with sandeels to feed their chicks, hidden in clifftop burrows. It's only when they land nearby that you realise just how small they are: barely 20cm tall and about the weight of a can of baked beans.

Lundy's puffin population of around 375 birds might not sound a lot, but it has grown from just ten pairs in 2000 when a project to eradicate puffling-munching rats began to reverse the bird's fortunes. Puffins were not the only seabirds to

↑ Lundy's dramatic coast, the church and Old Light at dusk; ↗ island aerial (William Gray; Paul White/Alamy)

benefit from pest control. During the same period, Manx shearwaters (another burrow-nesting species on the island) rocketed from 297 pairs to over 5,500.

You can't miss Lundy's puffins, but its shearwaters are much harder to spot. While one adult remains in the burrow, its partner feeds out at sea, banking on stiff, outstretched wings, plucking small fish from the surface. It's only under cover of darkness that they return to Lundy to feed their chicks. Step outside on a still night and you might hear their strange wheezy calls as they locate their burrows. It sounds a bit like someone stepping on a squeaky dog's ball.

It's still worth keeping your eyes peeled during the day for a glimpse of these soaring seabirds. You never know – you might spot something even more exciting. Around three pairs of peregrine falcons nest on Lundy. Even a close encounter with the pop-art puffin can't compete with a fleeting glimpse of this rakish raptor patrolling Lundy's granite-fortress cliffs.

With so much feathered finery on view, trying to convince your children to focus on looking for a cabbage might seem a lost cause. But this is no ordinary cabbage. Growing to around 1.2m in height, the yellow-flowering Lundy cabbage is not only endemic to the island (look for it alongside the cliff track), but it is also the host plant for the equally unique bronze Lundy cabbage flea beetle. Young nature detectives might want to bring a magnifying glass with them to study this minibeast in all its glory: 3mm of irreplaceable iridescence. Just imagine if Lundy had never been protected... Its puffins and peregrines might have found another home, but the cabbage and the beetle would have faced extinction.

→ Here comes the clown: puffin braced for landing (Hillebrand Breuker/S)

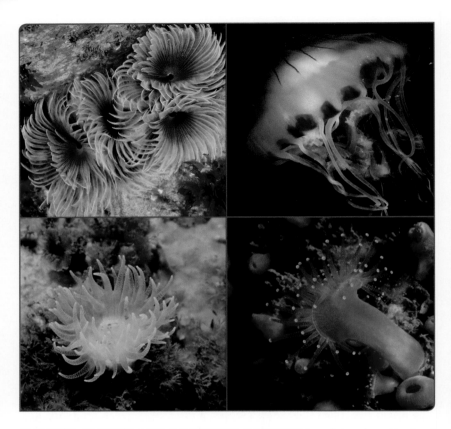

SNORKEL SAFARIS AND ROCKPOOL RAMBLES Lundy's only native land mammal is the pygmy shrew – 6cm long and rarely seen. Sika deer, Soay sheep and Lundy pony are all introduced. Wild marine mammals, on the other hand, are abundant. Grey seals are easily spotted from the clifftops while a vigilant sea watch might reward you with a glimpse of dolphins, harbour porpoise or, if you're extremely lucky, a minke whale or long-finned pilot whale.

The most rewarding sea-life encounters, however, are down at the shore. Head to Devil's Kitchen for wicked rockpooling in search of snakelocks, strawberry and jewel anemones, sea squirts and stalked jellyfish, hermit crabs, clingfish and cushion stars. The ultimate prize is to find the scarlet and gold star coral – one of five species of solitary cup coral found in the seas around Lundy. The other varieties tend to occur in deeper water. You could try your luck on a guided snorkel safari. Don't be surprised if your coral quest is distracted by the occasional swim-past from a curious seal. And even if you don't spot the rare but radiant sunset cup coral, you can still claim to have gone treasure hunting on Lundy. The island's living jewels are worth more than their weight in gold.

↑ **Clockwise from top left:** Tubeworms, compass jellyfish, sunset cup coral, jewel anemone (SS)

ACTION PLAN

ADVENTURE ESSENTIALS The 267-passenger *MS Oldenburg* sails to Lundy Island, March–October, from either Bideford or Ilfracombe, depending on tides. For timetables and fares, contact the Lundy Shore Office (✆ 01271 863636 🖰 lundyisland. co.uk). The voyage usually takes around two hours. Lundy Island is owned by the National Trust and managed by the Landmark Trust (✆ 01628 825920 🖰 landmarktrust.org.uk) which offers 23 historic buildings for self-catering holidays. Family options range from Bramble Villa and Castle Keep South (both sleeping four) to Millcombe House (with room for 12). You can also stay in the lighthouse keeper's quarters of the Old Light. The campsite on Lundy can accommodate up to 40 people. Lundy's shop sells fresh and frozen food, camping essentials, letterboxing packs and Lundy Island stamps, while Marisco Tavern serves daily meals. Lundy's warden organises guided walks, rockpool rambles and snorkel safaris. Lasting around an hour, snorkel safaris (minimum age 10) explore the shallow waters of Landing Bay and include wetsuit, hood, mask, fins, and snorkel.

MORE ADVENTURE Declared a Marine Conservation Zone in 2010, Lundy's seas are a magnet to divers, but you need to be highly experienced and able to cope with strong tidal races. Based in Ilfracombe, Wild Frontiers (✆ 07447 060036 🖰 wildfrontiercharters.co.uk) arrange dive charters and swim-with-seals trips.

ALSO CONSIDER Isles of Scilly See *Island-Hopping Adventure*, page 20; **Isle of Shuna** See *Hebridean Island Escape*, page 238.

↑ Accommodation on Lundy includes three cottages in the 13th-century castle (Jill Tate/Landmark Trust)

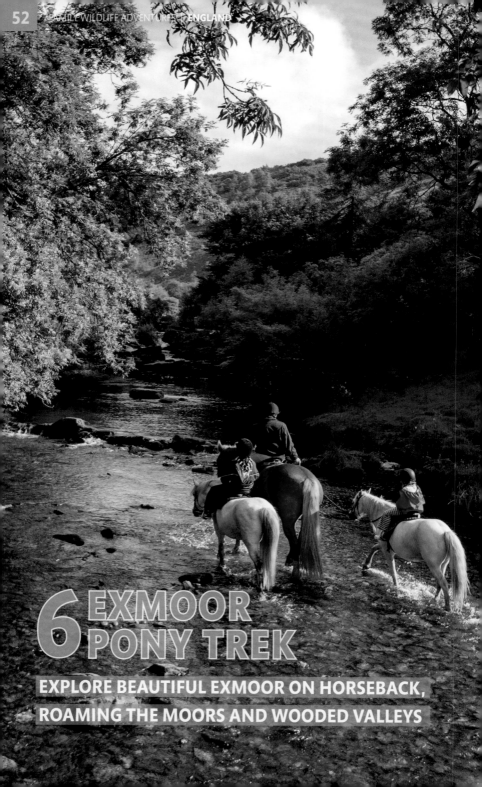

6 EXMOOR PONY TREK

EXPLORE BEAUTIFUL EXMOOR ON HORSEBACK, ROAMING THE MOORS AND WOODED VALLEYS

WHERE	Exmoor National Park, North Devon
WHEN	Although more limited in winter, horse treks are available year-round; visit in summer for moorland birds & Exmoor pony foals
HOW LONG	Horse treks last 1–5hrs depending on experience; 30min lead-rein walks for novices
WHO FOR	Rides are adapted to suit individuals; lead-rein walks are suitable for children under six
ADVENTURE POTENTIAL	Horseriding, hiking, camping, birdwatching, 4x4 safaris
WILDLIFE WISHLIST	Exmoor pony, red deer, buzzard, Dartford warbler, kestrel, merlin, stonechat & whinchat on moorland; fallow & roe deer, pied flycatcher, redstart & tawny owl in oak woodland; dipper, grey wagtail & kingfisher along rivers; fulmar, guillemot, kittiwake, peregrine & razorbill along coastal cliffs

Heather-cloaked moorland, a stream tumbling over rocks into tea-coloured eddies, grey wagtails dipping and dabbling among moss-covered boulders, and ponies grazing in riverside meadows. Doone Valley is quintessential Exmoor, and sitting pretty in the middle of it all is the National Trust's Cloud Farm Campsite (muffin.besotted.swims 01598 741190 nationaltrust.org.uk). You can pitch your tent right next to the burbling Badgworthy Water where kids will happily while away an afternoon netting water bugs, racing sticks through the rapids or paddling in one of the natural pools. Walk straight out of the campsite and you'll find yourself in the wilds of Exmoor – or saddle up at nearby Brendon Manor Stables (froze.beaks.cursing 01598 741246 brendonmanor.com) for a horse-powered adventure in one of Britain's most diverse national parks.

RIDE OUT ONTO THE MOORS Sit astride a horse and the connection with nature is instant and intense. The warmth, the restless movement, the earthy smell – it feels like a wildlife adventure even before you leave the stables, riding single-file on to the moors. Your horse seems to sense the wildness of these rolling uplands, its head nodding rythmically, like the prow of a ship butting feisty seas. A gentle nudge and you break into an easy trot. Swathes of pink heather stream beneath you as a rush of adrenaline flushes your cheeks.

Whether you're a beginner, wary of anything other than walking, or a more experienced rider chomping at the bit for a canter, horse trekking on Exmoor is not only exhilarating, it also feels completely in tune with the area. This is, after all 'wild horse country'. Although Exmoor ponies are not strictly wild (the 20 or so free-roaming herds are owned and managed), they are still Britain's most primitive horse – grazing the moors and forming an integral part of this ecosystem since

← Splashing though Badgworthy Water (William Gray)

pre-Roman times. When you encounter these hardy little ponies on horseback, look for the distinctive pale, fleshy rings around their eyes – designed to offer protection against wind-lashed rain. In winter, they grow a soft, insulating undercoat beneath a longer, water-shedding pelt; their ears are small to reduce heat loss, while large nasal passages warm frigid air before it reaches the lungs.

Out on the moors, you might also encounter red deer. Calves are usually born June–July, while autumn sees tensions (and testosterone levels) rise as stags prepare for the annual rut. Keep watch, too, for moorland birds. One of the most conspicuous is the stonechat – spot the black-headed, orange-breasted males perched on gorse bushes, flicking their wings and uttering a call that sounds like two stones being tapped together. With nothing but the wind and your horse's breathing to compete with birdsong, you could also hear the trilling of meadow pipits and skylarks, or a cuckoo calling from a nearby wooded valley.

On longer horse treks, or if the weather keeps you off the moors, you may head instead to one of Exmoor's sheltered oak woods. At Watersmeet (♥ EX35 6NT ✐ 01598 753348 ⊘ nationaltrust.org.uk), the East Lyn River flows through a wooded gorge – a leafy haven for a whole new cast of Exmoor wildlife. Spring migrants from West Africa, pied flycatchers nest in old trees, scouring the canopy for caterpillars to feed their young; roe deer skulk through the shade-dappled understorey, while dippers take the plunge, hunting mayfly and caddisfly larvae. A short distance downstream, the river reaches the sea at Lynmouth – gateway to the 59km stretch of coastline that fringes Exmoor National Park. It's no place for horses, but a boat trip beneath the 244m ramparts of England's tallest sea cliffs could reward nature lovers with sightings of peregrines, fulmars and guillemots.

Above: Exmoor pony (K Stuchelova/S); **opposite:** camping beside the river at Cloud Farm Campsite; male pied flycatcher (William Gray; Erni/S)

ACTION PLAN
ADVENTURE   ESSENTIALS

Brendon Manor Stables, Cloud Farm Campsite and Watersmeet are all in the northern part of Exmoor National Park (⌂ exmoor-nationalpark.gov.uk) between Oare and Lynmouth, and can be reached off the A39. Horse treks at Brendan Manor Stables are available for beginners and experienced riders, with a range of trips and routes from one to five hours, depending on your ability. Complete novices and young children can learn the basics on a lead-rein walk at the stables, before progressing to gentle walking rides further afield. All you need to bring is warm clothing, long trousers, showerproof jacket, gloves and suitable footwear (hiking boots, wellies or trainers). All riding equipment is provided. For safety and the welfare of the horses, the maximum weight for riders is 92kg. Tucked into the idyllic Doone Valley (11km from Lynmouth and 45km from the sandy beach at Woolacombe) and open late March–late October, Cloud Farm Campsite has 83 pitches, including ten electric hook-ups, a shop and a café. Catering for families with children of all ages, Exmoor Wildlife Safaris (✆ 07977 571494 ⌂ exmoorwildlifesafaris.co.uk) and Red Stag Safari (✆ 01643 841831 ⌂ redstagsafari.co.uk) operate Land Rover tours in search of Exmoor ponies, red deer and other species. Red deer rut and photography safaris can also be arranged.

MORE ADVENTURE Offering a wide range of boat trips along the Exmoor coast, Ilfracombe SeaSafari (📍 EX34 9EQ ✆ 07827 679189 ⌂ ilfracombeseasafari.co.uk) operates 12-seater, open RIBs. Its 25-minute Wave Rider powerboat experience is suitable for children aged ten and above. On the more leisurely two-hour voyages (for all ages) you head east along the North Devon coast, passing Combe Martin, Little Hangman and The Valley of the Rocks, searching for seals and seabirds. A four-hour voyage around Lundy Island (page 44) is also available, while dolphin safaris are possible May–October when common and bottlenose dolphins feed on shoals of mackerel.

ALSO CONSIDER **Derbyshire**
See *Bike Glamping in the Peak District*, page 122; **Yorkshire** See *Yorkshire Moors by Rail and Bike*, page 140.

7 ON THE NIGHT WATCH

ENTER THE TWILIGHT ZONE IN SEARCH OF OWLS BADGERS, BATS, NIGHTJARS AND GLOW-WORMS

WHERE	Devon Badger Watch near Tiverton; Bystock Pools Nature Reserve near Exmouth for bats, glow-worms & nightjars
WHEN	Spring–autumn for badger watching; warm summer evenings for bats & glow-worms
HOW LONG	You will need an evening for each of the wildlife adventures described here
WHO FOR	Nocturnal wildlife is easily spooked, so children need to remain still & quiet for long periods
ADVENTURE POTENTIAL	Badger watching, bat tracking, glow-worm spotting
WILDLIFE WISHLIST	Badger, various bats (including brown long-eared, common pipistrelle, Daubenton's & noctule), fox, hedgehog, nightjar, barn & tawny owl, glow-worm, plus numerous species of moth

As dusk falls, excitement levels rise on the two night-time adventures described here. In fact, you may need to reign in your children's enthusiasm as they prepare to enter the spooky twilight zone in search of strange nocturnal creatures and things that glow green in the night. With their acute night vision,

↑ Badgers live in groups of around six to eight adults (PhilipEllard/S)

hearing and sense of smell, many nocturnal species are easily disturbed, so stealth and silence are of the essence when it comes to tracking them down. You can improve your own night vision by using torches only when absolutely necessary. Wear long-sleeved clothing, hats and gloves, rather than dousing yourself in highly-scented insect repellent, and make sure jackets and trousers are as dark and rustle-free as possible.

Although Devon is the focus of the nocturnal forays described in this chapter, you can find badgers, bats and owls throughout Britain; glow-worms – quite rare in Scotland – are distributed across England and Wales, while nightjars are summer visitors, nesting in heathland mainly across southern England. Contact your local wildlife trust for organised events and night watches in your area.

A DATE WITH BROCK Staking out a sett can be rewarding throughout spring and summer, but badgers are particularly active feeding during September as they build up body fat in preparation for winter when they are less active. Devon Badger Watch (see *Action plan*, page 59) has been operating a purpose-built hide for several years. Tucked away in a bluebell wood near Tiverton, it offers close-up, ground-level views of badgers as they emerge from their sett around dusk. Waiting for the first black-and-white face to appear in the open, you'll tune in to the subtle sights and sounds that accompany the transition from day to night shifts: a blackbird singing, pheasants settling down to roost, a fox flowing like a wisp of russet smoke along the woodland edge… With luck, you'll hear tawny owls calling or glimpse the flickering shapes of bats.

If they feel safe, the badgers will emerge on to this twilight stage, raising their snouts to scent for possible danger before settling into their nocturnal routines. Food will be foremost on their minds. Earthworms typically comprise around half their diet, but badgers aren't fussy – they'll eat anything from birds, frogs, lizards and rodents to insects, seeds, bulbs and berries. As well as feeding, you could also observe them grooming and mating, or even doing a spot of housework, dragging out old bedding material from the sett and replacing it with fresh grass and leaves.

Cubs are usually born in February, venturing above ground for the first time at about 12 weeks of age. When they're not foraging, play-fighting or grooming, young badgers will be learning the importance of scent-marking. Each night, after an hour or two of busying themselves around the sett, most members of the clan usually shuffle off on their night patrols, visiting communal dung pits dotted along the boundaries of their territory. One moment, you're watching them a few metres away – stripes, snuffles and a shimmy of silvery fur – then they're gone, merging with the night. It's time for you to steal away from the hide, walking back through the woodland, your senses straining for any sound, any smell, that might be a clue you're not alone.

BYSTOCK POOLS NATURE RESERVE From the penetrating gaze of a tawny owl to a badger's constantly twitching muzzle, nocturnal creatures have developed a range of adaptions for life in the dark, but some species are pure genius. Take nightjars, for example. By day, they rest motionless on the ground, their plumage so impeccably cryptic that they're almost impossible to spot; only at dusk do they take flight, twisting and turning in hawkish pursuit of moths and other flying insects. The males attract mates by 'churring' – an oscillating techno-whirring, accompanied by loud clapping of the wings and flashing of white patches on the undersides. You can witness the almost supernatural spectacle at Bystock Pools Nature Reserve, near Exmouth (see *Action plan*, opposite) – try flapping a white handkerchief above your head to lure inquisitive birds nearer.

Nightjars are found on heathland, but down by the reserve's lily-pad-covered-lake, see if you can spot Daubenton's bats skimming across the surface, using echolocation to catch midges, gnats and mayflies. They can even use their feet to scoop up insects from the water. Common pipistrelle and noctule bats flicker around lakeside trees, while denser areas of woodland resonate with tawny owl chanting: territorial males uttering a long, mournful '*hooo*', followed by a brief pause, a softer '*hu*', then a final vibrato '*huhuhuhooo*'.

But it's the reserve's wildflower meadow that is home to perhaps Britain's most extraordinary nocturnal creature. Visit on a warm, still evening in June or July and you might witness the grasses flicker with green bioluminescense. Unremarkable beetles by day, glow-worms light up the night by producing a chemical reaction in their abdomens using a light-emitting enzyme called luciferase. The females put on the light show, luring the winged males (with their large, photosensitive eyes) to a romantic rendezvous. Only when mating is over do the lights go out. The larvae (which resemble the wingless adult females) feed on snails, delivering a toxic bite, then riding on their shells until they succumb. For molluscs, it's the stuff of nightmares.

↑ Master of disguise: a nightjar resting by day on heather-speckled heathland (Jordon Sharp/S)

ACTION PLAN

ADVENTURE ESSENTIALS Not far from Tiverton off junction 27 of the M5, Devon Badger Watch (℘ 01398 351506 ⚯ devonbadgerwatch.co.uk) operates Monday to Saturday from April to October. The exact location of the badger-watching hide is only revealed once you've booked. Although families are welcome, it may not be suitable for children under seven, as it's crucial that everyone remains quiet and still in the hide so as not to disturb the badgers. Children's events and photography evenings are available. Located a few kilometres inland from Exmouth and Budleigh Salterton, Bystock Pools Nature Reserve (▥ ally.regress.edit ℘ 01392 279244 ⚯ devonwildlifetrust.org) can be accessed off the B3179 – there's limited parking on the lane at the southern end of the reserve where a boardwalk leads around the lake towards the heathland and meadow.

MORE ADVENTURE

Before you venture into the great outdoors on a night watch with children, try a practice run in your garden, encouraging them to switch off torches and hone their night vision and hearing in order to locate bats and owls. Contact your local wildlife trust (⚯ wildlifetrusts.org) for details of organised events where experts use high-frequency detectors to identify bats. Another great way to engage kids with nocturnal wildlife is to set up a moth trap. Butterfly Conservation (⚯ mothscount.org) has tips on how to attract them by painting a sugary solution on tree trunks. Some 1,080 species of micro moth and 660 species of macro moth have been recorded in Devon alone.

ALSO CONSIDER Yorkshire See *Yorkshire Moors by Rail and Bike*, page 140; **Northumberland** See *Dark Sky Adventure*, page 150; **Cambridgeshire** See *Witness a Murmuration*, page 106; **Powys** See *Tree House Adventure*, page 188.

↑ **Top left:** tawny owl; **top right:** glow-worm; **above:** common pipistrelle bat (C Chambers, I Redding, R Zwerver/S)

8 JURASSIC COAST ADVENTURE

SET OUT IN SEARCH OF EVERYTHING FROM AMMONITES TO AVOCETS, BLENNIES TO BEAVERS

WHERE	Dorset & East Devon
WHEN	Year-round; summer for snorkelling at Kimmeridge Bay, winter for spotting avocets on the Exe Estuary
HOW LONG	Allow at least a weekend if you want to combine fossil hunting with a boat trip & other activities
WHO FOR	Any age, but you must be a confident swimmer to tackle the 400m snorkel trail in Kimmeridge Bay
ADVENTURE POTENTIAL	Fossil hunting, boat trips, snorkelling, rockpooling, beachcombing, birdwatching, sea kayaking
WILDLIFE WISHLIST	Beaver, otter, kingfisher, peregrine, wading birds (including avocet, little egret & curlew), plus various rockpool species

Rubbing shoulders with the Grand Canyon, the Jurassic Coast was declared a UNESCO World Heritage Site in 2002. A 185-million-year slice of earth history, this stretch of Dorset and East Devon shore is famed for its fossils. Spend a day on Charmouth beach, for example, and children are just as likely to end up with ammonites in their buckets as blennies or crabs. There's a fossil forest at

↑ Lower Jurassic ammonites from Lyme Regis (Mark Godden/S)

Lulworth Cove and dinosaur footprints on the Isle of Portland, while 27km-long Chesil Beach is one of the world's finest shingle banks – a panoply of pebbles.

You don't have to be a rock fan, however, to enjoy the Jurassic Coast. Wildlife highlights along the Dorset section include the rockpools at Kimmeridge Bay and the colony of nesting mute swans at Abbotsbury swannery. Crossing into East Devon, you can spot egrets and curlews on the Axe Estuary near Seaton, or try your luck for beavers and otters on the Otter Estuary, stretching inland from Budleigh Salterton. Boat trips from Exmouth, meanwhile, set out in search of avocets and other waders on the mudflats of the Exe Estuary.

TRAVEL BACK IN TIME Formed 250 million years ago, the oldest rocks on the Jurassic Coast are found in the west. Rich in iron oxide and evaporite minerals like gypsum and halite, the rust-coloured sediments in the cliffs and sea stacks at Ladram Bay were laid down in a hot, arid Triassic desert. Fossils are scant in these rocks, but just along the coast, Lyme Regis marks the start of the Jurassic Period when shallow seas and islands, teeming with life, dominated the prehistoric landscape. As sea levels rose and fell, rhythmic layers of mudstone, sandstone and limestone were deposited, entombing creatures destined to be exumed as fossils on the beaches of Dorset 145–200 million years later.

Charmouth is one of the most family-friendly fossil-hunting patches on the Jurassic Coast. Penny-sized, jewel-like ammonites (in shiny pyrite) can be plucked off the beach, along with bullet-shaped fragments of the squid-like belemnites. Start your fossil-hunting foray by visiting the excellent Charmouth Heritage Coast Centre (▦ crunchy.strikers.converter ✆ 01297 560772 ♂ charmouth.org) which not only has hands-on displays, but also runs guided fossil walks. An expert eye certainly helps, but if you decide to go it alone, remember to stay clear of the cliffs: they are extremely unstable and susceptible to landslides – and the best fossils are found on the beach. Serious fossil hunters should time their sorties to follow stormy weather when rain and heavy seas expose fresh fossils and wash them out. Look for shallow streams oozing from the base of the cliffs and spend some time sifting through the pools they form nearer the sea.

Once you've held the perfect ammonite, curled and glistening like a beetle grub in the palm of your hand, you'll never look at a beach the same way again. Although ammonites and belemnites are the most common finds, you might be lucky and discover a fragment of bone from an ichthyosaur or plesiosaur – the giant marine reptiles that terrorised Jurassic seas. Other rich pickings include fossilised sea urchins, clam-like brachiopods, shards of turtle carapace, corals and shark's teeth. Pop into the Lyme Regis Museum (♥ DT7 3QA ✆ 01297 443370 ♂ lymeregismuseum.co.uk) on Bridge Street to peruse a Jurassic treasure chest and find out about Lyme's legendary fossil hunter, Mary Anning, who discovered the first skeleton of a plesiosaur in 1823.

The museum runs fossil walks on Monmouth Beach, west of Lyme Regis harbour (♥ DT7 3JJ), and Black Ven and Church Cliffs, accessed from the promenade on the new sea wall at ▦ cycles.bought.mainframe. East of Weymouth, Ringstead Bay (park at ♥ DT2 8NQ) is another family-friendly location, rich in fossils, that can easily be combined with visiting Lulworth Cove (♥ BH20 5RQ) where a short walk around the bay leads to the fossilised remains of a prehistoric cypress swamp.

INTO THE SECRET FOREST

Venture into the Undercliffs Reserve (✆ 01308 807000 ♂ jurassiccoast.org), stretching 11km between Axmouth and Lyme Regis, and it can feel like you're stepping into a real-life Jurassic jungle.

← Ammonites, belemnites and a shark's tooth (AkemiO/S)

A rare slither of wilderness along Britain's south coast, the Undercliff was formed when waterlogged Cretaceous rocks broke away and slid downhill over the underlying, impermeable Jurassic clays. The landslide (which is still active) has created a 'hidden ravine' clogged with vegetation. Spears of hart's tongue fern and wild iris jostle for space beneath a wind and salt-gnawed canopy of ash and field maple, draped in coils of bramble and clematis. Allow at least three hours to follow the South West Coast Path through this wonderfully wild tangle. Occasionally, you'll glimpse the sea through chinks in the trees, or you might even cross paths with a grass snake or common lizard, thriving in the Undercliffs' warm, sheltered microclimate. Hazel dormouse and three species of shrew – common, pygmy and water – have also been recorded, while peregrines and ravens can often be seen patrolling the cliffs.

GOGGLE AT GOBIES A mesmerising window on the underwater world of the Jurassic Coast, the Fine Foundation Wild Seas Centre at Kimmeridge Bay (♥ BH20 5PF 𝒥 01929 481044 𝒹 dorsetwildlifetrust.org.uk) has interactive displays and aquariums where you can get nose-to-nose with tompot blennies, ballan wrasse and other local species. The best way to see the fishes, however, is to don mask, snorkel and fins. A self-guided snorkelling trail (May–September) has been laid out in a shallow, sheltered part of the bay where you can drift above swaying forests of rainbow wrack, searching for specialities like peacock's tail seaweed, Connemara clingfish and Montagu's blenny. Waterproof identification guides are available at the centre where you can also check tide information. Neap tides usually provide the best conditions for snorkelling, while low tide is the perfect opportunity for a guided rockpool ramble.

↑ Tompot blenny (Damsea/S)

WATCH THE WADERS Covering four reserves along the west bank of the Axe Estuary, Seaton Wetlands (♀ EX12 2SP ✐ 01395 517557 ⊘ wildeastdevon.co.uk) protects a marshy mosaic of habitats where you could spot anything from little egret and shelduck to kingfisher and curlew. As well as using the bird hides, you can go pond dipping or watch sand martins at the artificial nesting cliff.

Sand martins are summer visitors, but further west, on the Exe Estuary, you need to visit during winter to spot its elegant, long-legged avian superstar. RSPB emblem and icon of bird conservation, the avocet struts its stuff on the mudflats of this internationally important wetland between November and March, its piebald plumage and long, slightly upturned bill making it one of Britain's most striking and easily recognisable birds. Some 1,500 or so breeding pairs can be seen in coastal lagoons along the east coast of England, but the overwintering flocks on the Exe Estuary provide the unforgettable spectacle of seeing these gorgeous birds en masse. Boat trips with Stuart Line Cruises (✐ 01395 222144 ⊘ stuartlinecruises.co.uk) are accompanied by birdwatching experts who will help you spot a wealth of other waders, including black-tailed godwit, curlew, dunlin, grey plover, lapwing, oystercatcher and redshank – all drawn to the estuary to probe, pick and sift its invertebrate-rich mud (each cubic metre oozing with the same calorific value as fourteen Mars bars). Other birds to look out for include dark-bellied brent goose, goldeneye, pintail, teal and wigeon.

ON THE TRAIL OF THE BEAVER Following a successful reintroduction trial, a colony of beavers has been established on the River Otter in East Devon – the first to live wild in England since the species became extinct over 400 years ago. But it requires patience, detective work and luck to spot them. Following the riverside footpath upstream from the road bridge at Otterton Mill (♀ EX9 7HG), look for chewed willow stems and pathways trampled through the riverside grasses. The Otter is generally a shallow river, chuckling over pebbly shoals and slipping past low cliffs of red sandstone, riddled with the nesting holes of kingfishers and sand martins. If you come to a deeper pool, it may be a sign that beavers have constructed a dam and lodge nearby – although they also use natural holes in the riverbank, with an underwater entrance leading to a nesting chamber. Litters of up to six young are produced in May or June. Wait quietly, watching and listening, especially at dusk and dawn. Even if the beavers elude you, red-breasted mergansers are often seen feeding on the river. Otters are just as tricky to spot as beavers, but look for their spraints and tracks along the riverbank.

↑ Avocet (Maria Itina/S)

ACTION PLAN

ADVENTURE ESSENTIALS A boat trip along the Jurassic Coast is not only the best way to appreciate the geological sequence in the cliffs of the World Heritage Site, but it also offers the added opportunity for birdwatching, dolphin spotting or mackerel fishing. From east to west, operators include Jurassic Coast Cruises (✆ 07833 963785 ⌂ jurassiccoastcruise.co.uk) in Weymouth; Lyme Bay Boat Trips (✆ 01297 642044 ⌂ lymebayboattrips.com) and Lyme RIB Rides (✆ 07790 400300 ⌂ lymeribrides.com) in Lyme Regis, and Stuart Line Cruises (✆ 01395 222144 ⌂ stuartlinecruises.co.uk) in Sidmouth and Exmouth. An independent charity responsible for managing the Jurassic Coast World Heritage Site, the Jurassic Coast Trust (✆ 01308 807000 ⌂ jurassiccoast.org) has a range of downloadable walks from bus stops using the Jurassic Coaster service (⌂ firstbus.co.uk), plus suggestions for cycling sections of the coast.

MORE ADVENTURE Fore Adventure (✆ 01929 761515 ⌂ foreadventure.co.uk) runs sea kayaking, paddleboarding, coasteering and foraging activities from its base in Studland on the Dorset section of the Jurassic Coast. Suitable for children aged eight and above, its family kayaking tours explore the caves and sea arches of Old Harry Rocks – and there are options to combine kayaking with snorkelling or foraging. A half-day beach school (for ages six-plus) teaches children the importance of conservation and preserving the environment through activities such as rockpool rambles, seaweed scavenging, map making and shelter building. Forest-based bushcraft sessions (minimum age eight) are also available.

ALSO CONSIDER Isle of Wight See *Island Campervan Safari*, page 70; **Gower Peninsula** See *Gower Coast Adventure*, page 166; **Gwynedd** See *Journey to the Edge of Wales*, page 198; **Isle of Skye** See *Hike and Kayak on Skye*, page 270.

↑ Beaver in the River Otter (Cavan Images/S)

9 NEW FOREST REPTILE RAMBLE

TAKE A SLOW, STEALTHY HIKE THROUGH THE HEATHER IN SEARCH OF SNAKES AND LIZARDS

WHERE	New Forest National Park, Hampshire
WHEN	Spring to autumn; sunny mornings are best
HOW LONG	After a morning looking for basking snakes & lizards, visit the reptile centre in the afternoon
WHO FOR	Probably best for older children who can walk quietly & stealthily through the heathland
ADVENTURE POTENTIAL	Reptile spotting, birdwatching, hiking, cycling
WILDLIFE WISHLIST	Adder, common lizard, grass snake, sand lizard, slow-worm & smooth snake; fallow, roe, sika & red deer; brown long-eared & common pipistrelle bat; Dartford warbler, nightjar, stonechat & woodlark; green tiger & stag beetle; dragonflies & damselflies

Blink and you'll miss it: shiny scales, long, thin tail, head twitching from side to side – a lizard curled on a tree stump like a mislaid brooch. You freeze, hardly daring to breathe. But your footsteps have already sent tiny shockwaves through the heathland. The lizard sensed you long before you saw it. In a flash it's gone, darting into the thick cover of the heather.

Fortunately, in the New Forest, you have a good chance of further sightings. The national park is home to all six species of native British reptile, its large swathes of heathland providing the warm, dry, open habitat that many of them need. The best time to plan a reptile-spotting ramble is a sunny morning, anytime from spring to autumn. These are cold-blooded creatures – their body heat comes from the environment, and sun-baked sand is ideal. Basking lizards and snakes, however, are acutely sensitive to both movement and vibration, so you're going to need to move carefully, stealthily and quietly to stand a chance of seeing one. Stick to paths and don't be tempted to wade through the heather – not only will you scare off any reptiles, but you might also disturb birds that nest on or near the ground, like Dartford warbler, woodlark or nightjar.

Chances are your first sighting will be a common lizard. Look for the rows of dark-brown spots along its back. Easily spooked, a basking individual might return to a favourite rock, giving you a second chance to distinguish a male (with its orange or yellow undersides) from the paler, plain-bellied female. Also known as the viviparous lizard, it gives birth to live young, rather than laying eggs.

If you see a flash of green, you may well have been one of the lucky few to have spotted a rare sand lizard – or, to be more precise, a male sand lizard in its lime-green breeding finery. The sandy-coloured females are even harder to find. Restricted to dunes and heathland habitats, these exquisite lizards need bare patches of sand in which to lay their eggs and excavate burrows for night-time shelter and hibernation. A successful reintroduction programme is helping them recolonise the New Forest after they became extinct here in the 1970s.

← Sun-loving serpent: adders can be found basking in areas of open heath (Jamie Hall/S)

The more often you set eyes on a lizard, only for it to vanish in the next second, the more you start to appreciate how they're more than capable of catching fleet-footed prey like grasshoppers and spiders. But they also need to move fast when danger threatens. Predators include birds of prey, crows and foxes, but lizards have a neat trick to foil them – they can drop their tails, still twitching, as a decoy, and then make a quick getaway. A fully-functional replacement tail regenerates in about two months.

Lizards also have to be wary of other reptiles in the New Forest. Adders will ambush them if given the chance, but small mammals and ground-nesting birds, like skylarks and meadow pipits, are also on the menu for Britain's only venomous species of snake. Shy and secretive, adders are only likely to bite humans when provoked or accidentally trodden on. Although a bite can be painful and require immediate medical attention, the venom is rarely fatal. You can't mistake the zig-zag markings or steely red eye of this viper. Females are larger and more reddish-brown than the silvery-grey males. During spring, you might be lucky enough to witness males duelling, the rivals twisting around each other as they try to force their opponent's head to the ground in a writhing bout of reptilian wrestling.

Even adders have to watch their backs in the New Forest. Extremely rare and seldom seen, the non-venomous smooth snake not only hunts for lizards, rodents and birds, but will also eat young adders, constricting its prey like a python. Easily confused with an adder at first glance, the pale-golden snake lacks the vivid criss-cross pattern of its poisonous cousin.

That just leaves two species: the grass snake and slow-worm (which is actually a legless lizard). Both prefer cooler, damper spots in the New Forest, so look for them around woodland ponds and in wetter patches of heathland and meadow.

↑ **Clockwise from top left:** Common lizard, smooth snake, male sand lizard, young grass snake (Erni, Sandra Standbridge, BPpix, Jordon Sharp/S)

ACTION PLAN

ADVENTURE ESSENTIALS Focus your reptile search on south-facing heathery slopes, picking a sunny morning when they are more likely to be basking. Remember to keep to paths to avoid disturbing ground-nesting birds. About 5km west of Lyndhurst, the New Forest Reptile Centre (▥ oldest.brambles.bared 🖉 0300 067 4601 ⊘ forestryengland.uk) has low-walled, outdoor enclosures, allowing you to observe sand lizards, smooth snakes and adders. The centre also operates a 'Date with Nature' in partnership with the RSPB, where nestcams reveal intimate views of goshawks, buzzards and sparrowhawks. A 1.6km-long, family-friendly trail loops from the centre through the woods. For further information on the New Forest, see ⊘ newforestnpa.gov.uk.

MORE ADVENTURE A 5km drive from the New Forest Reptile Centre takes you to Bolderwood Deer Sanctuary (▥ stability.salon.quail) where an observation deck overlooks a forest-fringed meadow roamed by wild herds of fallow deer. The most commonly seen of the New Forest's five deer species, (the others being muntjac, red, roe and sika), they're fed daily by rangers between April and September, usually between 12:30 and 14:30. Most fallow deer have chestnut-brown coats with pale spots, although the colour can range from black through to sandy-white. The rut occurs during October and November.

ALSO CONSIDER Isle of Wight See *Island Campervan Safari*, page 70; **Kent** See *Wildlife Tracking and Bushcraft*, page 80; **London** See *A Day in the Urban Jungle*, page 86.

Above: fallow deer buck at Bolderwood; **right:** male Dartford warbler (William Gray; John Darcy/S)

ISLAND
10 CAMPERVAN
SAFARI

**HOP OVER TO THE ISLE OF WIGHT TO SEARCH FOR
RED SQUIRRELS, BUTTERFLIES AND... DINOSAURS**

dinosaur hunters have discovered eotyrannus (a small carnivore related to T-Rex), pelorosaurus (a gigantic sauropod, 24m in length) and Polacanthus (an armoured heavyweight covered in spikes). The best place to find their fossils is the 10km-long stretch of coast between Atherfield and Compton in the southwest of the island.

From your first night's camp near Sandown, drive south to Ventnor before following the coast road east towards Brighstone. You'll find a couple of options nearby for camping. Grange Farm Campsite is perched on a low cliff above Brighstone Bay, while Compton Farm Campsite nestles at the base of undulating downland with views of the chalk cliffs looming above Freshwater Bay. Plan on spending at least two nights in this area.

Dinosaur Expeditions (♥ PO30 4PG ✐ 01983 740844 ◌ dinosaurexpeditions. co.uk) organise fossil-hunting walks along wild, unspoilt beaches where experts train your eye to spot fossilised fragments of everything from turtles and pterosaurs to crocodiles and corals. With luck, you might crack open a flint to find a perfectly preserved sea urchin, or stumble upon a piece of petrified wood. Of course, what you're really after are fragments of dinosaur bone: black and shiny with a honeycomb texture. Who knows, the next big discovery might be just around the next headland. At Hanover Point you can follow in the footsteps of iguanodons – or at least admire their 50cm-wide, three-toed footprint casts that litter the beach at low tide.

BUTTERFLY BONANZA There's less detective work required for finding butterflies on the Isle of Wight. Around 40 of the UK's 59 species are resident here – and many of them can be found in the southwest of the island during summer, fussing over flower-speckled Compton Down. Simply walk from Compton Farm Campsite into the clover-rich folds of this rich habitat and you will begin seeing butterflies. Adonis blue, chalkhill blue and common blue are three of the most conspicuous species, flitting between patches of vetch and trefoil like wind-tossed confetti. The longer you look, though, the more species you begin to notice. Green hairstreak, dark green fritillary and grizzled skipper are often seen around areas of gorse, while the rare and exquisite Glanville fritillary prefers the coastal cliffs of Compton Bay.

→ Glanville fritillary (Kris Gillam/S)

Its southerly location means the Isle of Wight can stay sunny and warm well into September – so it's a great place to see late summer insects on the wing, including migrant butterflies such as the clouded yellow and painted lady.

BIRDS AND BUGS It's not only insects that are seduced by the Isle of Wight's balmy climate. Migrant birds also make a point of dropping by to rest and refuel on their southerly autumn migrations. The downs offer an excellent vantage from which to spot finches, larks and pipits, as well as migrant ospreys and honey buzzards. While gazing skyward, you might spot something even more spectacular: a white-tailed eagle soaring on a thermal, finger-tipped wings spread 2.5m wide. The last known breeding pair in England was recorded at Culver Cliff on the Isle of Wight in 1780 and now a reintroduction project hopes to tempt them back.

A short distance inland from Compton Bay, Mottistone Gardens (♀ PO30 4ED ✐ 01983 741302 ✇ nationaltrust.org.uk) is worth a visit to spot heath-loving birds like nightjar, Dartford warbler and yellowhammer. Get down on your hands and knees and you might encounter the green tiger beetle – no longer than your fingernail, but equipped with sickle-shaped mandibles more than capable of dispatching ants, flies and caterpillars.

From Compton Bay, it's a 20-minute drive to Camp Wight, a peaceful, leafy site close to Ningwood Common (✇ hiwwt.org.uk). A mixture of scrub, heath and woodland, this small nature reserve is a haven for red squirrels and hazel dormice. Get there early and you might hear nightingales singing, while a dusk visit can be accompanied by the soft churring of nightjars or the sight of a barn owl hunting. A few kilometres northeast of Camp Wight, Newtown National Nature Reserve (♀ PO30 4PA ✐ 01983 531785 ✇ nationaltrust.org.uk) protects a mosaic of mudflats, meadows and saltmarsh – great for butterflies in summer and wading birds in autumn.

Continuing east towards Newport on the A3054, turn right to Carisbrooke Castle and you will find the quirky Windmill Campersite where glamping options include a converted Westland Wessex helicopter. It's an ideal location for visiting Robin Hill (♀ PO30 2NU ✐ 01983 527352 ✇ robin-hill.com) – a woodland adventure park with everything from falconry displays and a canopy skywalk to gardens and forested areas dotted with squirrel feeding stations. Parkhurst Forest (♀ PO30 5UL ✐ 0300 067 4600 ✇ forestryengland.uk) is a quieter option. Park your campervan, enjoy a picnic beneath the pine trees, then set off on the Red Squirrel Walk. After 20 minutes, you reach a hide surrounded by feeders. Maybe, just maybe, this could be the red-furred finale to your Isle of Wight safari.

↑ Tiny terror: green tiger beetle (Henrik Larsson/S)

ACTION PLAN

ADVENTURE ESSENTIALS Isle of Wight ferries are operated by Hovertravel (𝒥 0345 222 0461 ⌀ hovertravel.co.uk), Red Funnel (𝒥 0238 001 9192 ⌀ www.redfunnel. co.uk) and Wightlink (𝒥 0333 999 7333 ⌀ wightlink.co.uk). Isle of Wight Campervan Holidays (𝒥 01983 642143 ⌀ isleofwightcampers.co.uk; see ad, page 317) offer classic 1970s and modern VW campervans for hire. With room for up to two adults and three children, each camper has a double bed, pop-top bunks, cooker, fridge and sink, plus bedding, camping table and chairs and even a standalone tent if you need more space. A six-berth motorhome is also available. For tourist information go to Visit Isle of Wight (⌀ visitisleofwight.co.uk). Around 3km from Sandown, Old Barn Touring Park (♥ PO36 9PJ 𝒥 01983 866414 ⌀ oldbarntouring.co.uk) has 60 pitches, showers, toilets and electric hook-ups. Park your camper right above the beach near Brighstone at Grange Farm Campsite (♥ PO30 4DA 𝒥 01983 740296 ⌀ grangefarmcamping.co.uk) or head to the nearby Compton Farm Campsite (♥ PO30 4HF 𝒥 01983 740215 ⌀ comptonfarm. co.uk) for a downland site close to the coast. Camp Wight (♥ PO41 0XP 𝒥 07748 844242 ⌀ campwight.co.uk) has composting toilets and solar showers, while the Windmill Campersite (♥ PO30 3DU 𝒥 07957 572221 ⌀ windmillcampersite.com) has a psychedelic shower shack and an equally eccentric pizza and potato oven.

MORE ADVENTURE Hire bikes in Yarmouth at Wight Cycle Hire (𝒥 01983 761 800 ⌀ wightcyclehire.co.uk) and set off on a two-wheeled adventure to Freshwater Bay, via the Needles and Tennyson Down.

ALSO CONSIDER West Sussex See *Rewilding Safari at Knepp*, page 76; **Cumbria and Lancashire** See *Motorway Stop Safari*, page 130; **Cumbria** See *Farm and Fell Safari*, page 146; **Isle of Mull** See *Eagle Island Adventure*, page 250.

↑ Oliver, a 1972 VW Campervan, sleeping four (Isle of Wight Campervan Holidays)

11 REWILDING SAFARI AT KNEPP

WITNESS THE REBIRTH OF A COUNTRYSIDE RICH IN WILDLIFE ON A WALKING SAFARI IN SUSSEX

WHERE	Knepp Castle Estate, near Horsham, West Sussex
WHEN	Apr–Oct
HOW LONG	Walking safaris last 3hrs; camping also available
WHO FOR	Minimum age 12 for safaris & camping
ADVENTURE POTENTIAL	Birdwatching, walking safaris, wildlife tracking
WILDLIFE WISHLIST	Free-roaming Exmoor ponies, longhorn cattle, fallow, red & roe deer, & Tamworth pig; numerous bird species, including cuckoo, great spotted woodpecker, kingfisher, little owl, nightingale, turtle dove & white stork; butterflies (purple emperor), plus bats, beetles, bumblebees...

Ask a child to paint a picture of the countryside and most will compose a neat and tidy scene of bright green fields dotted with cows. You probably won't see much in the way of tangled, sprawling hedgerows, deer-pruned scrub, beaver-dammed wetlands or meadows scuffed and snuffled by free-roaming herds of wild horses, longhorn cattle and feral pigs. And yet this is precisely the vision of a 'rewilded' countryside emerging at Knepp. Sprawling across 1,400

↑ Knepp is the focus of a white stork reintroduction project (William Gray)

hectares of Sussex Weald, the estate was devoted to traditional arable and dairy farming until 2001 when the focus was shifted to restoring nature as part of its pioneering Wildland Project. Knepp is still a farm – producing organic, pasture-fed meat from footloose herds – but nature-based tourism is now a key part of its revenue. Although, sadly, the minimum age is 12, this is a wonderful opportunity to show children that the British countryside doesn't have to be fields doused in fertiliser; where hedges are flayed to within an inch of their lives and fragments of woodland lie marooned in a sea of monoculture.

A WALK ON THE WILD SIDE Walking safaris were pioneered in Zambia by Norman Carr in the 1950s, and South Luangwa National Park is still one of the best places in the world to venture into the bush on foot. Knepp brings the same sense of anticipation to tracking down large mammals – but rather than elephant, giraffe and zebra, your sights are set on Exmoor ponies, deer, longhorn cattle and Tamworth pigs. When the estate turned its back on intensive agriculture, it wasn't simply abandoned to nature. The rewilding process has relied on these large mammals to shape the landscape and create a biodiverse patchwork of habitats.

As you follow your guide into the Knepp wilderness, the first thing you notice is birdsong – a rich, almost exotic, medley of interwoven calls. You recognise song thrush, blackbird and cuckoo, but your guide quickly deciphers the rattling outburst of lesser whitethroat and three or four other warblers. It's all about slowing down and fine-tuning your senses. This is a slow, stop-start nature ramble. Your patience is rewarded by the soft, distant purring of a rare turtle dove... Then another Knepp flagship species – the nightingale – stops you in your tracks with its quick-fire burst of whistles, chirps, guttural 'whoops' and insect-like buzzing. Studies have shown that nightingales can master over a thousand syllables – triple that of the skylark and ten times more than a blackbird. But you will rarely spot this drab, brown member of the chat family. It skulks in thorny scrub and overgrown hedges, thick with blackthorn, which it finds in abundance at Knepp.

One moment you're weaving between thickets of bramble, blackthorn and hawthorn whirring with nightingales, the next you're standing in the shadow of an old oak, surrounded by the woody wreckage of its fallen limbs. Your guide tells you that its hollow trunk is home to some of Knepp's 13 species of bats. Up in the canopy, a pair of white storks clatter their bills, reaffirming their mating bond atop a giant nest of twigs. Before these graceful birds successfully raised chicks at Knepp in 2020, the last reported record of white storks breeding in the UK was in 1416. Rewilding has given them a second chance.

→ Britain's largest population of purple emperors is found at Knepp (M Mierzejewski/S)

The estate is also the best place in Britain to watch purple emperor butterflies soaring and flitting through the woodland canopy, giddy on aphid honeydew and tree sap. Their success at Knepp is due to dense swathes of goat willow – the foodplant of the butterfly's caterpillar – that have been allowed to spill out of what were once tightly cropped hedgerows.

Like a blunt needle through tangled knots of twine, you ease yourself through dense, scratchy thickets for a glimpse of fallow deer browsing in the scrub beyond. A flash of red, black and white lifts your head as a great spotted woodpecker flies past. Seconds later you hear it drumming. Then you find yourself crouched around a patch of ground where pigs have been rooting for insect grubs. Already the disturbed soil has been colonised by a patchwork of flowering plants – a miniature meadow courtesy of the foraging activity of Knepp's living, snorting bulldozers.

Once established, introduced beavers will have an even more profound effect on the landscape at Knepp, their obsession with damming waterways leading to a mosaic of pools, flooded woodland and boggy pastures. The estate's ponds are already home to kingfishers, great crested newts and grass snakes – who knows what rarities will follow in the wake of the beavers' natural engineering?

The only thing missing from Knepp, of course, are large predators. Although foxes, badgers, weasels, stoats and polecats prowl the estate, the top of the natural foodchain – bear, lynx, wolf and wolverine – is absent. Remember, this is West Sussex, not Yellowstone, so humans have to take on the role of apex predator, culling large mammals to maintain their populations at a sustainable level. Exmoor ponies are substituted for wild horses, longhorn cattle for aurochs and Tamworth pigs for wild boars. This visionary approach to ecological restoration has not only thrown a lifeline to some of Britain's rarest species, like the nightingale, turtle dove and purple emperor butterfly, but it has also shown how failing or abandoned farmland can be transformed into a 'wilder countryside'. Wouldn't it be wonderful if children drew pictures of that in the future...?

↑ Fallow deer and Exmoor ponies at Knepp (William Gray)

ACTION PLAN

ADVENTURE ESSENTIALS Knepp Wildland Safaris (♀ RH13 8NN ✎ 01403 713230 ✐ kneppsafaris.co.uk) is based at New Barn Farm, Swallows Lane, and can be reached by taking the turning to Dial Post off the A24. A wide range of three-hour safaris is available, either vehicle-based or on foot, and there are also two-hour dawn and dusk safaris. April and May are the best months for the dawn chorus and to witness the arrival of cuckoos, nightingales and turtle doves, while mid-summer is best for seeing bats, butterflies and moths. Accommodation is available in various tree houses, shepherd's huts, tents and yurts, or you can pitch your own tent in the Wildland campsite. Each pitch has its own fire-pit and barbecue grill, with sustainable charcoal, firewood, kindling and eco-firelighters available on-site, along with Knepp Wild Range longhorn and venison sausages, steaks and burgers. As well as eco-friendly flushing loos, hot-water rain showers and open-air baths, facilities include an off-grid camp kitchen with solar lighting and wood-fired pizza oven. Safaris and camping at Knepp are suitable only for children aged 12 and over.

MORE ADVENTURE Just 16km from Knepp, heading south on the A24, then west on the A283, the RSPB Pulborough Brooks Reserve (♀ RH20 2EL ✎ 01798 875851 ✐ rspb.org.uk) protects a mosaic of wet grassland, pools, hay meadows and lowland heath in the Arun Valley. Birdwatching highlights include nightingales, nightjars, peregrines and large flocks of wintering ducks, geese and waders. During summer, green tiger beetles stalk the heathland, while dragonflies quarter the ponds and ditches. Family activities range from pond dipping and bug hunting to building dens in the woods.

ALSO CONSIDER London See *A Day in the Urban Jungle*, page 86; **Cumbria** See *Farm and Fell Safari*, page 146; **Dunbartonshire** See *Loch Lomond Farm Adventure*, page 234; **Scottish Highlands** See *Cairngorms Wilderness Adventure*, page 276.

↑ Around 30 pairs of nightingales nest at Knepp Estate (R Oksana/S)

WILDLIFE
12 TRACKING
AND BUSHCRAFT

LEARN HOW TO SURVIVE IN THE WOODS AND TRACK ANIMALS IN A LEAFY CORNER OF KENT

WHERE	A forest somewhere near Canterbury, Kent
WHEN	Easter holidays to October half-term
HOW LONG	Full-day bushcraft sessions or camping weekends, spending the night in your wilderness shelter
WHO FOR	Children aged five & above
ADVENTURE POTENTIAL	Bushcraft, wilderness survival, wildlife tracking
WILDLIFE WISHLIST	The emphasis is on animal tracks & signs, but you might see woodland species like badger, fox, great spotted woodpecker & tawny owl, plus various minibeasts & fungi

↑ Woodland retreat: building a shelter is the first rule of survival (William Gray)

In a world where technology is their future, what, you may ask, is the point of 'going bush' with your kids, roughing it in a rudimentary woodland shelter and learning how to make fire the prehistoric way? The simple answer is written all over James' face in the photograph above: it's fun. But there's more to this than simply mucking about in the woods. A day or two of bushcraft skills and wildlife tracking is not only an engaging way to reconnect children with the natural world – touching it, feeling it, smelling it, even sleeping in it – but it can also be an effective catalyst to boost self-confidence and encourage free thinking and environmental awareness.

Founded in 2002 by Hannah Nicholls, Natural Pathways (see *Action plan*, page 85) specialises in bushcraft and nature awareness, and offers several courses for families, ranging from a three-hour Mini Survival Adventure to a three-day Wilderness Camp. The rewilding of your children takes place in a remote patch of woodland somewhere between Canterbury and Dover (you're given the exact location when you book). Soon after you turn down the muddy track and enter the leafy embrace of oak and sweet chestnut, mobile phones and modern-day life are quickly forgotten as Hannah focuses your mind on the two fundamentals of woodland survival...

SHELTER AND FIRE Imagine you're lost in the woods; it's raining and you're cold and and wet. Your first priority is to take refuge from the elements, but you haven't got an axe or saw, let alone a tent. How do you create a shelter? The answer, it turns out, is lying all around you. With Hannah's guidance, you start collecting deadwood to build a debris shelter. A long ridge pole, kicked into the ground at one end and wedged into a V-shaped frame at the other, creates the basic tent shape. Smaller pieces of 'ribbing' wood are then arranged along each side before being covered in a meshwork of small conifer branches. Then all that's needed to make it snug and surprisingly weatherproof is a thick layer of dead leaves and a mattress of fresh bracken.

While you're collecting wood for your shelter, Hannah is already thinking ahead to your next survival essential: fire. She points out potential sources of tinder (the seed heads of thistles, clematis and rosebay willowherb) and dry kindling (the brittle twigs of 'standing deadwood' that you can find on old conifer trees). A few sparks from a handheld fire steel and you're soon coaxing flames to life.

With shelter and fire sorted, your next challenge is boiling water – and Hannah knows a trick for that too.... Carefully place an ember on top of a small block of wood and keep blowing it until it has burnt out a bowl-shaped depression; add water and a few hot stones from the fire and it will quickly boil – ready for a nettle, bramble-leaf or pine-needle brew.

TUNING IN TO NATURE Without realising it, all the survival skills you're learning are simultaneously honing your senses to the complex woodland habitat around you. While collecting bracken for your shelter, you find a badger latrine (the droppings full of seeds and berry pips); teeth marks on a fly agaric mushroom suggest there's a wood mouse about, while stripped fir cones are the calling cards of feeding squirrels. In full Bear Grylls mode, you might well use these clues to hunt for food. On a family bushcraft course, however, you're more likely to pop a banana, stuffed with chocolate, on the fire than a squirrel kebab. The emphasis is very much on wildlife observation and becoming a nature detective.

SCATS, SKULLS, PATHS AND PELLETS Britain's wild mammals are not easy to see, but a bushcraft expert like Hannah can teach you how to develop a 'sixth sense' – an ability to move stealthily through a woodland, keenly aware of the signs, smells and sounds around you. By imagining what it's like to be both predator and prey, you can thread yourself into the complex web of a forest ecosystem. You start to notice the narrow, trampled pathways of mice, shrews, rats and rabbits, along with their burrows and the scuffed patches of ground where they paused to forage for food.

Tree stumps are often used as feeding stations by small mammals to give them a clearer view of approaching predators, and it's worth checking them for discarded hazelnuts. Grey squirrels usually crack them in half, but other rodents gnaw holes in them. Only on closer inspection can you tell if it was a bank vole (a rough, irregular hole with few scratches or teeth marks) or a wood mouse (a rounder, neater hole, finely chiselled by tiny incisors).

Soft mud in a woodland clearing also draws your eye... it's the perfect medium for preserving the narrow slots left by fallow or roe deer. With luck, you might also decipher the dog-like tracks of a fox (four toes with claw marks) or the broader, five-toed prints of a badger. Mammal droppings are another gift for

↑ Skull collection (from top to bottom): badger, fox, weasel, rabbit, crow, rat and blackbird (William Gray)

nature detectives – whether it's the partly digested green pellets of a rabbit or the long, thin scat of a weasel, twisted at both ends and often containing bits of fur and bone. Owl pellets also provide clues both to the presence of predator and prey – gently tease one apart and you can usually identify the bird's last meal from the regurgitated, undigested parcel of bones.

Sometimes, you might come across a fresh kill: a pile of feathers could either be the aftermath of an ambush by a sparrowhawk or a fox – the raptor deftly plucks its victim, scattering intact feathers, whereas the canid rips and tears, breaking the delicate shafts in the process.

Skulls are rare, but if you do find one they can tell you a lot about the animal. The teeth, in particular, quickly sort the carnivores from the herbivores; rodents are well-equipped with sharp incisors, while badgers have a prominent sagittal crest running along the top of their skulls – an attachment point for strong jaw muscles. With bird skulls, it's all about the shape of the beak: you can easily tell apart a tree-boring woodpecker from a rabbit-hunting buzzard.

THE SIT SPOT So, you've found evidence that they're there, but what if you want to go beyond tracks and signs and actually lay eyes on these secretive and elusive woodland species? Most British mammals are largely nocturnal, so an overnight bushcraft experience provides an opportunity to glimpse badgers and foxes on their nightly patrols. It can be equally rewarding, though, to find a promising spot and simply sit quietly for 30 minutes or so. Naturalists call this wildlife-watching technique a 'sit spot', often returning to the same place on a regular basis. The idea is that by relaxing and tuning into nature – perhaps sitting with your back to a tree – you are not only more likely to notice the wildlife around you, but the animals themselves will be less wary of you. Just imagine the thrill of watching a badger shuffle past, a few metres from where you're sat, or hardly daring to breathe as a roe deer ventures from cover...

↑ **Above left:** roe deer; **above right:** learning how to use a fire steel (Daniel Opait/S; William Gray)

ACTION PLAN

ADVENTURE ESSENTIALS Family bushcraft and wildlife tracking courses are run by Natural Pathways (☎ 07828 316827 ⊘ natural-pathways.co.uk) at a woodland location near Canterbury, Kent. Options include a Skulls, Scats and Tracks Day where you learn how to become a nature detective, moving silently through the environment and deciphering the clues around you; a Survival in the Woods Bushcraft Day, covering the essentials of building a shelter and making a fire, and a choice of two- or three-day Bushcraft Camps where you spend a night or two in the woods, cooking on open fires, identifying plants and trees, making utensils and tracking wildlife. Although the minimum age is five, these are family courses where parental supervision (and participation) is encouraged. Children aged ten and over can also join flint-knapping workshops with prehistoric man, Will Lord, and staff-making days with wizard whittler, Andrew Duncan.

MORE ADVENTURE The headquarters of the Kent Wildlife Trust, Tyland Barn (📍 ME14 3BD ☎ 01622 662012 ⊘ kentwildlifetrust.org.uk) is located 5km north of Maidstone and offers a range of family workshops and discovery days throughout the year, including Nature Tots for pre-school ages and Nature Explorers for children up to 11. Paths weave past ponds and through woodland and wildflower meadows – home to everything from orchids to stag beetles and dragonflies.

ALSO CONSIDER Devon See *On the Night Watch* page 56; **South Devon** See *Foraging along the Devon Coast* page 40; **Yorkshire Dales** See *On the Trail of the Red Squirrel*, page 134; **Powys** See *Tree House Adventure*, page 188; **Moidart** See *On the Trail of the Otter*, page 256.

Above: bushcamp fire; **right:** red fox (William Gray)

13 A DAY IN THE URBAN JUNGLE

FROM RED DEER AND RARE WATERBIRDS TO THE SECRET LIFE OF ANCIENT OAKS, LONDON IS ALIVE!

WHERE	London
WHEN	Year-round; visit in autumn for the deer rut, winter for mass gatherings of ducks & geese, & late spring for duelling stag beetles
HOW LONG	This adventure describes a day at the London Wetland Centre & Richmond Park, but add a few London Wildlife Trust sites to make it a full weekend
WHO FOR	Any age
ADVENTURE POTENTIAL	Birdwatching, deer watching, pond dipping, nature walks
WILDLIFE WISHLIST	Red & fallow deer, water vole, bittern, common tern, green woodpecker, kingfisher, lapwing, peregrine, ring-necked parakeet, sand martin, tawny owl, tufted duck, stag beetle

↑ Golden stag: red deer in Richmond Park (William Gray)

Two bittern, a peregrine, 12 snipe, a kingfisher, 100-plus teal, 234 tufted duck, 46 lapwing and a bearded tit… You might think that such an impressive list of bird sightings from a single day in January could only have come from some remote watery wilderness – a sprawling nature reserve on the Norfolk coast perhaps. But the London Wetland Centre flexes its muscles against the urban sprawl of England's capital with a wealth of wetland habitats that's irresistible to birds – as well as wildlife lovers in search of a different kind of city break.

A wildlife adventure in the middle of London? Absolutely! Just because there are around 5,700 people per km^2 in the capital (with boroughs like Islington and Tower Hamlets recording over 16,000), it doesn't mean there's no room left for wildlife. Far from it. Declared the world's first National Park City in 2019, London is home to 14,000 species. Around 47% of the capital is green, thanks to 3.8 million gardens, 30,000 allotments, 3,000 parks and countless patches of woodland. And then there's 850km of rivers, canals and streams...

Delve into Greater London's 1,572km^2 of urban jungle and you can discover two National Nature Reserves, 1,400 Sites of Importance for Nature Conservation, 142 Local Nature Reserves, 37 Sites of Special Scientific Interest and three Special Areas of Conservation. Together they form London's living landscape. In a single day, walking, cycling or using public transport, you can easily visit dozens of wildlife-rich green spaces.

LONDON WETLAND CENTRE A brilliantly boggy bit of Barnes, the London Wetland Centre (♀ SW13 9WT ☎ 0208 409 4400 ⊘ wwt.org.uk) is the perfect place for families to embark on a wildlife adventure. The moment you step foot on the network of paths that thread through its mosaic of lakes, pools and wildlife gardens, the city hubbub fades away. Quivering reeds draw a green veil around you; sparkling water catches your eye and the air is filled with the contented babble of ducks and geese.

Winter is one of the best times to visit. It's when some of the biggest concentrations of wildfowl can be seen. Gadwall, pochard, pintail, shoveler, teal, tufted duck and wigeon speckle the main lake and sheltered lagoons. You'll need more time and patience to spot camouflaged wading birds like snipe and water rail. The latter can sometimes be glimpsed dashing for cover, uttering a cry that's said to resemble a piglet squealing.

Stake out the reedbeds from one of the wetland centre's hides for a chance to see a bittern. Several usually overwinter on the reserve, but their cryptic plumage can render them almost invisible as they stand motionless in the shallows. Keep focused and watch for movement – that patch of reeds you've been staring at might suddenly transform into one of these secretive, skulking herons.

During spring and summer, other species enter the limelight. Sand martins arrive in April to nest, taking up residence in a specially created sand bank, rigged with CCTV to offer intimate views inside their burrows. Common terns also return to the wetland centre each spring, nesting on purpose-built rafts, while the surrounding reedbeds and willow trees whir and chatter with the songs of migrant willow, sedge and grasshopper warblers, blackcaps and whitethroats. For budding ornithologists this is the perfect place to boost a fledgling tick list, whether you're visiting in summer for lapwing, little ringed plover, yellow wagtail and great crested grebe, or autumn for migrant waders like black-tailed godwit, greenshank and green sandpiper. You can enjoy numerous exotic species in the collections – from American wood duck to Hawaiian goose.

But it's not just birds that benefit from this wetland wilderness. Find a quiet spot to sit and wait, or slowly stalk along the balance beams that squeeze through dense patches of reeds and you might just glimpse a water vole. Rare and secretive, these chestnut-brown rodents have suffered a 94% decline in range, but conservation organisations like the Wildfowl and Wetlands Trust are providing much-needed

↑ On reflection: female tufted duck, London Wetland Centre (William Gray)

havens for their recovery. Play the nature detective and look for signs of 'Ratty': piles of nibbled stems (bitten off at a distinctive 45-degree angle) or latrines of cigar-shaped droppings. Often, by slowing down and looking hard for details like this, you will begin to notice other small wonders, such as orchids, dragonflies, grass snakes and frogs.

RICHMOND PARK From one of Britain's smallest mammals to its largest, a day in the urban jungle can find you tracking water voles one moment and red deer the next. Only a few miles from the London Wetland Centre, as the ring-necked parakeet flies, Richmond Park (✆ 0300 061 2200 ☝ royalparks.org.uk) has been home to red and fallow deer since 1637. The National Nature Reserve is now home to free-roaming herds comprising over 600 individuals.

During autumn, red deer stags and fallow deer bucks compete for females, displaying to rivals with deep-throated roars and barks. Two males will often parallel-walk to assess each other's size and condition. Sometimes, they will thrash about in bracken to create leafy headdresses to big themselves up. The weaker of the two is usually chased away, but if neither backs down, they will lock antlers in tests of strength to decide who will hold the biggest harems.

The deer rut is one of Britain's greatest wildlife spectacles. You can experience it in several places covered in this book – from Exmoor National Park to Scotland's Galloway Forest – but it seems particularly remarkable to witness it in Richmond Park, against the backdrop of the Shard and London's city skyline.

Taking heed of the precautions on page 91, this is a family wildlife adventure best undertaken on foot. Treat it as if you're on a walking safari: moving slowly, senses alert. The first thing you might notice is that all of the trees have a distinctive 'browse line' created by the deer eating all vegetation up to about 1.5m above the ground. Pick your way towards any of the large, gnarled oaks – Richmond Park has about 1,200 ancient trees, some of which are thought to be 750 years old. Spend some time studying one of these venerable giants. Many

have crevices and hollows: dark, hidden worlds that are ideal roosts for some of the park's eight species of bat. Dead wood provides decaying riches for fungi and the grubs of stag beetles. The males of this endangered species lock antlers, like red deer, to fight for territory. Growing up to 7cm in length, it's Britain's largest native ground-dwelling beetle and it relies on ancient woodland. The best time to see them is from May until late July – but this is just one of 1,350 species of beetle to discover in Richmond Park. Study one of its oaks and you may also spot some of its 139 spider species or 700 moths. Each oak is, quite literally, a 'tree of life'.

Train your binoculars at the canopy and you might spot purple hairstreak butterflies flitting through sunlit chinks. You'll almost certainly hear the shrill screech of ring-necked parakeets. The UK's only naturalised species of parrot, this green, long-tailed bird was a popular pet in Victorian times, but it started breeding in the wild in 1969 and there are now at least 8,600 pairs in southeast England. Richmond Park's ancient oaks offer plenty of natural nesting holes. It's not the only eye-catching green bird to be seen here though. The park's old, undisturbed grassland is dimpled with ant hills – a favourite feeding ground for green woodpeckers.

Pack a picnic and spend a few hours in the shade of a mighty oak; listen to parakeets squabbling through the treetops and imagine the vast web of insect life all around you; rest your back against ancient, wrinkled bark and gaze across grassland lorded over by strutting red deer stags. Yes, this really is London.

↑ **Top:** regal in Richmond – a stag with his harem; **above:** male stag beetle (William Gray; Cynoclub/S)

ACTION PLAN

ADVENTURE ESSENTIALS Located in Barnes, the London Wetland Centre is easily reached by public transport. Catch a bus from Barnes or Hammersmith and alight at the Red Lion Pub on Castlenau, a five-minute walk to the centre, or take a train to Barnes Bridge Station, a 15-minute walk away. You can also cycle there along Sustrans Cycle Route 4. At 1,012 hectares, Richmond Park (the largest of London's eight Royal Parks) is accessible by bus and train – Richmond Station is served by the District Line and National Rail. The London National Park City website (⊘ nationalparkcity.london) has details of events, places to visit and how to become a volunteer ranger. The Urban Good London National Park City Map (⊘ urbangood.org) highlights the capital's green and blue spaces, revealing hills and valleys, parks and commons, walks and public transport, as well as various outdoor activities.

Remember that Richmond Park's red deer are wild animals. They are not there to be fed, petted or hashtagged in selfies. Always keep at least 50m away and keep alert to their movements to ensure you never get between a mother and her calf or two rutting males. Ticks are found in Richmond Park, so avoid walking through dense vegetation, tuck trousers into socks and use insect repellent.

MORE ADVENTURE Other wildlife hotspots in London include several nature reserves managed by the London Wildlife Trust (⊘ 0207 261 0447 ⊘ wildlondon.org.uk), including Camley Street Natural Park (♀ N1C 4PW), a fabulous mini-mosaic of woodland, grassland and wetland between King's Cross and St Pancras, and Sydenham Hill Wood (♀ SE26 6LS) for stag beetles, tawny owls, fungi and bluebells. Located on the Thames estuary, the RSPB Rainham Marshes Reserve (♀ RM19 1SZ ⊘ 01708 899840 ⊘ rspb.org. uk) is a haven for birds, water voles and dragonflies.

CONSERVATION HEROES One of Britain's most inspiring young nature writers and conservationists, Kabir Kaul (⊘ kabirswildsideoflondon.blogspot.com) has created an interactive map of over 1,000 nature reserves and wildlife sites in London.

ALSO CONSIDER **West Sussex** See *Rewilding Safari at Knepp*, page 76; **Essex** See *Wetland Wonders Adventure*, page 92; **Cumbria and Lancashire** See *Motorway Stop Safari*, page 130; **Scottish Borders** See *Tree Climbing Adventure*, page 218.

↑ Ring-necked parakeet (Huw Penson/S)

14 WETLAND WONDERS ADVENTURE

**GLIMPSE A KING AND HUNT FOR DRAGONS IN
THE POOLS AND MEADOWS OF LEE VALLEY PARK**

WHERE	Lee Valley Park, Essex & Hertfordshire
WHEN	Spring for water vole & orchids; summer for breeding birds & dragonflies; autumn for migrant waders; winter for bittern & wildfowl
HOW LONG	Allow a few hours to visit one reserve, or spend a day or more exploring the entire Lee Valley
WHO FOR	Any age
ADVENTURE POTENTIAL	Birdwatching, cycling, canoeing, train journeys
WILDLIFE WISHLIST	Otter & water vole are present, but hard to spot; birds include common tern, great crested grebe & kingfisher, as well as raptors (barn owl, hobby, kestrel & peregrine), wading birds (bittern, common & green sandpiper, grey heron, lapwing, little egret, little ringed plover, redshank & snipe) & wildfowl (gadwall, goldeneye, goosander, shoveler, smew & teal); also look for brown & migrant hawker, broad-bodied chaser & emperor dragonfly, banded demoiselle & red-eyed damselfly; bee, common spotted, early marsh & pyramidal orchid; grass snake

It was once London's neglected 'backyard' – a derelict, unloved mire of gravel pits, sewage works, rubbish dumps and factories. Then, in 1967, the Lee Valley began its remarkable transformation into a verdant oasis – a green vein, pulsing with life, stretching 42km from London into Essex and Hertfordshire. Take the train north from Liverpool Street in the heart of the city and you can hop off at several stations along the line to find yourself within walking distance of an orchid-speckled meadow, a nature reserve bustling with nesting terns, herons, waders and warblers, or a wetland dancing with damselflies and dragonflies. See the *Action plan*, page 97, for details of train stations and access to each of the reserves described below.

WALTHAMSTOW WETLANDS After weaving through Bethnal Green, Hackney and Clapton, the first stop on your 'wildlife train odyssey' is Tottenham Hale – gateway to Europe's largest urban wetland reserve. Built over a period of 70 years by the East London Waterworks, the ten reservoirs at Walthamstow Wetlands are a magnet to wildfowl during winter. Large congregations of gadwall, pochard, shoveler, teal, tufted duck and wigeon can be seen, while bittern often overwinter in the reedbeds. In spring and summer, the 210-hectare wetlands are also brimming with life. Set off on the reserve's Touchstone Trail and one of the first things you'll see is the island heronry – grey herons have nested in the treetops here since 1930, but it's only in more recent years that little egrets have joined them. The islands on Reservoir 5 are daubed with guano from nesting

cormorants, while artificial rafts attract breeding common terns. Keep an eye out for kingfishers, which have nesting holes on the islands, and linger by the reedbeds where you may also spot a reed bunting perched atop the swaying stems of phragmites. The males are well turned out with black cap, white collar and drooping moustache, while females go for a streaky-brown, understated look. If you hear a long, slightly frantic outpouring of churring and chirping rising from the reedbeds, it's probably the song of a reed warbler – more rythmic and fluid than the sedge warbler, which likes to improvise its repertoire with random phrases. Usually hidden deep in the reedbeds, both species are difficult to spot, but if you do get a sighting, reed warblers are plain brown above, with a short eye stripe, while sedge warblers have dark streaks on their heads and backs, and a broader, more prominent eye stripe. Following the trail to Lockwood Reservoir in the northern part of the reserve, look for waders like green sandpiper, lapwing and little ringed plover, before looping back to the entrance where the Victorian-era Engine House now hosts a visitor centre and a 24m-tall swift-nesting tower built in the shape of the building's original chimney.

CORNMILL MEADOWS A few stops along the line from Tottenham Hale, Waltham Cross is the nearest train station to this mishmash of river channels, ditches, pools and floodplain grassland. Of the 42 resident species of breeding dragonflies and damselflies in Britain, around half can be found here – and a warm, sunny day in August gives you a good chance of spotting several of them. Follow the circular, 3km Dragonfly Discovery Trail and one of the first species you're likely to spot is the emperor dragonfly. This 8cm-long, kingfisher-blue 'hawker' quarters open water, snatching prey midair and devouring it on the wing. Also look for black-tailed skimmer, brown hawker, broad-bodied chaser and ruddy darter resting on waterside plants or nearby fence posts, warming their bodies in the sun before taking flight. Migrant hawkers sometimes form large

↑ Secretive songster: sedge warbler (Sander Meertins/S)

feeding swarms along the sanctuary's woodland glades, while common darters can be seen well into late summer – you might spot a mating pair, flying in tandem, the female dipping to the water's edge to lay her eggs. Less frenetic, the damselflies at Cornmill Meadows include dainty beauties like the banded demoiselle and red-eyed damselfly. Unlike their bold cousins, they flutter rather than prowl, and perch with their wings folded back (dragonflies hold them wide open). Using binoculars you'll also notice that a damselfly's eyes are small, spherical and widely spaced, whereas dragonflies have huge bulging eyes that meet in the middle. If you're extremely lucky, you may witness these spellbinding predators become prey as a hobby falcon deftly snatches one in its outstretched talons. The flooded meadows at Cornmill are also prime hunting territory for barn owls and kestrels.

TURNFORD & CHESHUNT PITS The next stop north from Waltham Cross, Cheshunt station provides access to a mosaic of lakes at the heart of the River Lee Country Park. Aim for Fishers Green – a 2.5km waterside walk – to find the Wildlife Discovery Centre with its observation tower overlooking Seventy Acres Lake. Anything is possible here, from lazy rafts of wildfowl to a kingfisher's electrifying fly-past. You might even spy an otter slipping into the water, or a bittern tiptoeing furtively through the reedbeds. The scrubby woodland around the lake is full of birdsong during spring. Listen carefully... what you initially think is an over-exuberant blackbird or song thrush might actually be a nightingale, performing its rich chorus of high and low notes sung in quick succession. During May and June, see if you can find the pink spires of common-spotted and pyramidal orchids scattered through damp meadows. Later in the summer, the grasslands are alive with grasshoppers and crickets, including Roesel's bush-cricket – its song (or stridulation) is reminiscent of a hot day in the Mediterranean and easily confused with the song of the rare Savi's warbler. Out on the lake, meanwhile, the common terns and black-headed gulls will be fledging their young from the floating rafts.

↑ Here be dragons: common darter and migrant hawker dragonflies (William Gray)

SILVERMEADE A short walk from Broxbourne station, the quiet backwaters and reed-choked channels of this small reserve offer a leafy refuge for Britain's most rapidly declining mammal. The water vole has been lost from over 94% of its former range, with habitat loss and predation by American mink largely to blame. Blunt nose, small ears and a furry tail distinguish this endearing rodent from the brown rat, but you'll need to play the (silent) detective to spot one. Telltale signs include neat little piles of nibbled leaves and stems by the water's edge. Use your ears too. You might just hear the 'plop' as one of these furballs dives into the water. Spring is the best time to look, when vegetation is less dense and water voles are actively asserting their territories. But don't worry if you visit in summer and 'Ratty' eludes you: there are plenty of other discoveries to be made, from swimming grass snakes to shimmering damselflies.

RYE MEADS NATURE RESERVE Rye House station is close to the entrance of this wildlife-rich reserve where three short trails link numerous hides. Nothing has been spared to make birds feel at home here. Special rafts have been anchored in the lagoons to entice breeding common terns; shallow scrapes attract lapwing, sandpipers and snipe, while reedbeds have been created to offer shelter for bitterns, water rails and flocks of starlings in winter, and dense nesting sites for warblers and buntings during summer. There is even an artificial sandbank for kingfishers to excavate their nesting burrows. Extending up to 90cm in length, the entrances to these tunnels are just 6cm in diameter and end in a bare chamber where two or three broods are raised in quick succession, starting in early April. From the Kingfisher Hide at Rye Meads, you can watch the adults diving to catch minnows and sticklebacks, before flying back to their favourite perches, striking the fish and swallowing them head first. This is probably the best place in the entire Lee Valley to see these gorgeous birds.

↑ Water vole (Mark Bridger/S)

ACTION PLAN

ADVENTURE ESSENTIALS Although this wildlife adventure is based on train travel, all sites are also accessible by car (see individual websites for directions). General information on the Lee Valley Park can be found at ⊘ visitleevalley.org.uk. To spread the adventure over a couple of days or more, there's a wide range of family-friendly places to stay in the area, such as Lee Valley Camping and Caravan Park, Edmonton (♥ N9 0AR ⊘ 0300 003 0625) and Lee Valley Almost Wild Campsite, Broxbourne (♥ EN10 6TD ⊘ 0300 003 0619) – of which the latter has a minimum age of 12.

Walthamstow Wetlands (♥ N17 9NH ⊘ 0203 989 7448 ⊘ wildlondon.org.uk) is a 10-minute walk from Tottenham Hale station to the entrance on Ferry Lane/Forest Road. Cornmill Meadows (⧟ rate.cool.voter ⊘ 03000 030 610 ⊘ visitleevalley.org.uk) can be accessed from Waltham Cross station by walking around 3km, passing the Lee Valley White Water Centre and Waltham Abbey Gardens along the way. To reach Turnford and Cheshunt Pits and the Wildlife Discovery Centre (⊘ visitleevalley.org.uk), take the train to Cheshunt Station, then walk around 2.5km to Fishers Green and Seventy Acres Lake. The nearest car park is Fishers Green at Stubbins Hall Lane (⧟ pages.patio.frozen. Silvermeade (♥ EN10 7AX ⊘ 0300 003 0610 ⊘ visitleevalley.org.uk) is tucked down Mill Lane, a 10-minute walk from Broxbourne station, via Station Road and Churchfields towards Broxbourne Old Mill and Meadow. RSPB Rye Meads Nature Reserve (♥ SG12 8JS ⊘ 01992 708383 ⊘ rspb.org.uk) is only 400m from Rye House Station, turning right towards Rye Meads and following a footpath to the visitor centre.

MORE ADVENTURE Lee Valley Canoe Cycle (♥ EN10 7AX ⊘ 01992 676650 ⊘ lvcc.link) can set you up with everything you need for a pedalling or paddling adventure. As well as single and double kayaks, you can hire Canadian canoes with room for two adults and two children. Adult and children's bicycles, as well as tag-alongs, are also available to rent. Setting out from their base in Broxbourne, you can spend a few hours or a full day exploring the rivers, lakes and trails, heading north towards Rye Meads, or south to Fishers Green.

ALSO CONSIDER **London** See *A Day in the Urban Jungle*, page 86; **Norfolk** See *Canoeing on the Broads*, page 110; **Yorkshire** See *Yorkshire Moors by Rail and Bike*, page 140.

↑ Grey heron (William Gray)

15 COTSWOLD WATER PARK SAFARI

GET WET 'N' WILD COMBINING WATERSPORTS WITH BIRDWATCHING AND DRAGONFLY SPOTTING

WHERE	Gloucestershire & Wiltshire
WHEN	Year-round
HOW LONG	At least a day for watersports & a nature reserve
WHO FOR	Age limits may apply to some watersports
ADVENTURE POTENTIAL	Birdwatching, dragonfly spotting, canoeing, paddleboarding, cycling
WILDLIFE WISHLIST	Otter, water vole, bittern, common tern, great crested grebe, hobby, kingfisher, little & great white egret, nightingale, reed bunting, sand martin, various warblers & ducks, plus butterflies, damselflies & dragonflies

Glance at a map of the Cotswold Water Park and it resembles crazy paving – except the 'slabs' are 180 lakes spread over more than 100km². Venture into this giant wetland mosaic and, one moment, you could find yourself walking beside a lake where a speedboat is towing an inflatable ring full of screaming children and, an hour later, be crouched in a hide gazing across waters barely rippled by flotillas of ducks, coots and grebes.

↑ Common blue damselfly (William Gray)

Sand and gravel extraction began in the area around 50 years ago – and still continues today. Once a pit is exhausted, pumps are switched off and it naturally fills with water. A little bit of restoration work – contouring the lakebed, adding crinkly edges and planting reedbeds – helps to create varied habitats for wildlife. Over 20,000 waterbirds spend the winter here, while spring and summer sees the lakeshores dancing with damselflies and buzzing with breeding warblers and waders. Just don't expect a total wilderness. The Cotswold Water Park is as much for wakeboarders as it is for reed warblers. That's what makes it such a perfect location for a family wildlife adventure: spend the morning enjoying watersports, then take the kids to a quieter lake in search of dragonfly-hunting hobby falcons, plunge-diving common terns or the balletic courtship displays of great crested grebes.

THE REALLY WILD SIDE OF THE WATER PARK Make your first stop the Gateway Centre (see *Action plan*, page 101) to pick up a copy of the *Leisure Map* – or download it beforehand. A five-minute drive south, Waterhay Car Park (🔲 magnitude.flock.scales) is the starting point for a circular walk exploring the Cleveland Lakes Nature Reserve – an ideal introduction to the water park's wetland habitats and wildlife. The path skirts the southern shore of Lake 68, before bearing left to a hide overlooking a reedbed and Lake 74. Scan the broad expanse of water through binoculars and you should see large rafts of waterfowl. Several species, including coot, gadwall, great crested grebe, mallard, mute swan and tufted duck, are resident year-round, but during autumn and winter their numbers burgeon with the arrival of goldeneye, pochard, shoveler, smew, teal and wigeon.

On a still winter's day, you may be able to hear the whistling *"weee-ooo"* cries of the wigeon echoing across the mist-covered water. In summer, the lake's soundtrack is likely to be dominated by the splashing of bad-tempered coots chasing each other, or the gruff croaks of grey herons nesting in the trees visible from the Reed Hide at Lake 74. Look closely at this heronry and you may be able to spot little egrets – bright splashes of white – nesting among their larger cousins. In recent years, two other species of heron have also started breeding in the Cotswold Water Park. Almost the size of a grey heron, the great white egret is slowly gaining a toehold in Britain after a pair was first recorded nesting in Somerset during 2012. Widely distributed, the species was almost exterminated in North America during the late 1800s following the fashion industry's insatiable

→ Male reed bunting (Erni/S)

demand for the long, white plumes of its breeding plumage. At first glance, the bittern might seem rather dumpy and drab, but if you're lucky enough to spot this rare heron you'll be spellbound by its exquisite camouflage as it stalks through dense reeds. Wetland drainage and hunting led to its extinction in Britain by the late 19th century and it's only through reedbed restoration that this enigmatic bird has started to reclaim its wetland realm. You're more likely to hear them – the males' distinctive 'booming' (used to attract a mate) sounds like someone blowing over the top of an empty bottle.

Cleveland Lakes might also reward you with the riveting sight of a hobby dashing after dragonflies, the kestrel-sized falcon more than equal to the aerial acrobatics of Odonata. Prey is snatched mid-air and eaten on the wing. Sand martins and swifts weave equally dizzy flightpaths across the lakes as they feed on gnats, while blackcaps, chiffchaffs, reed buntings and sedge warblers fuss through the reedy fringes and willow carr.

A ten-minute drive west from Waterhay, Lower Moor Farm Nature Reserve (⊞ sweetened.resorting.pursue ♂ wiltshirewildlife.org) links with Clattinger Farm, Oaksey Moor Farm Meadow and Sandpool nature reserves to form a lush patchwork of lakes, ponds and wetland scrapes laced with boardwalks, ancient hedges, woodland and meadows. Wait quietly beside Flagham Brook for a chance to spy a water vole or otter. Sort your migrant hawkers from your emperor dragonflies, or simply fall under the spell of the hypnotic flight of banded demoiselles. Visit Clattinger Farm in late April to discover a meadow blushed with the nodding flowerheads of a host of snake's-head fritillaries; try winter for lapwing and snipe, or explore Sandpool for everything from herons and willow warblers to barn owls and bats.

Other nature hotspots include Coke's Pit Nature Reserve (site of a large nesting colony of black-headed gulls), North Meadow (a National Nature Reserve near Cricklade that's home to 80% of Britain's snake's-head fritillaries) and Shorncote Reedbed (where a hide provides a good vantage for spotting secretive birds like bittern, reed bunting, reed warbler and snipe).

Between Fairford and Lechlade, Whelford Pools Nature Reserve (⊞ dimes.bathtubs.busy ♂ gloucestershirewildlifetrust.co.uk) provides a refuge for overwintering flocks of pochard, tufted duck and wigeon. From February through to late summer, it's also a good location to observe the elaborate breeding behaviour of great crested grebes. Pairs reaffirm their bond with synchronised swimming, head-shaking, ruff-fanning and the presentation of waterweed bouquets. With their striking black-and-white-striped heads, the chicks abandon the nest of floating sticks and weed soon after hatching, often riding on their parents' backs.

↑ Snake's-head fritillary (William Gray)

ACTION PLAN

ADVENTURE ESSENTIALS Easily accessed by following the A419 south from Cirencester, the western section of the Cotswold Water Park (⌖ waterpark.org) sprawls over a wide area. Visit the Gateway Centre (♀ GL7 5TL) for information on activities and places to visit. To reach the smaller eastern section of the water park, head east from Cirencester on the A417. The Cotswold Lakes Trust (⌖ cotswoldlakestrust.org) manages several sites in the water park, including nature reserves, country parks and car parks. As well as supporting conservation projects, such as water vole recovery, membership entitles you to free parking at Neigh Bridge Country Park, Clayhill, Bridge, Lakeside, Waterhay and Riverside Park. Good options for family accommodation in the water park include the Hobourne Cotswold Holiday Park (✆ 01285 860216 ⌖ hoburne.com) and Lower Mill Estate (✆ 0333 241 6616 ⌖ habitatescapes.com).

MORE ADVENTURE The Cotswold Water Park is awash with activities, including adrenaline-charged watersports like inflatable rides and wake boarding. If you want to combine watersports with wildlife watching, however, choose something more peaceful. Operators offering SUP, canoeing and kayaking include 4 Lakes (✆ 07572 113220 ⌖ 4lakes.co.uk), CWP Hire (✆ 01285 860086 ⌖ cotswoldwaterparkhire. com), Cotswold Canoe Hire (✆ 01367 252303 ⌖ cotswoldcanoehire.co.uk) and South Cerney Outdoor (✆ 01285 860388 ⌖ southcerneyoutdoor.co.uk). With its network of trails and quiet lanes, the Cotswold Water Park is also perfect for a cycling adventure. Bike hire is available from Go-By-Cycle (✆ 01285 862152 ⌖ go-by-cycle.co.uk).

ALSO CONSIDER London See *A Day in the Urban Jungle*, page 86; **Essex** See *Wetland Wonders Adventure*, page 92; **Norfolk** See *Canoeing on the Broads*, page 110; **Dunbartonshire** See *Loch Lomond Farm Adventure*, page 234.

↑ Courting great crested grebes (Denis Vesely/S)

16 A PADDLE ALONG THE RIVER WYE

LAUNCH A CANOE AND EMBARK ON A RIVER TRIP SPICED WITH WILDLIFE AND MILD WHITE WATER

WHERE	Wye Valley, Herefordshire
WHEN	Canoe hire is generally available Apr–Sep
HOW LONG	From a few hours to multi-day paddles
WHO FOR	Children under 14 must be supervised 1:1 by an adult; canoes can carry up to three people, or be lashed together to form a catamaran carrying four. Paddling is easy with a few gentle (Grade 1) rapids
ADVENTURE POTENTIAL	Canoeing, birdwatching, camping, riverside picnics
WILDLIFE WISHLIST	Secretive riverside mammals like otter & water vole are occasionally seen; birds include cormorant, dipper, goosander, grey heron, kingfisher, mute swan, peregrine & sand martin

Rising in the Cambrian Mountains of mid-Wales, the River Wye flows south for some 240km to meet the Severn Estuary at Chepstow. Between Hay-on-Wye and Whitney, the river is young and exuberant, rushing beween the Black Mountains and Radnorshire Hills. But as it approaches Hereford, it begins to calm down, unravelling in lazy meanders across broad floodplains before snaking through the steep wooded gorges at Symonds Yat. This gentler section of the Wye is perfect for a family canoeing adventure – several operators offer canoe hire or guided trips, and you can choose various stretches of river depending on how much time you have. This adventure describes a two-day paddle between Hoarwithy and Symonds Yat – around 38km in total, with a night camping at Ross-on-Wye about half-way through.

GOING WITH THE FLOW After loading our Canadian canoes with a picnic and basic camping gear, we pushed off from the riverbank a short distance downstream from the small village of Hoarwithy. Almost immediately, you feel the ripple of excitement that comes from river travel – the canoe carried along at the whim of the current; your whole perspective suddenly focused on the channel ahead and what lies beyond the next bend. There's time to practise your paddling technique, or simply go with the flow... the Wye a smooth green slick, streaked with tendrils of weed; balsam-blushed riverbanks slipping past.

This is perfect otter territory. Look for their tracks in muddy areas – the five-toed footprints are similar to mink, but much larger (up to 9cm long and 6cm wide) with a prominent impression of the rear pad. You might even be able to make out the shallow groove of a 'tail drag'. When the river is running low in summer, shingle shoals appear. Stop to explore these ephemeral islands for otter spraints – easily recognised by their crumbly texture and undigested fish scales.

About 3km south from Hoarwithy, a footbridge invites a short shore excursion to Sellack, renowned for its striking 14th-century church of St Tysilio.

← Peregrine's view of the Wye (Steve D/S)

Then it's back on the river, drifting past overhanging willow branches – each one a potential perch for kingfishers. Other birds to keep watch for include grey wagtails catching gnats near the water's edge, or goosander hunting fish, using their 'sawbills' to snatch anything from stickleback to salmon.

Beyond Sellack, the River Wye flows through a hairpin bend, almost doubling back on itself before settling on a southerly dawdle towards Ross-on-Wye. We landed at the rowing club, hauled our canoes ashore and pitched tents in the camping field next to the clubhouse. There's no shortage of places to stay in the town itself, but this is the best option for staying close to the river – and nature.

RAPIDS AND RAPTORS

Get an early start the following morning to maximise your chances of spotting wildlife before it gets busy with other canoeists. From Ross-on-Wye you continue south, paddling through beautiful Herefordshire countryside. Goodrich Castle (♥ HR9 6HY ✎ 01600 890538 ⊘ english-heritage.org.uk) looms ahead, the crumbling sandstone towers of the 12th-century fort clinging to a wooded hill.

Beyond the next bend, you pass under Kerne Bridge. Forget castles and kingfishers for a moment – your first set of rapids lies ahead and you'll need to concentrate on keeping to the main channel and avoiding any large rocks. A few hundred metres later, you can haul out at the Inn on The Wye (✎ 01600 890872 ⊘ innonthewye.co.uk) for a rest and a pub lunch. Otherwise, push on past Lower Lydbrook to Welsh Bicknor where there's a lovely picnic spot near the church and youth hostel (a former rectory).

Not far from here, the river sweeps past the limestone ramparts of Symonds Yat Rock (✎ 0300 067 4800 ⊘ forestryengland.uk). As you drift beneath the 120m-tall cliffs, crane your neck for a glimpse of peregrine falcons. They've been nesting high on the Coldwell Rocks every year since 1982. A clifftop viewpoint operated by the RSPB (♥ GL16 7NZ ✎ 01767 693777 ⊘ rspb.org.uk) offers your best chance of a sighting, but you might spot one of these breathtaking raptors from the river – soaring high above the Forest of Dean or plummeting at up to 320km/h on an unsuspecting pigeon. Goshawk, sparrowhawk and buzzard are also seen here, making it one of the best places in Britain for raptor viewing.

The River Wye coils north from Symonds Yat Rock before looping south again to your take-out point at the Wyedean Canoe & Adventure Centre. But if you're not quite ready to give up the river life, you can always camp nearby and spend a third day paddling to Monmouth.

↑ Peregrine (Alec Taylor/S)

ACTION PLAN

ADVENTURE ESSENTIALS Canoes, paddles, buoyancy aids, helmets and drysacks can be hired from several operators, including Canoe the Wye (✆ 01600 891100 🖱 canoethewye.co.uk), Monmouth Canoe (✆ 01600 716083 🖱 monmouthcanoe.co.uk), Ross-on-Wye Canoe Hire (✆ 01600 890470 🖱 thecanoehire.co.uk), Symonds Yat Canoe Hire (✆ 01600 891069 🖱 canoehire.com) and Wyedean Canoe Hire (✆ 01600 891376 🖱 wyedean.co.uk). Some also offer guided canoeing trips. Alternatively, you could launch your own kayak or canoe. The public right of navigation on the River Wye extends for approximatey 160km from the Severn Estuary to Hay Town Bridge, but remember that some launch and landing sites require permission from landowners. The *Canoeists' Guide to the River Wye* can be downloaded at 🖱 wyevalleyaonb.org.uk. Camping is available at Ross Rowing Club (🖱 rossrowingclub.co.uk).

MORE ADVENTURE A great way to round off a canoeing adventure on the River Wye, pitch your tent at one of the many campsites in the Forest of Dean and spend a few days exploring the vast network of walking and cycling trails. Forest centres like Beechenhurst Lodge (📍 GL16 7EL ✆ 0300 067 4800 🖱 forestryengland.uk) are a good place to start.

ALSO CONSIDER South Cornwall See *River Fowey Adventure*, page 36; **Norfolk** See *Canoeing on the Broads*, page 110; **Moidart** See *Sea Kayaking in Arisaig*, page 262; **Isle of Skye** See *Hike and Kayak on Skye*, page 270.

↑ Easy paddling on the River Wye (William Gray)

17 WITNESS A MURMURATION

SEE STACKS OF STARLINGS AND LOTS OF KNOTS
IN A MASSED WINTER WHIRRING OF WINGS

WHERE	This adventure focuses on Fen Drayton Lakes in Cambridgeshire & Snettisham in Norfolk, but superflocks can be seen throughout Britain
WHEN	Autumn and winter
HOW LONG	Murmurations are unpredictable and may only last a few minutes – just before dusk for starlings, or when rising tides force knots from mudflats
WHO FOR	There's a lot of standing around on cold evenings waiting for things to happen, but children will love the drama
ADVENTURE POTENTIAL	Birdwatching
WILDLIFE WISHLIST	Starling murmurations & huge flocks of knot are your main targets, but also look out for migrant geese

W hen clouds gather over the reedbeds of RSPB Fen Drayton Lakes Reserve next to the River Great Ouse in Cambridgeshire, birdwatchers hold their breath in anticipation. These are no ordinary clouds. Pulsing, swirling and

↑ All of aflutter: starling murmuration at Shapwick Heath (Richard Evans/S)

wheeling against the fading light of dusk, they are created by birds – tens of thousands of starlings – massing in sinuous superflocks as they prepare to roost.

Some people compare the spectacle (known as a murmuration) to a vast shoal of fish, coursing one way, then another. It's almost as if a single force is controlling the movements of each individual – an invisible magnet drawn back and forth through a haze of iron filings.

Wrap yourselves up – starling murmurations take place during autumn and winter, but December is a prime month, with migrant birds doubling the UK population to 16 million. Some of the most transfixing displays are in clear, calm, cold conditions. Find a good spot (reedbeds and piers are favoured roost sites), aim to get there an hour or two before dusk, then wait for the show to begin.

Sometimes nothing much happens. Roosts are mobile and can change location from month to month, or the starlings may simply arrive in dribs and drabs, flying straight to their roost. Don't worry – you'll still have witnessed a rare moment of tranquility as twilight settles over a reedbed. But with luck, you'll witness a full-blown murmuration – the flock swelling in size until you can actually hear the purr of thousands of tiny wingbeats. Your children may be unable to suppress an urge to stretch out their arms and conduct the performance. And why not?! This is, after all, one of nature's most spellbinding shows. If anything is going to inspire a lifelong love of birds, this is it.

THE MYSTERY OF MURMURATIONS The reedbeds at Fen Drayton Lakes provide a safe overnight refuge from predators and harsh weather, but why starlings gather in such numbers is not fully understood. There's certainly safety in numbers – peregrine falcons, for example, find it hard to pick out one bird from a bewildering flock of thousands. The starlings may also be seeking communal warmth, or a chance to socialise. Some researchers have suggested that settling down for the night en masse provides an ideal opportunity to have a chatter about where all the best local feeding sites are, while others have observed starlings using roosts to reassert pecking orders.

Whatever the science behind the gatherings, the hypnotic aerial ballet can end abruptly as the starlings suddenly cascade into the reedbeds. There's usually a noisy period of avian gossip before the birds settle down for the night. Despite the mesmerising displays, however, the flocks are actually just a fraction of what they used to be. Starling numbers have crashed by 66% since the mid-1970s – cause for more than a murmur of concern.

WHEELING OVER THE WASH If the starlings at Fen Drayton prove compulsive viewing, there's a binge-worthy sequel to be enjoyed at another RSPB reserve, 90 minutes' drive north along the A10. During winter, throngs of wading birds mingle on the mudflats of The Wash at Snettisham – but when a spring tide inundates the worm-riddled ooze, the whole lot are put to flight. Imagine a superflock of 140,000 knot, peppered with oystercatcher and dunlin, streaming across the vast, uncluttered seascape of this tidal wilderness: a maritime murmuration on a massive scale.

Snettisham even has its very own rival blockbuster – 40,000 pink-footed geese stitching V-shaped skeins across the dawn-blushed skies of Norfolk as they head inland to feed for the day. Winter visitors from Iceland and Greenland, the geese might not murmurate, but the sight of a large flock lifting off – as one – from a saltmarsh or grazing pasture still ranks as one of Britain's most breathtaking natural spectacles.

↑ Knot at Snettisham: multiply by around 100,000 (Brian Kushner/S)

ACTION PLAN

ADVENTURE ESSENTIALS Clearly signposted off the A14, RSPB Fen Drayton Lakes Reserve (✆ 01954 233260 ⊘ rspb.org.uk) is located on Fen Drayton Road (♥ CB24 4RB). The Busway (⊘ thebusway.info) has a request stop here, while National Cycle Route 51 passes through the centre of the reserve. To reach RSPB Snettisham Reserve (✆ 01485 210779 ⊘ rspb.org.uk) follow the A149 Snettisham and Dersingham bypass and turn off at Beach Road (♥ PE31 7RA). Fen Drayton Lakes is just one of Britain's choice sites for witnessing a starling murmuration. Other RSPB reserves, such as Ham Wall (Somerset), Leighton Moss (Lancashire), Newport Wetlands (Gwent) and Strumpshaw Fen (Norfolk), can prove equally rewarding. Exe Reedbeds (Devon), Gretna Green (Dumfries & Galloway) and Teifi Marshes (Pembrokeshire) are also good locations. Even manmade structures, like West Pier at Brighton and Royal Pier at Aberystwyth, are magnets for mass roosts. Check out the Starling Murmuration Roost Map (⊘ starlingsintheuk.co.uk/roost-map) to find out where the action is.

MORE ADVENTURE A trip to witness the knot flocks at Snettisham combines well with a wildlife-themed tour of the North Norfolk coast. Around 10 minutes' drive north along the A149, you reach Hunstanton where Searles Sea Tours (✆ 01485 534444 ⊘ seatours.co.uk) run seal-watching boat trips. Nearby Brancaster Beach has miles of unspoilt sand, as well as an area of saltmarsh that's often teeming with winter waders. Head 20 minutes east to explore the coastal wilderness of Holkham National Nature Reserve before continuing to Blakeney Point (page 118).

ALSO CONSIDER Powys See *On the Trail of the Kite*, page 180; **Solway Firth** See *Wild Winter Goose Chase*, page 206; **Firth of Forth** See *Bass Rock Boat Trip*, page 228.

↑ Pink profusion: starling murmuration in Scotland (Keith K/S)

18 CANOEING ON THE BROADS

PADDLE THROUGH BRITAIN'S LARGEST WETLAND, EXPLORING HIDDEN CHANNELS RICH IN WILDLIFE

WHERE	Broads National Park, Norfolk & Suffolk
WHEN	With the right clothing you can canoe year round, but late spring & summer are best for birds, butterflies, dragonflies & damselflies
HOW LONG	Spend a day paddling or camp overnight
WHO FOR	All ages who are confident on the water; canoes are stable with room for one or two non-paddling children to sit in the middle
ADVENTURE POTENTIAL	Canoeing, camping, birdwatching
WILDLIFE WISHLIST	Otter, water vole, bittern, Cetti's warbler, crane, cuckoo, great crested grebe, kingfisher, marsh harrier, reed warbler, sedge warbler, azure damselfly, banded demoiselle, emperor dragonfly, Norfolk hawker, swallowtail butterfly

Paddle into a quiet backwater of the Norfolk Broads and you are in among the damselflies and dragonflies: electric blue and iridescent green, dancing and dipping above the thick mesh of water plants; some linked together mating, others quartering back and forth in search of prey. Reeds tower above you. In the narrower channels it feels like you're drifting into a whispering canyon. A puff of wind rustles the tightly packed stems, ruffling their feathery seed heads 2m or more above where you sit, hunkered down in your canoe. It's so peaceful that your ears fine-tune to the plop of a leaping fish, the distant churring of an unseen sedge warbler and the chuckle of water beneath your hull. A piping cry, a flash of turquoise and orange… your first kingfisher flies past, low and straight – a dazzling jewelled dart in this watery wilderness. It's a fleeting glimpse, unlike the marsh harrier that drifts lazily overhead; dark, broad wings flexing and twisting as the raptor effortlessly embraces the shifting breeze.

You imagine what lies beyond that wall of reed stems. It's all part of the adventure, the sense of exploration when you paddle a canoe through the Broads. This is Britain's wetland wonder – our mini-Okavango; a little piece of the Pantanal. You won't find hippos or caimans, but there's still that tingle of anticipation about what might lay around the next bend… Was that splash just a fish, or something more exciting? An otter perhaps?

GETTING AFLOAT Glance at a map of the Broads and you'll find a maze of channels, canals, lagoons, rivers and lakes. This vast network of waterways seeps across 300km² of Norfolk and Suffolk. So where do you choose to paddle? With seven rivers, 63 broads and around 200km of navigable waterways, the region seems awash with possibilities. For a family wildlife adventure, however, you want a quiet spot, away from the main pleasure-cruiser routes – somewhere

← Blazing paddles (William Gray)

where you're more likely to see wildlife and synch with the subtle rhythm of this extraordinary ecosystem.

Hickling Broad is ideal. A haven for wetland species, the National Nature Reserve is also less visited than other parts of the Broads. You can rent canoes and get afloat at the village of Hickling Heath on the broad itself, but we made for Martham Boats instead. Well off the beaten track (but offering canoe hire if you need it), this small boatyard on the River Thurne is located south of Hickling Broad, raising the tantalising prospect of a mini-expedition, navigating your way through a reedy labyrinth. We brought our own inflatable kayaks and paid a small fee to launch them.

Paddling briefly along the Thurne, we turned left into a winding channel leading to Duck Broad. Occasionally, a small motor boat or traditional wherry (with its distinctive gaff-rigged sail) would slip past – but otherwise we had the place to ourselves. A foray into Meadow Dyke enveloped us in dense reedbeds and provided our first sightings of marsh harriers and kingfishers. After an hour of easy paddling, the narrow channel opened into the wide, glittering expanse of Horsey Mere. We kayaked up to the five-storey windmill (the Horsey Windpump) that stands at its far end, before backtracking along Meadow Dyke and veering right to enter Hickling Broad.

WINGED WONDERS With no outboard engine putting wildlife to flight, exploring Hickling Broad by canoe is silent and stealthy. It also sits you just above the water level, providing a swan's eye perspective of the life around you. Stow your paddle, let yourself drift and glance down. Chances are you'll begin to notice some of the 13 species of dragonflies and damselflies that are found in the Broads National Park. Resting on reed stems with its wings spread open, a brown dragonfly with large green eyes could be a Norfolk hawker – look for the distinctive yellow triangular spot near the top of its abdomen. In flight, this rare species zips back and forth along dykes and ditches, snatching gnats, mosquitoes, butterflies and even smaller dragonflies. Vibrant blue and green, the more commonly sighted emperor dragonfly is another stealth hunter.

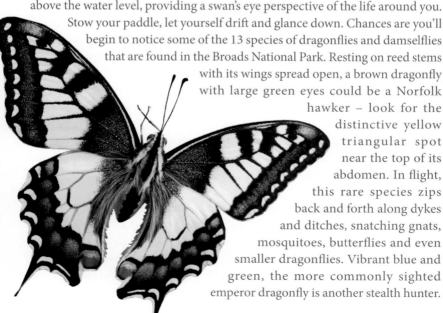

← Swallowtail (Luca Kikina/S)

The closely related damselflies rest with their wings closed, or partially folded, and are far daintier in flight. Look for azure damselflies flickering like blue sparks above the water surface, or banded demoiselles fluttering through the reeds – the metallic-green males flashing their distinctive dark wing patches to attract mates.

Hickling Broad is also one of the best places to spot swallowtails. Your eyes are not deceiving you: this beguiling butterfly really is a native species. Confined to the Norfolk Broads, it is Britain's sole representative of the Papilionidae family – over 560 species of brightly coloured butterflies that are more usually found fluttering through forests in the tropics. The strong-flying adults (with wingspans of 9cm) sip nectar from thistles, ragged robin and other fen-loving plants, while the caterpillars feed exclusively on milk parsley. Swallowtail butterflies emerge between late May and early July, with a second brood appearing in good years from late August to early September.

↑ Banded demoiselle (Marek Mierzejewski/S)

FLIGHTS OF FANCY Swallowtails are exotic and eye-catching but it's the kingfisher – dazzling in its electric-blue and orange plumage – that everyone wants to see. Listen for its shrill whistle, often repeated several times in flight. If you can quickly locate its source you stand a good chance of spotting the bird as it zips past, fast and low above the water. With luck, paddling quietly around the fringes of Hickling Broad, you might steal up on one, perched on an overhanging branch or reed stem, staring intently at the water. Kingfishers feed on small fish, like minnows and sticklebacks, or aquatic invertebrates, such as freshwater shrimps and dragonfly larvae. After plunge-diving on a victim, the bird returns to its perch, knocking the prey senseless against the stem before swallowing it. Kingfishers nest in burrows (up to 90cm long) that they excavate in steep, sandy banks – something you're more likely to find along rivers than reed-fringed broads, which explains why this bejewelled bird is not as common at Hickling as you might expect.

One species you'll almost certainly see, however, is the marsh harrier. Easily recognised by its light, almost butterfly-like flight, with wings held aloft in a shallow V-shape, this graceful raptor can often be spotted drifting slowly above the reedbeds, hunting frogs, small mammals and waterbirds. During the breeding season, you might witness the marsh harrier's sensational 'sky dance'. Males

(paler than the chocolate-brown females and with distinctive black wingtips) climb high into the sky before swooping towards the ground and performing a series of tumbles. Sometimes the female will fly up and lock talons with him in a mesmerising display of avian acrobatics. Don't be disappointed if the harriers aren't in the mood for courtship – just to catch a fleeting glimpse of this bird is enough to make your heart soar. In 1971, after years of persecution and habitat loss, only one nesting female remained in the whole country. To see one of the 400 pairs nesting in the UK today is a real privilege.

Another conservation success story in the Norfolk Broads, the common crane was once widespread across East Anglia, but died out during the 17th century as hunting and wetland drainage took their toll. Since 1979, however, a small breeding population has been nurtured and it's possible, once again, to spot this flamboyant, 1.2m-tall bird gracing the marshes and wet grasslands.

Winter is the best time to see cranes at Hickling Broad when up to 30 individuals, along with similar numbers of marsh harrier and even a few hen harrier and merlin, gather to roost at Stubb Mill. A viewing platform overlooking the roost can be accessed from the visitor centre at Hickling Broad National Nature Reserve. Located on the northern edge of the broad, this superb site also has several trails and boardwalks leading to hides and an observation tower.

↑ Kingfisher (Martin Bouwhuis/S)

PADDLING AND PITCHING It's a full day's paddling to Hickling Broad and back. We hauled out on grassy banks or islands of stunted oak, birch and willow to stretch our legs and have a picnic. By the time we returned to Duck Broad and the boatyard on the River Thurne, the sun was laying a tangerine path across the water; common terns were making their final fishing forays, while squadrons of cormorants and skeins of geese swept overhead to roost. As we dragged our kayaks up the slipway, there was a brief murmuration in a nearby reedbed as starlings settled down for the night.

You can combine your canoe adventure with an overnight camp near Hickling Heath at the northwest tip of Hickling Broad. The campsite is about 1.5km away, so you would need to drive to the waterside village to launch your canoes.

For a more straightforward canoe-camping option, Salhouse Broad, near Wroxham, has a campsite right at the water's edge. After hiring a canoe here, you can explore the Wherry Cut, an abandoned channel of water off the main broad, before paddling along the River Bure to Horning. Allow three hours for the return trip and be prepared for this stretch of river to be busy during summer. With a full day, you could push on to the mooring and café at Malthouse Broad. From there, a boardwalk probes a tangle of flooded 'carr' woodland (Norfolk's very own Everglades) before delving into the dense reedbeds of Ranworth Broad. After a short stroll (keeping your eyes peeled for swallowtail butterflies) you reach a floating visitor centre packed to the rafters with hands-on activities for children. Catch a water taxi back to Malthouse Broad before canoeing back to camp.

↑ Dusk on the River Thurne (William Gray)

ACTION PLAN

ADVENTURE ESSENTIALS Hickling and Ranworth Broad are managed by the Norfolk Wildlife Trust (☏ 01603 625540 ☌ norfolkwildlifetrust.org.uk). Visitor centres at both locations are open daily March–October. Hickling Broad is 4km south of Stalham off the A149, while Ranworth Broad is 3km west of Acle. Visit the Broads (☌ visitthebroads.co.uk) works with the Norfolk Broads Authority (☏ 01603 610734 ☌ www.broads-authority.gov.uk) to manage the national park. For Hickling Broad, you can rent Canadian canoes at Martham Boats (☏ 01493 740249 ☌ marthamboats. com) located off Cess Road (📍 NR29 4RF) on the River Thurne, or at Whispering Reeds Boats (☏ 01692 598314 ☌ whisperingreeds.net) at Staithe Road, Hickling (📍 NR12 0YW). For paddling adventures along the River Bure to Horning and Ranworth Broad, you can hire canoes at Salhouse Broad (☏ 01603 722775 ☌ salhousebroad.org.uk). Park on Lower Street, Salhouse (📍 NR13 6RX) and walk through the village to the broad. You can also catch a bus from Wroxham or the train from Norwich. It's possible to launch your own canoe – a small fee is payable locally and you will need to obtain a Short Visit Toll permit from the Norfolk Broads Authority.

Barely a kilometre from Whispering Reeds (see above), Hickling Campsite (Heath Road, Hickling 📍 NR12 0AU ☏ 07811 440280 ☌ hicklingcampsite.co.uk) offers generous pitches, toilets and showers, plus shepherd's huts and a pod for rent. Camping at Salhouse Broad (see above) is more basic with chemical toilets and a drinking water standpipe.

MORE ADVENTURE The Canoe Man (☏ 07873 748408 ☌ thecanoeman. com) offers guided canoeing adventures in the Norfolk Broads (including day trips and overnight camping), as well as 'Swallows and Amazons' days combining canoeing and bushcraft. Norfolk Wildlife Trust (see above) offers guided wildlife boat tours, exploring the backwaters of both Hickling and Ranworth Broad.

ALSO CONSIDER **South Cornwall** See *River Fowey Adventure*, page 36; **Herefordshire** See *A Paddle along the River Wye*, page 102; **Moidart** See *On the Trail of the Otter*, page 256; **Moidart** See *Sea Kayaking in Arisaig*, page 262; **Isle of Skye** See *Hike and Kayak on Skye*, page 270.

↑ Marsh harrier (William Gray)

19 SEAL SPOTTING IN NORFOLK

TAKE A BOAT TRIP TO BLAKENEY POINT, HOME TO ENGLAND'S LARGEST GREY SEAL COLONY

WHERE	Blakeney Point, North Norfolk Coast
WHEN	Boat trips operate daily Apr–Oct, plus regular departures throughout winter; grey seals pup Nov–Dec, harbour seals pup Jun–Aug
HOW LONG	Boat trips last roughly an hour
WHO FOR	All ages; a gentle adventure in small, open boats
ADVENTURE POTENTIAL	Boat trips, beach walks, birdwatching
WILDLIFE WISHLIST	Grey & harbour seal, summer terns (Arctic, sandwich, common & little), oystercatcher, ringed plover, winter wildfowl (brent goose, teal, pintail & wigeon)

With their large, round eyes, soft fur and helpless expressions, few animals are more appealing to children than grey seal pups. They'll love you for taking them to see dozens of the endearing little fuzz-balls at Blakeney Point – the largest breeding grey seal colony in England. Open boats chug out to the end of the 6km-long spit of sand and shingle from Morston Quay. The seals see

↑ Grey seals frolic in the shallows at Blakeney Point (William Gray)

you coming. Naturally inquisitive, one or two will almost certainly surface near your boat, long before you reach the main haul-out and realise that the beach is littered with sausage-shaped bundles of fluff and blubber. Look closely and, depending on the time of year, you'll see cream-coloured pups lying among the darker, speckled adults.

Grey seals didn't start breeding here until the late 1980s, but now over 3,000 pups are born each winter. What's so special about Blakeney Point? Conservationists believe it gets a seal of approval due to its remote location and the sheltered, gently sloping beach (on rocky shores, seal pups are easily washed away in storms).

It's not only grey seals that breed here. Harbour (or common) seals give birth during summer. At any time of year, you can see both species and one of the best ways to tell them apart is by peering at their noses – grey seal nostrils are like parallel lines, while harbour seals have V-shaped nostrils that meet at the bottom. As well as being larger overall, grey seals also tend to have a flatter head than harbour seals, and longer, more pronounced 'Roman' noses.

Blakeney Point is also an internationally important nesting site for four species of tern – Arctic, common, little and sandwich. Spot them hovering over the sea, diving on small fish, then flying back to feed their partners or chicks at the shallow scrapes they've excavated in the shingle bank. Other summer nesting birds include oystercatchers and ringed plovers, while October sees the arrival of winter visitors like brent geese.

HORSEY SEALS About an hour's drive southeast along the coast, Horsey hosts another large colony of grey seals. Be sure to remain behind the roped-off path in the dunes to avoid disturbing the seals on the beach below – and keep dogs on short leads. To find out more about responsible seal watching, visit Friends of Horsey Seals (⊘ friendsofhorseyseals.co.uk) Following birth, grey seal pups suckle for around three weeks, before spending another few weeks shedding their fluffy white coats and replacing it with something more waterproof that allows them to venture safely into the sea. This is why you can see grey seals and their white pups at places like Blakeney Point and Horsey for several months over winter. Harbour seal pups are far less dependent. They can swim and dive within a few hours of birth, which explains why this species can breed on tidal sandbanks that are only uncovered for a short part of the day.

PUP RESCUE If you think you've found an abandoned seal pup, do not approach it – you could easily scare it back into the sea and cause more harm than good. If the pup looks healthy (fat and with no visible neck, like a furry maggot), monitor it from a safe distance for 24 hours – seal pups are weaned at three to four weeks old and may not have been abandoned. If, however, you think the pup is injured or distressed, contact the RSPCA (⊘ 0300 1234 999) or Norfolk's Seal and Shore Watch (⊘ 07498 597448).

↑ **Top:** Arctic tern; **above:** grey seal pup at Blakeney Point (William Gray; Kieran Am/S)

ACTION PLAN

ADVENTURE ESSENTIALS Blakeney Point is part of the Blakeney National Nature Reserve managed by the National Trust (⌂ nationaltrust.org.uk) and is accessed by boat trips from Morston Quay (♀ NR25 7BH, off the A149 Cromer to Hunstanton road). The Coast Hopper bus stops in Morston village, a five-minute walk to the quay. Don't try to walk to see the seals at Blakeney Point. Seal-watching boat trips are available with Beans Boats (✆ 01263 740505 ⌂ beansboattrips.co.uk), Bishop's Boats (✆ 01263 740753 ⌂ bishopsboats.co.uk), Ptarmigan Seal Trips (✆ 01263 740792 ⌂ blakeneypointsealtrips.co.uk) and Temples (✆ 01263 740791 ⌂ sealtrips.co.uk). Lasting around an hour, some trips spend an additional 30–60 minutes landing on Blakeney Point where you can walk to bird hides and the old lifeboat station. Most trips operate in traditional clinker-built boats with little protection from the elements, so remember to take warm, weatherproof clothing – and don't forget binoculars for birdwatching.

MORE ADVENTURE Both the Norfolk Coast Path and cycle route NCN30 run along this section of coast, so you could include a seal watching trip in a cycling or walking weekend. Alternatively, make it part of a Norfolk wildlife odyssey, touring nearby nature reserves like Cley Marshes and Holkham.

ALSO CONSIDER Isles of Scilly See *Island-Hopping Adventure*, page 20; **Northumberland** See *Farne Islands Boat Trip*, page 156; **Pembrokeshire** See *On the Trail of the Puffin*, page 170; **Isle of Shuna** See *Hebridean Island Escape*, page 238.

↑ Wrap up warm for a Blakeney Point boat trip during winter (William Gray)

20 BIKE GLAMPING IN THE PEAK DISTRICT

CYCLE BACKROADS AND TRAILS THROUGH THE FLOWER MEADOWS OF THE DERBYSHIRE DALES

WHERE	Peak District National Park, Derbyshire
WHEN	Easter holidays to October half-term
HOW LONG	Allow two full days with a night's glamping
WHO FOR	Trips are tailor-made to suit your experience & how far you want to cycle
ADVENTURE POTENTIAL	Mountain biking, glamping, butterfly spotting
WILDLIFE WISHLIST	Buzzard, kestrel, little owl, skylark, yellowhammer, butterflies (including common blue, dark-green fritillary & small skipper), moths, grasshoppers & bush-crickets

↑ Easy riding: many of the trails follow former railway lines (William Gray)

Pete and Alice McNeil know a thing or two about cycle touring – they pedalled 20,000km from Britain to New Zealand on their honeymoon. Since returning home, their passion for two-wheeled travel has been channelled through Adventure Pedlars, inspiring others to set out on their own free-spirited journeys. Most children love cycling, but this adventure transforms the humble bicycle into a full-blown expedition machine. Although Adventure Pedlars offer more basic and challenging bike-packing trips, the bike glamping option will appeal to most families. Your self-guided route is tailor-made to suit your experience, the ages of your children and how far you want to ride. Bikes, luggage and gear

(including an easy-to-follow GPS gizmo) are all included – you just need to turn up with sleeping bags, spare clothes and cycling helmets. Accommodation is in a luxury bell tent, with camp beds, cooker and a hamper full of local produce.

GETTING KITTED OUT Our weekend bike glamping through the Derbyshire Dales in the southern tip of the Peak District National Park began – and ended – in Ashbourne. By the time we arrived at the pre-arranged meeting point, Pete had our bikes ready and was brewing fresh coffee over a camp stove for our briefing.

Just as you'd expect, the mountain bikes were lightweight with chunky tyres and plenty of gears, but what set them apart was the array of storage devices cleverly attached to their frames. We stuffed our sleeping bags into a dry sack attached to the handlebars; spare clothes and other overnight items were cajoled into another dry bag behind the saddle, while two additional storage pouches had space for a pump, puncture repair kit, mobile phone, sun cream, waterproofs and snacks. There was still room left for two water bottles, while the GPS unit – with our 65km route for the weekend – simply clipped on to the handlebars.

↑ **Clockwise from top left:** summer meadows teem with insects, including common blue and small skipper butterflies, Roesel's bush-cricket and field grasshopper (William Gray)

↑ Cycling the High Peaks Trail (William Gray)

UP HILL AND DOWN DALE To start with, we followed the Tissington Trail…
easy riding along the gentle incline of a former railway line that once supplied
milk to London and limestone to nearby industrial centres. The trail was created
after the railway closed in 1967 and now offers a 21km cycling or walking route
between Ashbourne and Parsley Hay. But our cycling adventure promised more
than a pilgrimage to Victorian engineering prowess.

As we pedalled north, shady woodland gave way to the open, rolling hills of the
Derbyshire Dales; cuttings in the old railroad became streaked with the pink and
white-speckled spires of common spotted orchids, rising through a colourful tangle
of bird's-foot trefoil, cranesbill, harebell, lesser knapweed and scabious. Whenever
we stopped for a break, or to admire the views, the air was filled with a rapid
ticking sound – not unlike a freewheeling bicycle – as grasshoppers stridulated,
unseen, in the trailside meadows. Yellowhammers called from the hedgerows,
their song once rendered by Enid Blyton as 'a-little-bit-of-bread-and-no-cheese'
– stuttering at first, then drawn out into a long, thin, final note. Along with the
liquid warbling song of skylarks and the scratchy percussion of grasshoppers,

↑ Adventure Pedlars' glamping site in Middleton (William Gray)

it formed a treasured soundtrack to Britain's bygone countryside – an uplifting chorus that took you back 50 years to a time when intensive farming practices were yet to take their toll on many of our best-loved countryside species.

The limestone grasslands, hay meadows and flower-rich roadside verges of the Peak District breathe life into the rural landscape, but some of the best places to discover its wildlife are the abandoned, rewilded quarries that have since become local nature reserves.

INSECT LIFE CYCLES After bearing right from the Tissington Trail at Biggin, and cycling along gravelled drovers' tracks through gently undulating fields, we joined the High Peak Trail – originally one of the world's first railway lines, built in the 1820s to link the Peak Forest and Cromford canals. Minninglow loomed ahead, its hilltop ring of beech trees concealing a Neolithic burial chamber and Bronze Age barrows, but we had our sights set on other treasures.

A few kilometres further, we chained our bikes to a gate and walked down a half-hidden path to Hoe Grange Quarry Nature Reserve (♥ DE4 4HX ✐ 01773 881188 ∂ derbyshirewildlifetrust.org.uk). Well off the beaten track and easily overlooked, what was once a dusty limestone quarry is now a flower-swathed hollow, flickering with insects. Managed jointly by Butterfly Conservation and the Derbyshire Wildlife Trust, the scars of extraction have been fuzzed over by 156 species of plants, many of which provide food for the reserve's kaleidoscope of butterflies. Walk slowly and get down on your hands and knees, careful not to flatten the flowers, and you'll spot common blues – the males with striking, metallic blue upper wings, and both sexes sporting delicately patterned silvery-brown underwings, woven with orange and black spots. Their caterpillars feed on the yellow, slipper-shaped flowers of bird's-foot trefoil. Harder to track down, small skippers are flighty, orange-brown butterflies which, at first glance, resemble moths when they're actively feeding. Once you get your eye in, you could tick off 29 butterfly species at Hoe Grange, including brown argus, dark-green fritillary and holly blue. Visit at dusk and you'll be in moth heaven – the quarry is home to the exotic-looking wood tiger, its wings splodged with chocolate-brown and cream – and the grey, ghostly chalk carpet which rests by day, perfectly camouflaged on mottled patches of limestone.

During the heat of a midsummer's day, rocks and boulders are good places to search for grasshoppers. Both roughly 2cm in length, the species you're most likely to find are the green meadow grasshopper and brown field grasshopper – the latter

↑ Soundtrack of the Derbyshire Dales: skylark singing in flight (Gallinago Media/S)

often sporting a flash of orange on the top of its abdomen. While grasshoppers generally prefer rough, dry grass, the closely related bush-crickets lurk in dense, longer grass. An easy way to tell them apart is to look at their antennae – short and thick in grasshoppers, long and wispy in bush-crickets.

The profusion of insect life at Hoe Grange doesn't go unnoticed – little owls can be seen hunting at dawn and dusk, dropping from a favourite perch on to an unsuspecting grasshopper or beetle. By contrast, kestrels are masters of aerial hunting, often seen hovering above fields and roadside verges in the Peak District. Although it certainly helps them to detect the movement of potential prey in the grasses below, it's now known that hovering kestrels are just as likely to be looking for the urine trails of voles – telltale traces that fluoresce and catch the raptor's eye.

COMPLETING THE LOOP If you still have the energy after a day's cycling, there's plenty of wildlife to spot at Adventure Pedlars' glamping meadow in Middleton. Sitting in deck chairs around the campfire, you might spot treecreepers or woodpeckers in the surrounding woodland, or buzzards pirouetting over the distant crags of the Black Rocks.

The following morning, saddle-sore but well-rested, our return route to Ashbourne took us west along the shores of Carsington Water. The reservoir is a magnet to autumn migrants, with anything from golden plovers to great northern divers dropping by. During summer, however, the sparkling expanse of water is more likely to be dotted with great crested grebes, tufted ducks and mute swans. Head to the Visitor Centre's RSPB shop (♀ DE6 1ST ✆ 01629 541842 ✆ rspb.org.uk) for tips on where to spot kingfishers.

From Carsington, we pedalled back into the hills, rejoining the Tissington Trail before coasting back to Ashbourne – fresh converts to the free-spirited world of bike glamping. Pete was waiting to meet us; we handed back the bikes and drove home – the countryside passing in a blur, strangely silent and detached.

↑ **Above left:** male kestrel; **above right:** little owl (William Gray; Rudmer Zwerver/S)

ACTION PLAN

ADVENTURE ESSENTIALS Based in the village of Middleton, about halfway between Carsington Water and Matlock in the Derbyshire Dales, Adventure Pedlars (✆ 07960 991254 ⌚ adventurepedlars.com) offer a range of cycling escapes in the Peak District National Park. Two-day, tailor-made bike glamping adventures include a night in a luxury bell tent (pitched in a private meadow with camp toilet and shower), dinner, breakfast and treats, all bike, luggage and camping equipment (including camp beds, pillows and towels), expert tuition in preparation for your ride, plus a bespoke GPS route for you to follow. As well as waterproofs, cycle helmet and a change of clothes, you need to bring your own sleeping bag. No previous off-road cycling or mountain biking experience is required – Adventure Pedlars track your progress and are always on hand to offer assistance if you need it. The 21km Tissington Trail and 28km High Peak Trail are part of the recreational network of former railway lines managed by the Peak District National Park (✆ 01629 816200 ⌚ peakdistrict.gov.uk). Visitor centres are located in Bakewell (◉ DE45 1DS), Castleton (◉ S33 8WN), Edale (◉ S33 7ZA) and Upper Derwent (◉ S33 0AQ).

MORE ADVENTURE If you prefer two feet to two wheels, Natural Derbyshire Tours (✆ 07989 218860 ⌚ naturalderbyshiretours.uk) offer a range of expert-led wildlife walks in Derbyshire and the Peak District. Full-day options from April to July include High Peak in search of iconic moorland species, such as mountain hare, meadow pipit, merlin, peregrine, red grouse, ring ouzel and whinchat. Dippers, redstarts and various warblers are the focus for spring and summer walks in the limestone dales of White Peak, while rutting red deer take centre-stage during September and October on the Eastern Moors. Shorter walks are also available in search of everything from swifts to water voles.

ALSO CONSIDER Devon See *Exmoor Pony Trek*, page 52; **Yorkshire** See *Yorkshire Moors by Rail and Bike*, page 140; **Inner Hebrides** See *Isle of Islay Adventure*, page 246.

↑ Off-road cycling towards the tree-topped hill of Minninglow (William Gray)

21 MOTORWAY STOP SAFARI

TAKE A WILD DIVERSION WHEN YOU NEED A BREAK FROM DRIVING AND DISCOVER NATURE'S SERVICES

WHERE	This mini-adventure focuses on two options for breaking a long journey on the M6 at either Wreay Woods Nature Reserve in Cumbria or Brockholes Nature Reserve in Lancashire.
WHEN	Year-round
HOW LONG	This depends on your travel schedule, but try to allow at least a couple of hours
WHO FOR	Any age
ADVENTURE POTENTIAL	Birdwatching, woodland walks, pond dipping
WILDLIFE WISHLIST	Brown hare, otter, roe deer, bittern, buzzard, dipper, great crested grebe, grey wagtail, hobby, kestrel, kingfisher, lapwing, sand martin & swift, plus various butterflies & dragonflies

This family wildlife adventure is really an add-on to any of the others in this book. Although it delves into two small nature reserves off the M6 in northwest England, it works just as well for breaking any long journey you might need to take. It's simply a case of finding the right kind of motorway stop. Of course, if you need to refuel or check your tyre pressure, then a service station is going to be more useful than an ancient woodland. And while one or two motorway-side nature reserves have a visitor centre with restaurant and toilets, most will only have a small parking area and, if you're lucky, a picnic table.

Why not simply stretch your legs at the next motorway services? Well, you'd be amazed at how many easily accessible wildlife hotspots you whizz past on Britain's motorways. The Wildlife Trusts manage over 2,000 nature reserves and, although many require a long detour from the nearest motorway, there are plenty just a short drive away.

Take the M6, for example. You're driving northbound between Manchester and Preston. You've already been on the road for hours and there are ominous signs of a backseat revolt. The question is: do you nip into Charnock Richard Welcome Break, breathe a sigh of relief and succumb to Starbucks and a Burger King? Or do you push on for another 15km and come off at Junction 31 where Brockholes Nature Reserve (♥ PR5 0AG ✆ 01772 872000 ⌂ brockholes.org) offers 100 hectares of wetland, a floating visitor centre and lakeside café?

BROCKHOLES THROUGH THE SEASONS It's almost inconceivable that this mosaic of reed-fringed lagoons, marsh and woodland was once a dusty quarry, supplying sand and gravel for building the M6. Since 2007, the Lancashire Wildlife Trust has performed a rewilding miracle. Well over 200 different types of bird have been recorded, and each year the number edges upwards as more species discover the reserve's potential for nesting or overwintering.

← M6 escape route: Wreay Woods Nature Reserve (William Gray)

Stop by in spring and you can use one of Brockhole's hides to spy on nesting lapwing, oystercatcher, redshank and snipe on Boilton Marsh, where 17,000m³ of quarry spoil has been remodelled to create a wetland paradise for waders. Over on Number 1 Pit – a shimmering lake where once there was a gravel pit – look for great crested grebe and diving ducks. Around its edges, reedbeds twitch with buntings and warblers. Floating rafts have been installed to attract nesting terns, and there's also an artificial sand martin wall. On the adjacent Meadow Lake, a platform has been erected to tempt transient ospreys to nest.

During summer, escape your stuffy car – even for just half an hour – to stand on the deck of Brockhole's floating visitor centre to watch swifts, martins and swallows twist and turn above the lake catching insects. Occasionally, a dragon-hunter joins them. Summer visitors to Britain, the hobby uses its rapier wings and aerial skills to outwit dragonflies and damselflies, snatching them mid-air in mustard-yellow talons. Come winter and the dashing little falcon (with its peregrine-like mask and distinctive rufous breeches) is long gone, back to Africa. But migrant waders take its place. Keep your eyes peeled and you may even spot an overwintering bittern, tiptoeing through the reeds.

WREAY WOODS NATURAL SERVICES Not all motorway stop safaris have to be rewarded with a long list of wildlife sightings. Simply getting out of the fast lane on to a woodland path and re-tuning your senses to nature can do wonders for traffic-shredded nerves or fractious children.

About 137km north of Brockholes, Wreay Woods Nature Reserve (♀ CA4 0BT ✆ 01228 829570 ♂ cumbriawildlifetrust.org.uk) is located just off Junction 42 of the M6. Take the exit to Dalston off the motorway roundabout, then (after a few hundred metres) bear left into a small parking area. As you bundle out of the car, ask your children what they can hear. Lorries? Cars? The constant roar of traffic? Certainly not much else.

A footpath passes under the motorway before entering a grassy glade, framed by wooded slopes to your left and the shallow River Petteril to the right. After less than 2km, the path burrows into woodland as you enter the nature reserve. Ask the kids what they can hear now. A chuckling river? The rustle of leaves? Stop for a moment and you'll also hear birds – wrens, dunnocks and great tits chattering in the leafy shadows of oak and birch. You might even be lucky enough to hear the short, sharp whistles of a kingfisher and glimpse the bird flashing by in a streak of blue. Sit quietly by the river and you may well see grey wagtail poking about in mossy pebbles, or dipper hunting caddisfly larvae in the tea-coloured shallows. Occasionally otters are seen here. It's hard to imagine that only an hour ago you were bored out of your mind on the M6, and now you're in a secret wood surrounded by nuthatches, jays, roe deer and red squirrels.

ACTION PLAN

ADVENTURE ESSENTIALS There's a small fee for parking at Brockholes, but entry to the reserve is free. As well as family-friendly bird hides, walking trails, a play area and programme of nature activities, you'll find the impressive floating Visitor Village complete with wildlife-themed gift shop and the Kestrel Kitchen restaurant. Wreay Woods Nature Reserve has no facilities.

MORE ADVENTURE Plan your own motorway stop safari by searching the map at ⊘ wildlifetrusts.org/nature-reserves. Located just 8km from junction 25 of the M1, the Attenborough Nature Reserve (♀ NG9 6DY ✆ 0115 972 1777 ⊘ nottinghamshirewildlife. org) sprawls over 205 hectares of lake, reedbed, grassland and woodland next to the River Trent. As well as a visitor centre with a lakeside café and shop, the reserve offers activities for children, such as pond dipping and nature art, while teenagers can help out with conservation management. Several trails wind through the reserve, leading to hides where you can spot a wide range of birds, including bittern, Cetti's warbler, kingfisher, sand martin, water rail and various ducks and waders. A short drive from junction 13 or 14 of the M5, Slimbridge Wetland Centre (♀ GL2 7BT ✆ 01453 891900 ⊘ wwt.org.uk) is another excellent option for a wildlife-themed motorway stop. Several National Trust properties (⊘ nationaltrust.org.uk) are also worth considering.

ALSO CONSIDER **Essex** See *Wetland Wonders Adventure*, page 92; **Scottish Borders** See *Tree Climbing Adventure*, page 218.

↑ Master of disguise: a bittern in the reeds (Mati Kose/S)

22 ON THE TRAIL OF THE RED SQUIRREL

SPOT BRITAIN'S NATIVE SPECIES OF SQUIRREL IN THE WOODLANDS OF THE YORKSHIRE DALES

WHERE	Yorkshire Dales National Park
WHEN	Year-round
HOW LONG	The Snaizeholme Red Squirrel Trail can be completed in a few hours, but allow at least a full day to explore other areas as well
WHO FOR	All ages, as long as they can stay quiet & patient!
ADVENTURE POTENTIAL	Squirrel tracking, birdwatching, hiking
WILDLIFE WISHLIST	Red squirrel, roe deer, chiffchaff, coal tit, great spotted woodpecker, nuthatch, spotted flycatcher, treecreeper

↑ Bright-eyed and bushy-tailed – red squirrels also have distinctive ear tufts (William Gray)

S low down! Red Squirrels. You see the road warning signs everywhere in the Yorkshire Dales, but how do you actually go about spotting Britain's native nutkins? Snaizeholme in the northwestern corner of the national park is one of 17 red squirrel refuges in northern England where woodlands are managed to stem the decline of this increasingly rare and elusive species.

Following the introduction of the North American grey squirrel in the 1800s, the smaller red squirrel – a flash of auburn fur in our forests for some 10,000 years – has retreated north, unable to compete with its larger, more robust cousin. Today, greys outnumber reds in the UK by 2½ million to 140,000. Once widespread, only isolated populations of red squirrels exist south of Scotland, clinging on in places like Anglesey, the Isle of Wight and Kielder Forest. The Yorkshire Dales contingent survives on the 'frontline' between the reds and greys. Pockets of forest west of Hawes and north of Kirkby Lonsdale provide isolation from grey squirrels, which are not only twice the size of reds, but are also more efficient at digesting seeds with a high tannin content, such as acorns. Grey squirrels can also transmit a squirrelpox virus – deadly if passed on to reds.

THE RED SQUIRREL TRAIL When Hugh and Jane Kemp moved to Mirk Pot Farm over 40 years ago, their plan to grow Christmas trees in the Snaizeholme valley was a gift for red squirrels. As the conifers matured, the squirrels took advantage of the new habitat and abundant food supply. The Kemps now manage the woodland specifically for the russet rodents and have worked with the Yorkshire Dales National Park Authority to create a walking trail and viewing area.

You may well spot your first red squirrel nibbling a nut from the feeder on the farm's gatepost. The circular 4km trail starts by descending steeply through shady forest, scattered with fallen limbs and mossy stumps, before emerging into the open where stepping stones cross a swathe of marshy ground. A few hundred metres ahead lies the squirrel viewing area, but take your time – the drystone wall on your right is used as a highway for squirrels to move from one patch of forest to another. Crouch down on the stepping stones and wait quietly... with patience you might be rewarded with the unforgettable sight of a red squirrel bounding along the stony parapet straight towards you. Out in the open, their fur catches the light and you can watch them leaping gaps in the wall.

After following the stepping stones into the next area of forest, the viewing area is nearby. Logs have been strung between trees to create an arboreal walkway to a feeder that's regularly filled with a mixture of nuts and seeds. Again, patience is key. You also need eyes in the back of your head, as the squirrels are just as likely to appear behind you, foraging among the ferns and tree stumps. Finches and tits flit through the forest and you may see a nuthatch or great spotted woodpecker raiding the feeder.

"Crouch down on the stepping stones and wait quietly... with patience you might be rewarded with the unforgettable sight of a red squirrel bounding along the stony parapet straight towards you"

↑ Rocky road – a red squirrel uses a drystone wall as a highway (William Gray)

HOW TO BECOME A SQUIRREL DETECTIVE Now that you've followed the Snaizeholme Red Squirrel Trail and learnt a bit about their habitat and behaviour, it's time to put your newfound squirrel tracking skills to the test by seeking them out in other parts of the Yorkshire Dales.

Mixed broadleaf and conifer woodland provides a year-round supply of food: wych elm seeds and beech mast in late spring, acorns and hazelnuts in autumn; pine seeds (and other stashed food) in winter. Check stumps for hazelnuts split in half, or pine cones that have been stripped to their core – a sure sign that squirrels are about.

We followed the A684 between Hawes and Sedburgh and found a promising patch of woodland just beyond Garsdale where Blea Gill meets the Clough River. Download the What3Words app (⊘ what3words.com) and you can find the precise spot by entering the unique combination of ⧄ solicitor.baker.couple. Using the car as a hide, we spotted our first squirrel running along the roadside wall before leaping into a sycamore growing by the river. On closer inspection, we discovered that the moss on the wall had been flattened and worn smooth by the tiny patter of red furry paws.

Walking into the woodland, the canopy drew a thick green veil overhead. We tried listening for the squirrels' distinctive chattering, but it was the sudden movement of a branch (on a windless day) that focused our gaze on a lone individual, high in a wych elm, plucking the tree's paper-thin seeds.

During times of plenty, red squirrels will hoard food by burying nuts and seeds in the ground, so remember to scan the woodland floor for signs of activity. Their dreys, meanwhile, are constructed high in trees – a football-sized nest of twigs and bark strips, lined with leaves and moss. Red squirrels don't hibernate, so you can see them year-round. Mating chases begin in January, with the first litter of three or four kittens born in March. The young begin to venture from the maternal drey at about seven weeks old. If there is enough food available, the female may have a second litter in July.

ACTION PLAN

ADVENTURE ESSENTIALS The Snaizeholme Red Squirrel Trail can be reached by following the B6255 about 4.5km west from Hawes, but don't just turn up – you need to either prebook one of the two parking spaces at Mirk Pot Farm or purchase a ticket from the Little White Bus Company, which runs from the Dales Countryside Museum in Hawes to the start of the trail. Both can be arranged through the Hawes National Park Centre (♥ DL8 3NT ✆ 01969 666210 ♂ yorkshiredales.org.uk) which will give you detailed instructions for finding Mirk Pot Farm if you're driving there. Allow around 40 minutes to reach the squirrel viewing area. The route includes a couple of steep sections and can be muddy in places. Remember to take midge repellant and binoculars, but don't be tempted to bring food for the squirrels. If you're serious about snapping red squirrels, Paul Fowlie Photography (♂ paulfowliephotography.co.uk) operates a dedicated hide near Hawes. It takes away the thrill of tracking them on your own, but it's a reliable, if pricey, option for getting close-up views and pictures.

MORE ADVENTURE Buckden Farm Campsite (♥ BD23 5JA ✆ 07786 896985 ♂ buckdencamping.co.uk) might not be in the Yorkshire Dales' red squirrel hotspot, but it makes an excellent base for exploring the national park's spectacular Wharfedale Valley. Located on a working farm owned by the National Trust, the campsite lies at the hub of numerous walking trails, including a 10km jaunt to Cray (renowned for its petal-packed meadows of buttercups, cranesbill, daisies, knapweed, ragged robin and orchids), returning to Buckden via a riverside track. As well as tent pitches, the campsite offers pods sleeping up to five people.

ALSO CONSIDER Isle of Wight See *Island Campervan Safari*, page 70; **Dumfries & Galloway** See *Seeing Red in Galloway*, page 210; **Moidart** See *On the Trail of the Otter*, page 256; **Scottish Highlands** See *Cairngorms Wilderness Adventure*, page 276.

Left: stripped fir cones; **above:** red squirrel feeding on wych elm seeds; Wharfedale Valley (William Gray)

23 YORKSHIRE MOORS BY RAIL AND BIKE

EXPLORE THE ESK VALLEY: TRAIN ONE WAY, CYCLE THE OTHER, WITH BIRDWATCHING INBETWEEN

WHERE	North York Moors National Park, Yorkshire
WHEN	Summer is best: the weather is kinder & the heather flowers late Jul–Sep, but a spring or autumn visit can also be rewarding
HOW LONG	A weekend at least, but you could easily fill a week
WHO FOR	Any age: simply adapt the cycling & walking parts of the adventure to suit your children
ADVENTURE POTENTIAL	Rail journey, cycling, hiking & birdwatching on the moors with bushcraft & nocturnal wildlife spotting in the forest
WILDLIFE WISHLIST	Iconic moorland birds (curlew, golden plover, lapwing, merlin & red grouse), plus badger, tawny owl & other forest species

One of Britain's most varied national parks, the North York Moors has over 44,000 hectares of heather-blushed heathland, but this is only one-third of an intricate tapestry that also includes secluded dales, tumbling streams and shady woodland. Consisting of two parts, this wildlife adventure takes you on an

↑ Pretty in pink: swathes of heather on the North York Moors (Helen Hotson/S)

exploration of the glorious Esk Valley by train and bicycle – the slow and green way to go – followed by a night or two spotting wildlife in the ancient woods of Dalby Forest. See *Action plan*, page 145, for details of the Esk Valley Railway, bike hire, accommodation and wildlife activities, as well as ideas for exploring the coastal treasures of 'God's own country'.

TRACKING DOWN THE 'FEATHERED FIVE' Connecting Middlesbrough and Whitby, the 56km Esk Valley Railway weaves through the North York Moors National Park, stopping at 18 stations along the way. You could, of course, simply sink into your seat and fall under the spell of the passing scenery, arriving at the end of the line 90 minutes later. Or you could pick somewhere to hop off and walk to the next station, before catching a later train for your onward journey (three or four usually operate each day). At Egton Bridge, for example, you can walk to the settlement of Delves before following a riverside path through Arncliffe Woods to Glaisdale. The 3km trail, which includes sections of ancient pathway paved with stone slabs, known as *trods*, ends at Beggar's Bridge. The single-span stone arch, built in 1619 for packhorses, is right by the station.

For something more adventurous, hire bikes in Whitby, take them on the train to Danby (around 40 minutes), then cycle the exhilarating 24km route back again. Start by pedalling up Briar Hill, then follow Lodge Lane down a steep hill to reach the Moors National Park Centre (♥ YO21 2NB ♪ 01439 772737 ♂ northyorkmoors.org.uk). If you haven't already downloaded them from the website, this is the place to pick up a route map and directions for the cycle back to Whitby. Inside there are also excellent displays on the natural history of the North York Moors, including its famous 'feathered five': the curlew, golden plover, lapwing, merlin and red grouse. Once you've honed your ID-skills for these quintessential moorland birds, it's time to get back in the saddle and head out on to the moors to see if you can spot them.

From the visitor centre, cycle along Lodge Lane and Park Bank before taking a steep left turn, signposted to Danby Beacon – the remains of an early warning radar built prior to the World War II. The views from here are spectacular – the North Sea shimmering in the distance; swathes of heather rolling away in all directions. The cycle route continues along a track signposted to Lealholm, climbing gently to cross another moor.

The first signs of birdlife you notice might well be the wind-shredded cries of a curlew – an evocative trilling, rising on the second note, like a wild spirit let loose on the moors. Beautifully camouflaged among tufts of sedge and rough grass, the long-billed wader is easily distinguished from golden plover – a summer visitor from Iceland with a black belly and gold-flecked back. Look for adults standing proud on tussocks, keeping watch for predators, like the merlin. Britain's smallest raptor also nests in the heather, strafing the moors for pipits, skylarks and wheatears to feed its chicks. Lapwing will fiercely defend their nests from attack, the adults launching into noisy flight, twisting and tumbling, flashing their black-and-white wings. Red grouse – last of the 'feathered five' – are more secretive, skulking through the heather, or flying low and fast when disturbed.

Opposite, clockwise from top left: moorland birds include golden plover, lapwing, curlew and red grouse; **above:** hunter in the heather – merlin usually prey on smaller birds like pipits (C Mckie, Coatesy, S Ward/S)

Take your time cycling across Lealholm Moor, stopping often to look and listen, then freewheel down narrow lanes into the Esk Valley, gliding through wooded gills and pedalling through farmland to reach the village of Egton. A short diversion south will take you to Egton Bridge and densely wooded stretches of the River Esk – an opportunity to spot dipper and kingfisher. This is Yorkshire's only salmon river (the fish can be seen jumping October–December) and there's also a healthy, but elusive, population of otters. Continuing east towards Aislaby and Ruswarp, you finally reach Whitby – for well-earned fish and chips.

WHEN NIGHT FALLS IN CROPTON FOREST Cloaking the southern flanks of the North York Moors, Dalby and Cropton forests are a complete contrast to the big-sky country of the open moors. A dense canopy of oak, ash and birch casts dappled shadows over an understory of hazel – a secretive world where wildlife is not easily seen. Signposted off the A169 between Whitby and Pickering, Dalby Visitor Centre (♥ YO18 7LT ✐ 01751 460295 ♂ forestryengland. uk) is a hub for walking and cycling trails. The 4km Dalby Beck Walk passes a hide where you can watch for tits, woodpeckers and nuthatches. Venture into areas of conifer plantation and you enter the haunt of crossbill and goshawk. For your best chance of spotting woodland wildlife, though, try to spend a night in nearby Cropton Forest where guided evening walks can reveal a range of nocturnal species.

Following your forest ranger into the twilight world of an ancient wood, you're conscious of every twig and leaf crackling beneath your feet. Tawny owls call and you freeze. There it is again: the male's long, vibrato hoot, answered by the female's terse '*keewik*'. They're somewhere in the trees ahead. Peering through night-vision optics you glimpse bats weaving between pale tree trunks, hunting moths. There's also something moving on the forest floor. Probably a wood mouse, whispers the ranger, and you wonder whether the owls have seen it too. Later, you spot a lone roe deer, a ghostly shape tiptoeing though a stand of pines, but the highlight is your badger encounter. With night vision, you clearly see the black-and-white-striped muzzle and the shimmy of silvery fur as it ambles across your path.

← Tawny owl (Mark Caunt/S)

ACTION PLAN

ADVENTURE ESSENTIALS Usually three to four trains run daily between Middlesbrough and Whitby on the Esk Valley Railway (☏ 07584 419114 ⌂ eskvalleyrailway.co.uk) stopping at all 18 stations along the 56km, 90-minute line. Bike hire is available in Whitby at Trailways (☏ 01947 820207 ⌂ trailways.info) and you can take your bikes on the train at no extra charge. Another way to avoid using your car, the Moors Bus (☏ 01751 477216 ⌂ moorsbus.org) connects numerous destinations, including the forest sites of Cropton and Dalby and the national park visitor centres at Danby and Sutton Bank (☏ 01845 597426 ⌂ northyorkmoors.org.uk). Forest Holidays (☏ 0333 011 0495 ⌂ forestholidays.co.uk) offer stylish cabins with log burners and outdoor hot tubs in the heart of Cropton Forest. On-site activities include ranger-led nocturnal walks and forest survival sessions.

MORE ADVENTURE Stretching from Boulby to Cloughton, Yorkshire's Heritage Coast is a spectacular succession of rocky coves, sweeping bays and towering cliffs, rich in Jurassic fossils. Scour the beach at South Landing for the teeth of prehistoric sharks and marine reptiles, as well as sea urchins and ammonites. Robin Hood's Bay is a good spot for both fossil hunting and rockpooling, while the RSPB Bempton Cliffs Reserve (♀ YO15 1JF ☏ 01262 422212 ⌂ rspb.org.uk) is home to around half a million seabirds, from March to October, including gannets, guillemots and puffins. During summer, Yorkshire Coast Nature (☏ 01723 865498 ⌂ yorkshirecoastnature.co.uk) runs boat trips from Staithes in search of seabirds, dolphins, porpoises and minke whales.

ALSO CONSIDER **Derbyshire** See *Bike Glamping in the Peak District*, page 122; **Gwynedd** See *Snowdonia Wilderness Adventure*, page 192.

↑ Leafy refuge: Forest Holidays lodge at Cropton Forest (William Gray)

24 FARM AND FELL SAFARI

SEARCH HIGH AND LOW FOR RED SQUIRRELS, OSPREYS AND OTHER LAKE DISTRICT WILDLIFE

WHERE	Lake District National Park, Cumbria
WHEN	Year-round, but Apr–Sep for ospreys
HOW LONG	At least a weekend
WHO FOR	Any age
ADVENTURE POTENTIAL	Hiking, canoeing, mountain biking, birdwatching, farm tours, red squirrel spotting
WILDLIFE WISHLIST	Otter, pine marten, red & roe deer, red squirrel; buzzard, peregrine, raven, ring ouzel & whinchat on the fells; nuthatch, pied flycatcher & redstart in oak woods; goldcrest & siskin in conifer woods; dipper, goosander, osprey & red-breasted merganser on rivers & lakes, along with bog bush-cricket, golden-ringed dragonfly & white-clawed crayfish

Rucked up into more than 200 fells and glinting with dozens of lakes, meres and tarns, England's largest national park sprawls over 2,362km² – an area the size of Northamptonshire. Hike to a lofty ridge above mountain slopes of wind-jostled bracken and juniper and you can't fail to notice the patchwork of

↑ Fell walking in the Lake District's Langdale Valley (William Gray)

fields on the valley floors, or the drystone walls snaking through the folds and creases of this rugged landscape. Glaciation may have laid down the bones of the Lake District, but it's also been shaped by thousands of years of human activity. A wildlife adventure here can take you from mountaintop to hay meadow, ancient woodland to sheep-speckled pasture – each with its own cast of species.

LIFE ON A HILL FARM When the Lake District was declared a World Heritage Site in 2017, it was in recognition of the combined influences of people and nature – and there's no better way to appreciate this than on a farm safari. John Temple has been farming in the Lake District all his life and now offers wildlife tours at his traditional Lakeland hill sheep farm (CA13 9XA 01768 770204 lakedistrictwildlifewalks.co.uk), nestled between Buttermere and Crummock Water, a 30-minute drive south from Keswick. Spend the night in the farm's traditional camping barn (sleeping up to eight) and you can make an early start in the morning, helping John with a few chores around the farm and spotting local wildlife. As well as red squirrels, roe deer and brown hares, John has recorded well over 100 species of birds, from goldcrest and redstart to golden plover and raven. On full-day tours, the mountains beckon, tracking red deer in the nearby Borrowdale Fells, learning about the region's iconic Herdwick sheep and discovering what life as a hill farmer is really like. Back at Cragg House Farm, John can take you on a night walk in search of badgers and bats.

THE ENNERDALE EXPERIMENT Loop round into the next valley south of Buttermere and you'll find Ennerdale where an innovative rewilding project is allowing native forest, heathland and bog to develop with minimal human intervention. The Wild Ennerdale partnership (⊘ wildennerdale.co.uk) weaves its slow magic through a 15km-long valley, which you can explore by hiking, cycling or canoeing. Venturing into this remote and secluded tract of the Lake District, snug between the 800m-plus fells of High Stile and Pillar, it can sometimes feel like you've been transported to the Scottish Highlands or Scandinavia. Since 2002, when the project started, red squirrel numbers have risen in leaps and bounds to around 150 individuals; native oak woods support nesting pied flycatchers and wood warblers during summer, while a successful reintroduction project has established one of England's largest populations of the rare marsh fritillary butterfly.

OSPREYS AND PEAT BOGS A few kilometres north of Keswick, Bassenthwaite Lake became the focus of one of the national park's most high-profile conservation success stories in 2001 when ospreys returned to breed for the first time in over 150 years. Migrating to the lake from their overwintering grounds in Africa, the birds have successfully raised at least one chick every year since. A 10-minute drive from Keswick on the A591, Dodd Wood (♀ CA12 4QE ✆ 01768 778469 ⊘ forestryengland.uk) has viewpoints offering sightings of the magnificent fish-eating raptors between April and September. The forest trails, meanwhile, are worth exploring for red squirrels.

The number of nesting ospreys in the Lake District is slowly increasing. Another reliable spot to see them, Foulshaw Moss Nature Reserve (♀ LA11 6SL ✆ 01539 816300 ⊘ cumbriawildlifetrust.org.uk) is also renowned for its rare and precious peatbog. Boardwalks cross a mishmash of sphagnum mosses, carnivorous sundews, cranberry, bog-rosemary and cotton grass. Crouch down next to a moss-fringed pool and you'll see dozens of dragonflies during summer, including – with luck – the rare white-faced darter. Adders, toads, common lizards and bog bush-crickets also lurk in the squelchy mire.

↑ Osprey (Dennis Jacobsen/S)

ACTION PLAN

ADVENTURE ESSENTIALS John Temple's Lake District Wildlife Walks are based at Cragg House Farm (☏ 01768 770204 ⌂ buttermerecottage.co.uk) near Buttermere. You can reach it by either following the B5289 south from Keswick to Borrowdale and then crossing Honister Pass, or by heading west out of Keswick towards Braithwaite and then driving south over Newlands Pass. Continue up the hill past the Bridge Hotel in Buttermere and the farm is just before the National Trust car park. The 77/77A Honister Rambler bus (⌂ stagecoachbus.com) connects Keswick and Buttermere. As well as a self-catering cottage sleeping two, the farm has a basic eight-bed camping barn with toilet, shower and kitchen. Ennerdale Bridge lies near the entrance to the Ennerdale Valley and can be reached by following signs off the A5086 between Cockermouth and Egremont. The Gather Café and Shop (♥ CA23 3AR ☏ 01946 862453 ⌂ thegatherennerdale.com) serves locally sourced food and has information on visiting Ennerdale. Several paths start from the Bowness Knott and Bleach Green car parks, including a 10.5km trail around Ennerdale Water. Halfway up the valley, Ennerdale YHA (♥ CA23 3AX ☏ 0345 371 9116 ⌂ yha.org.uk) has private and dorm rooms, as well as a camping barn. To reach Dodd Wood, take the A591 from Keswick towards Bothel. The entrance is opposite Mirehouse and the osprey viewpoint can be accessed on paths from the car park.

MORE ADVENTURE Setting out from their base near Windermere, Fell Pony Adventures (⌂ fellpony.co.uk) offer day treks with packhorses. Wild camping trips (lasting one to three nights) are also available, travelling up to 12km a day along old packhorse trails and little-trodden routes in the fells and woods of the Lake District. The sturdy fell ponies carry all the basic equipment, from pots and pans to tents and sleeping bags.

ALSO CONSIDER **West Sussex** See *Rewilding Safari at Knepp*, page 76; **Dunbartonshire** See *Loch Lomond Farm Adventure*, page 234.

↑ **Above left:** goldcrest; **above right:** golden-ringed dragonfly (Nick Vorobey; Wild Media/S)

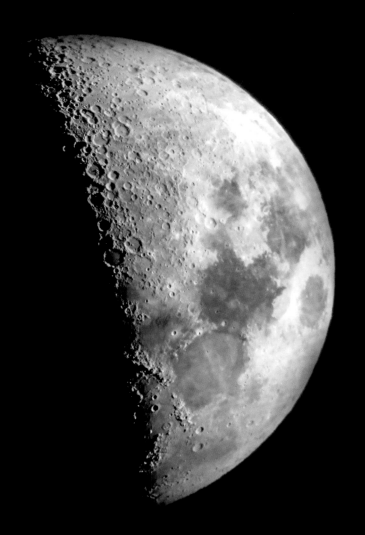

25 DARK SKY ADVENTURE

DISCOVER LIFE IN KIELDER FOREST AND GAZE DEEP INTO THE COSMOS AT ITS DARK SKY OBSERVATORY

WHERE	Kielder Forest, Northumberland
WHEN	Year-round
HOW LONG	Allow at least a weekend, with one night at a stargazing event at Kielder Observatory; coincide your visit with a new moon to ensure the darkest night skies for stargazing – or go when the moon is visible to study the lunar landscape
WHO FOR	There are family events at the observatory for children as young as four, but the main astronomy evenings often last until midnight & are more suited to older children
ADVENTURE POTENTIAL	Stargazing, hiking, cycling, birdwatching, watersports
WILDLIFE WISHLIST	Otter, roe deer, red squirrel, crossbill, goshawk, osprey, siskin, treecreeper, winter wildfowl, adder, wood ant

Wildlife watching and stargazing are natural partners. The best views of the cosmos are from places where night skies are dark, far from the lurid glow of artificial light pollution from our towns and cities. You're not trying to spot life on Mars during this adventure in Kielder Forest, but you will find yourself deep in the wilderness of Britain's greatest dark sky reserve, surrounded by wildlife-rich woodland. By day, you can hike trails in search of rare species, such as red squirrel; by night you can peer through the telescopes at Kielder Observatory, equally captivated by the lifeless, pockmarked surface of the Moon – or wondering just how many of the estimated one trillion stars in our neighbouring galaxy, Andromeda, might have a planet like ours orbiting around it...

TO BOLDLY GO... Covering 1,592km², the Northumberland International Dark Sky Park (𝄐 darksky.org) is the second largest area of protected night sky in Europe (after Cévennes National Park in France). Perched on stilts, Kielder Observatory is surrounded by a green tide of conifers. You can only visit during one of its astronomy evenings, bumping along 2.5km of rough forest track to emerge at the summit of Black Fell, where the contemporary, almost otherworldly, building of spruce and larch suddenly looms out of the twilight.

Stargazing evenings usually start with astronomers giving an audio-visual presentation on the wonders of the universe, covering everything from stars and planets to galaxies and nebulae – but the real journey of discovery begins when you get the chance to look through the observatory's large-aperture telescopes. If the Moon is visible, you'll be able to see the lunar surface in extraordinary detail, including the dark patch known as the Sea of Tranquillity where Neil Armstrong stepped from the *Eagle* on 20 July 1969, uttering the immortal words, "That's one small step for man, one giant leap for mankind."

← The moon's 'terminator' line divides lunar night from day; the darkest patch in this view is the Sea of Tranquillity – landing site for the Apollo 11 mission (William Gray/Kielder Observatory)

During summer, one of the first stars to emerge is Arcturus, a red giant located just 37 light years away in the Boötes constellation. In the east, you'll see the so-called 'Summer Triangle' of Altair, Deneb and blue-white Vega, the brightest star in the Lyra constellation. Look deeper into Lyra and you might just spot the Ring Nebula – a glowing halo of gases surrounding a dying star, known as a white dwarf. Winter is the best time to see deep-space objects, like the Andromeda Galaxy (2½ million light years away), but you might still be able to make it out on a moonless night in summer.

Look southeast on a dark summer's night and you'll be treated to the magical sight of our own galaxy, the Milky Way, rising above the horizon, its glowing, elongated core peppered with stars, nebulae and cosmic dust. From around mid- to late-August, perfectly timed for the school summer holidays, shooting stars from the annual Perseid meteor shower streak overhead, while four planets – Venus, Mars, Jupiter and Saturn – form bright spots in the night sky. Prepare to be amazed as the astronomers at Kielder Observatory focus its telescopes on Jupiter's iconic Great Red Spot (a perpetual storm twice as wide as Earth) or the rings of Saturn (billions of fragments of rock and ice from shattered moons and comets).

BACK DOWN TO EARTH Kielder Forest is riddled with hiking and cycling trails, but for wildlife watching, head to Bakethin Nature Reserve, located at the northwestern tip of Kielder Reservoir near the village of Butteryhaugh (♀ NE48 1HF). From the car park, the family-friendly, 2.2km Wild Walk leads through dense forest, heady with pine scent. Walk quietly and slowly, keeping an eye out for mixed flocks of coal tits, chaffinches, chiffchaffs and siskins feeding through the trees. They might be joined by a treecreeper – a small, brown-speckled bird with a white belly that scuttles up tree trunks, winkling insects from the crevices of pine bark using its narrow bill. A short distance along the trail, you'll find a small clearing with a bug hotel and various wildlife activities for children.

↑ Perseid meteor and Milky Way above Kielder Observatory during August (Dan Monk/Kielder Observatory)

↑ The wildwoods of Kielder at Bakethin Nature Reserve (William Gray)

Nearby, the Bakethin Hide is divided into two sections, offering a window on the forest as well as the reservoir. You should see common waterbirds, like grey herons and cormorants, but keep your fingers crossed for an osprey. They started breeding at Kielder in 2009, using special nesting platforms, including the one on the island in front of the hide.

Retracing your steps, be sure to stop at the small pond, teeming with frogs, palmate newts and dragonfly nymphs. It's also worth checking any tree stumps you come across for pine cones that have been stripped of their seeds. Kielder is a stronghold for red squirrels (displaced from much of England by the introduced grey squirrel) and the moss-covered stumps are sometimes used as feeding posts.

Apart from midges – and on some days in early summer it can feel like they outnumber the stars in the Andromeda Galaxy – one of the most striking insects you might encounter is the hairy wood ant. Scan the forest floor for large domes of pine needles and twigs, up to a metre across, swarming with ants. Observe from a safe distance: wood ants defend themselves by squirting formic acid at intruders – some birds, like jays, 'bathe' in the nests, relying on the burning barrage to rid themselves of lice and mites. But there's also a gentler side to these formidable insects. While 10% of their diet comes from devouring caterpillars, beetles and other ants, the vast majority is honeydew 'milked' from aphids high in the pine trees. They are also superb engineers. Far from a scruffy wood pile, each nest – a seething citadel of up to 400,000 inhabitants – contains an intricate network of tunnels leading to food stores and a special 'royal chamber' for the 12mm-long queen. The surface thatch is carefully arranged to act like a solar panel, warming the nest, while tunnel entrances can be opened or closed to regulate the internal temperature and humidity. Wood ants are also 'keystone' species, controlling outbreaks of pests, dispersing seeds and channelling nutrients into the soil. When it comes to the forest floor, they really are the masters of their universe.

↑ **Top:** the alien empire of a wood ant nest; **above left:** worker ant (William Gray; Manfred Ruckszio/S)

ACTION PLAN

ADVENTURE ESSENTIALS Don't rely on satnav to locate Kielder Observatory (📞 0191 265 5510 ⌖ kielderobservatory.org) – instead use 🅦 tickles.path.tangling to pinpoint the astronomy centre deep in Kielder Forest. Events run each night from about 19:00 for three hours and cover a range of themes, including *Jewels of the Universe*, *Discovering New Worlds* and *The Secret Lives of Stars*. Some evenings focus on the moon, aurora borealis or annual cosmic events, such as the Geminid and Perseid meteor showers. The observatory also runs late-night stargazing sessions at weekends and earlier family events. *Young Explorers* and *Space Kids: Searching for Aliens* are suitable for budding astronomers aged seven and above, while *Space Kids: Rockets* is perfect for getting four- or five-year-olds fired up about space travel. All events must be booked in advance. Kielder Water and Forest Park (📞 0345 155 0236 ⌖ visitkielder.com) offers a wide range of activities, from hiking and cycling to canoeing and sailing. Get your bearings at Kielder Castle Visitor Centre (📍 NE48 1EP) or Tower Knowe Visitor Centre (📍 NE48 1BX) – both of which offer access to the 42km Lakeside Way. Watersports are available at Kielder Waterside (📍 NE48 1BT), while accommodation ranges from luxury lodges at Calvert Kielder (📞 01434 250232 ⌖ calvertkielder.org.uk) to camping at Kielder Campsite (📞 01434 239257 ⌖ kieldercampsite.co.uk).

MORE ADVENTURE A 2-hour drive west of Kielder Forest, Scotland's Galloway Forest Park also has International Dark Sky Park status (page 213), while a 2½-hour drive south will take you to the International Dark Sky Reserve of the North York Moors (page 140). Other national parks recognised for their dark skies include the Cairngorms and Snowdonia. Visit ⌖ nationalparks.uk/dark-skies for details of stargazing events.

ALSO CONSIDER Dumfries & Galloway See *Seeing Red in Galloway*, page 210; **Scottish Highlands** See *Cairngorms Wilderness Adventure*, page 276.

↑ **Above left:** treecreeper; **above right:** red squirrel (Tasha Bubo/S; William Gray)

26 FARNE ISLANDS BOAT TRIP

WITNESS 'LIFE ON THE LEDGE' IN NORTHUMBRIA'S CROWDED, CAPTIVATING SEABIRD ARCHIPELAGO

WHERE	Farne Islands, Northumberland
WHEN	Year-round, but May–Jul for nesting seabirds, Oct–Dec for seal pups
HOW LONG	Allow 1½–2hrs for a typical boat trip sailing around the islands & 3–4hrs for trips that include landings on Inner Farne &/or Staple
WHO FOR	All ages, but be prepared for dive-bombing Arctic terns when walking on the islands
ADVENTURE POTENTIAL	Birdwatching, boat trips, island walks, seal & dolphin spotting
WILDLIFE WISHLIST	Bottlenose dolphin, grey seal, harbour porpoise, cormorant, eider, fulmar, guillemot, various gulls (including black-headed, kittiwake & lesser black-backed), puffin, razorbill, shag, Arctic, common & sandwich tern & oystercatcher, plus rarer sightings of minke whale, roseate tern & basking shark

↑ Longstone Lighthouse rears above the guillemots and gulls of the Outer Farnes (William Gray)

Twenty minutes. That's all it takes to chug out of the harbour at Seahouses and find yourself bobbing around in the Farne Islands surrounded by 200,000 nesting seabirds and their chicks. There probably isn't a bigger, more easily accessible and family-friendly wildlife spectacle anywhere in Britain. And if you miss the feathered frenzy in summer, then a boat trip during October half-term will reward you instead with a thriving colony of grey seals – in a good year, over 2,800 pups are born on the islands.

A TICKET TO SEABIRD HEAVEN Like any boat trip to a seabird colony, the Farne Islands experience slowly gains momentum as you travel from the mainland. Around 4km from Seahouses as the gull flies, the islands crouch low on the horizon, rising to a modest 19m above sea level. A red-and-white-hooped lighthouse towers above Longstone, the most easterly of the 28 islands.

Even from a distance, you can see a pepper-storm of seabirds above the scraps of land – a tantalising sign of things to come. You pass a few guillemots swimming at the surface, but they quickly duck underwater – a typical dive can take these auks to depths of over 60m, using their stubby wings for paddles as they pursue shoals of fish. As you approach a bigger raft, the birds scatter, running on water, furiously beating their wings to get airborne. A flash of colour and your eyes are drawn to a flight of puffins, their orange, yellow and blue bills crammed with silvery sandeels as they scud overhead, their wings whirring at over 400 beats per minute. Fulmars play it cool, gliding effortlessly in the boat's wake, teasing the surface with their wingtips. And all the while, you hear the murmur of seabird gossip steadily building. As the nearest island, Inner Farne, looms ahead, its low, dark cliffs and rocky pedestals morph into a living, seething mass of seabirds: a monotone melee of guillemots, gulls, razorbills and shags. The garrulous clamour of a seabird metropolis now fills your ears, and the sea air is heady with the pungent odour of guano.

The boat eases to within a few metres of the shore until you almost feel part of the colony. Your eyes flick from one seabird melodrama to the next... squabbling guillemots standing shoulder-to-shoulder on every ledge; pairs of courting puffins rubbing their bills together; a shag tending its scrawny chick atop a nest of dried seaweed... Air traffic is severely conjested as seabirds stream overhead, to and from the island; predatory gulls loiter with intent, while Arctic terns swarm over their nesting grounds.

→ The Farne Islands have a breeding population of around 43,750 pairs of puffins (William Gray)

GOING ASHORE As well as cruising around the archipelago, visiting seal haul-outs and landmarks like Longstone Lighthouse, where Grace Darling launched her famous rescue of the stricken steamship *Forfarshire* in 1838, some boat trips include landings on Inner Farne or Staple. Rugged, exposed and festooned with guillemots, razorbills, kittiwakes and puffins, Staple Island is a must for serious ornithologists. Also teeming with birds, Inner Farne is a better option for families, with its circular walking path, visitor centre and toilets. St Cuthbert spent over ten years living here as a hermit until his death in AD687 – a chapel now stands on what was once a much larger monastic site.

You won't get far on Inner Farne before meeting its infamous Arctic terns. Several colonies of the islands' total population of around 1,130 pairs nest on the island and – being highly territorial – they take exception to daytrippers walking past the shallow scrapes in which they lay between one and three eggs in May or early June. Expect to be dive-bombed. Wearing a hat offers some protection, or you could gently wave an arm above your head. Don't get agitated – these tireless birds have just completed a round-trip migration of

↑ **Clockwise from top left:** fulmar, shag with chick, puffin, female eider on nest (William Gray)

Arctic terns swarm around the beacon tower on Brownsman Island (William G

"Your eyes flick from one seabird melodrama to the next... squabbling guillemots standing shoulder-to-shoulder on every ledge; pairs of courting puffins rubbing their bills together; a shag tending its scrawny chick atop a nest of dried seaweed..."

↑ Guillemots crowd the shores and clifftops of Staple Island (William Gray)

some 30,000km to Antarctic waters and back in order to raise their young in the Farne Islands. As you walk from the chapel towards the lighthouse, see if you can spot the small nesting colony of sandwich terns. They're larger than Arctic terns, with a yellow tip to their black bills.

A track to the left of the lighthouse leads to a viewpoint over cliffs thronging with guillemots, kittiwakes and shags. Look closely at the guillemots – you might spot the bridled form: identical to the others except for a thin white 'spectacle' line around its eyes and face. Guillemots don't bother with a nest and simply lay a single, large egg on the bare rock. The pyriform, or pear-shaped, design might be the reason why it doesn't simply roll into the sea. Come fledging time in July, however, three-week-old guillemots are actively throwing themselves off the cliffs – the so-called 'jumplings' are accompanied by adult males, which continue to feed the chicks out at sea until they can fly and fend for themselves.

Looping back towards the chapel, a boardwalk crosses land riddled with the burrows of puffins. Known locally as the 'Tommy Noddy', puffins are auks, just like guillemots and razorbills. Returning to the Farne Islands in late April, they clean out their burrows before laying a single egg. After an incubation period of around 40 days, the pufflings spend another six weeks developing in their burrows before waddling to the entrance and seeing the ocean for the first time in their lives. By late July, most, if not all, have made their way to the water's edge and slipped away. They won't return to land for another two years – and most won't find a mate and start breeding until they're five.

SEAL SPOTTING When all but the fulmars, kittiwakes and shags have left the Farne Islands in late July and early August, the archipelago's wildlife spectacle continues throughout autumn, thanks to its thriving population of grey seals – one of the largest colonies in England. October is a prime month for pupping on Brownsman, Staple and North and South Wamses. Look for mothers suckling young (conspicuous in their white fur) and dominant males patrolling shoreline territories. Until they are independent at around three weeks of age, pups remain on land at the mercy of autumn and winter storms when they can be washed away and perish. However, a good supply of food saw the number of pups born in the Farne Islands swell from 1,740 in 2014 to 2,823 in 2020.

ACTION PLAN

ADVENTURE ESSENTIALS The harbour at Seahouses (♥ NE68 7RN) is the departure point for boat trips to the Farne Islands with Billy Shiel's (✆ 01665 720308 ⊘ farne-islands.com) and Serenity (✆ 01665 721667 ⊘ farneislandstours.co.uk). A wide range of options are available, from 1½–2-hour trips that focus on seabirds and seals to 2½–3-hour cruises that include a 1-hour landing on either Inner Farne or Staple. Some longer trips combine both islands or head further offshore in search of cetaceans and pelagic seabirds like shearwaters and skuas. The Farne Islands are owned and managed by the National Trust (✆ 01289 389244 ⊘ nationaltrust.org.uk) – non-members need to pay a landing fee for going ashore. Wardens occasionally organise rockpooling events for visitors to Inner Farne.

MORE ADVENTURE Covering 64km of coastline between Berwick-upon-Tweed and the Coquet Estuary, the Northumberland Coast Area of Outstanding Natural Beauty (✆ 07774 715744 ⊘ www.northumberlandcoastaonb.org) not only includes Lindisfarne, or Holy Island (reached by driving across the tidal causeway), but it is also notched with long, sweeping bays, offering everything from surfing to beachcombing. Children can model their sandcastles on the real thing: the medieval ramparts of Bamburgh Castle (♥ NE69 7DF ✆ 01668 214208 ⊘ bamburghcastle.com) loom above a magnificent beach, while further south, Dunstanburgh Castle (♥ NE67 3TW ✆ 01665 576231 ⊘ english-heritage.org.uk) presides over the scimitar curve of Embleton Bay. At low tide, many beaches reveal rockpools, while the sand dunes at Beadnell Bay are good places for spotting reed buntings, skylarks, stonechats and wheatears.

ALSO CONSIDER West Cornwall See *Cornish Coast Wildlife Safari*, page 28; **Pembrokeshire** See *On the Trail of the Puffin*, page 170; **Firth of Forth** See *Bass Rock Boat Trip*, page 228; **Shetland Islands** See *Journey to the End of Britain*, page 300.

Left: grey seal on the rocks; **above:** when puffins overdo the sandeels (William Gray)

WALES

↑ Red kite at Gigrin Farm (William Gray)

27 GOWER COAST ADVENTURE

DISCOVER LIFE BETWEEN THE TIDES ON A ROCKPOOLING EXPEDITION TO WORM'S HEAD

WHERE	Gower Peninsula, Wales
WHEN	Late spring to early autumn
HOW LONG	Plan rockpooling for 2–3hrs either side of low tide; coasteering sessions usually last 3–4hrs
WHO FOR	Rockpooling should always be supervised for young children; minimum age for coasteering is 7–8 years
ADVENTURE POTENTIAL	Rockpooling, coasteering, surfing, boat trips
WILDLIFE WISHLIST	Grey seal, harbour porpoise, fulmar, gannet, kittiwake, Manx shearwater & turnstone, plus numerous rockpool species

The next time you crouch next to a rockpool with your children and watch tiny gobies flicker through layered salads of amber and pink seaweed, spare a thought for Theia – a Mars-sized proto-planet that crashed into the embryonic Earth over four billion years ago. Without this chance collision, there would have been no gigantic explosion and no mass-ejection of vaporised debris that would eventually coalesce to form our moon. Without the moon there would be no tides;

↑ Worm's Head at Rhossili (Richard Whitcombe/S)

without tides there would be no rockpools. The daily ebbing and flowing of tides not only nurtures these exquisite little pools of biodiversity, but it also gnaws away at the coast, creating one of Britain's most dynamic and exciting environments. Experiencing life between the tides is an essential rite of childhood – whether you're a handheld toddler wide-eyed over your first hermit crab, or a wetsuit-clad teenager cavorting like a seal on a coasteering expedition.

THE WONDERS OF WORM'S HEAD Just 26km from head to toe, the Gower dangles into the Bristol Channel, its rocky southern shore crinkle-cut with sublime sandy bays like Caswell, Oxwich and Three Cliffs. Continue to the tip of the peninsula, however, and you reach Rhossili, the crowning glory of the Gower Heritage Coast and a prime spot for rockpooling.

Try to resist the temptation to head straight down onto the spectacular 5km-long sweep of sand – the rockpools are to be found on Worm's Head, a spindly promontory that's accessed from the clifftop path. Before setting off, it's essential that you check the tide times. The rocky causeway that links Worm's Head to the mainland is submerged at high tide. To avoid being cut off you must plan your trip to coincide with 2–3 hours either side of low tide. If in doubt, seek advice at the National Trust shop (SA3 1PR 01792 390707 nationaltrust.org.uk).

With Rhossili Bay to your right, follow the coast path west, passing a series of mounds that hints at an Iron Age fort. Glance inland and you'll see the banked hedges of 12th-century strip fields, now managed as traditional hay meadows seething with ox-eye daisies, knapweed and yellow rattle – a petal paradise for pollinating insects and nesting skylarks. Some of the fields are planted with sunflowers – molten yellow in summer for the bees, and black with seed in winter for hungry flocks of finches.

About 1.2km from Rhossili, you'll reach a small coastguard hut where you can double-check tide times before descending on to the causeway. Save your rockpooling for the walk back; cross the causeway (keeping watch for turnstones and oystercatchers foraging along the exposed shore), then follow the path over the first, flat-topped, hump of the Worm (a name that's thought to be derived from *ormr* – the Old Norse word for dragon). It certainly feels more dragonlike as you cross the rock arch of Devil's Bridge to reach the next ridge. Scan the cliffs for kittiwakes and fulmars, the latter wheeling over the sea on stiff, outstretched wings, but don't be tempted to scale the outermost headland,

↑ Turnstone (William Gray)

which is a sanctuary for breeding seabirds. You may be lucky and spot the fulmars' close relatives – Manx shearwaters – flying offshore, banking low over the waves; our very own 'mini-albatrosses'. Gannets are more conspicuous and you might spot the odd puffin. Keep an eye out, too, for grey seals, harbour porpoises and common dolphins – although you'll stand more chance of spotting cetaceans on a boat trip (see *More adventure*, opposite).

ROCKPOOL STARS OF THE GOWER Retracing your steps to the causeway, you can now spend the remainder of your 'safe window' on Worm's Head focused on rockpools. The limestone is riddled with them. Following the rockpooling code (page 13), stake out a promising spot and start by simply keeping still and watching. Easily spooked by your approach, skittish gobies and blennies may start to venture back into the open. Gently lift stones and seaweed (carefully replacing them afterwards) and use a bucket and your hands to gently catch specimens, rather than a net that can easily rip seaweed off rocks, entangle crabs and damage soft-bodied creatures like anemones. Keep one animal in your bucket at a time, try to identify it, then return it to the same pool.

So, what might you find? One of the most widespread rockpool fish, the common goby is easily identified by its twin dorsal fins. If you find a chunkier fish with one long dorsal fin and fat lips, it's probably a common blenny, also known as a shanny. But look closely at its head – a flamboyant pair of feathery antennae are the telltale signs of a tompot blenny, while shorter tufts might indicate an even rarer Montagu's blenny. One of the most bizarre rockpool fish, the clingfish has a modified pelvic fin that allows it to 'stick' to seaweed and the undersides of rocks, while other hard-to-find species include pipefish and butterfish.

Worm's Head rockpools are also home to strawberry anemones and green-and-purple snakelocks anemones (as well as the common 'red blob' beadlet variety). The humble limpet also has a more exotic cousin in the form of the blue-rayed limpet – look for clusters on kelp fronds. Other little rockpool beauties include cushion stars, purple topshells and mustard-yellow periwinkles. You'll see bucketloads of shore crabs, but see if you can find their feisty cousin – the red-eyed velvet swimming crab. Bonus points for a spiny squat lobster (just over 10cm long, but with a snazzy blue-and-orange carapace), porcelain crab (barely 2.5cm across, with broad, flattened claws) or sea hare (a well camouflaged, seaweed-browsing mollusc). Bonus-points-with-bells-on for an octopus or small-spotted catshark.

← Rockpool rarity: Montagu's blenny (Macronatura/S)

ACTION PLAN

ADVENTURE ESSENTIALS Drive to Swansea on the M4 and you're at the threshold of the Gower. The B4436/A4118 provides the best access to bays along the south coast of the peninsula. Once you reach Scurlage, it's just 6km to Rhossili on the B4247. There are also regular bus services from Swansea to Rhossili with First Cymru (✆ firstbus.co.uk). Visit the National Trust shop and visitor centre at Rhossili to check tide times and buy last-minute essentials, like sun cream. It's also worth taking an ID guide with you, such as *The Rocky Shore Name Trail* from the Field Studies Council (✆ field-studies-council.org). There are a few cafés in the village, including The Bay Bistro (✆ 01792 390519 ✆ thebaybistro.co.uk). With plenty to fill a weekend or longer, the Gower Peninsula boasts several excellent camping options, such as Skysea (📍 SA3 1NN ✆ 01792 390795 ✆ porteynon.com) right on the beach at Port Eynon.

MORE ADVENTURE If rockpooling seems too tame, you could supercharge your intertidal experience with a coasteering expedition, traversing the rocky shore using a combination of swimming, scrambling and heart-pounding ledge jumps. You'll gain a vivid insight into the challenges of living in the tidal zone, and you might encounter a curious seal. Providing wetsuits and all safety gear, Big Blue Adventures (✆ 07985 368956 ✆ explorebigblue.com) and RipnRock (✆ 07815 784122 ✆ ripnrock.co.uk) both offer 3–4-hour expert-led tours at Rhossili. Gower Coast Adventures (✆ 01792 348229 ✆ gowercoastadventures.co.uk) operates 2-hour boat trips from Oxwich Bay to Worm's Head to observe the resident colony of grey seals and encounter other marine wildlife, including common dolphins, which often visit the Gower during June-August.

ALSO CONSIDER **Isles of Scilly** See *Island-Hopping Adventure*, page 20; **East Devon and Dorset** See *Jurassic Coast Adventure*, page 60; **Moidart** See *On the Trail of the Otter*, page 256.

↑ Seaweed smorgasbord in a Gower rockpool (William Gray)

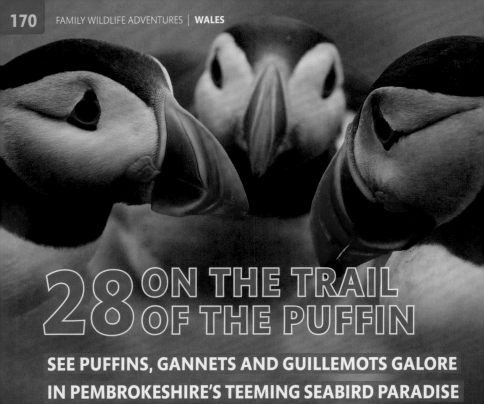

28 ON THE TRAIL OF THE PUFFIN

SEE PUFFINS, GANNETS AND GUILLEMOTS GALORE IN PEMBROKESHIRE'S TEEMING SEABIRD PARADISE

WHERE	Skomer, Skokholm, Grassholm & Ramsey, Pembrokeshire
WHEN	Summer for the seabird breeding season; puffins arrive to nest in April, leaving again by late July
HOW LONG	Allow 5hrs for visiting Skomer, including the 15min boat rides; overnight stays are also possible; cruises to the other islands last 1–2hrs
WHO FOR	All ages, but height restrictions for under-10s on some sea safaris using high-speed RIBs
ADVENTURE POTENTIAL	Boat trips, birdwatching, island walks, seal spotting, whale watching
WILDLIFE WISHLIST	As well as seabirds (including cormorant, fulmar, gannet, guillemot, kittiwake, Manx shearwater, puffin, razorbill & shag), keep watch for chough, peregrine & short-eared owl, marine mammals (bottlenose, common & Risso's dolphin, grey seal, harbour porpoise & rarer sightings of minke whale), the endemic Skomer Island vole, as well as basking shark, sunfish & jellyfish (blue, compass, lion's mane & moon)

↑ Three's a crowd: puffins usually breed with the same mate every year (Will Hall/S)

E very child's favourite seabird, the plucky little puffin with the pop-art beak arrives to breed on Skomer Island in early April. Some 35,000 of them take up residence in their nesting burrows, rear their pufflings, then leave again by late July – just as the school summer holidays are getting going. It's the same with the guillemots, razorbills and many of the other seabirds that nest on Skomer, a National Nature Reserve that lies just off the tip of Pembrokeshire's Dale Peninsula. A visit during the May half-term holiday, or a weekend in June, is ideal. Not only will you see the puffins, but the whole island is ablaze with bluebells, red campion and thrift. Stay overnight (there's basic self-catering accommodation in the island's Old Farm) and you can witness one of Britain's greatest wildlife spectacles when – each dusk – a myriad Manx shearwaters return to their nesting burrows under cover of darkness, having fed all day out at sea. A staggering 350,000 pairs of these ocean wanderers are thought to breed on Skomer, their chicks fledging in late August. Grey seals can be seen year-round (with pups in September), while other avian highlights include choughs and short-eared owls.

About 90,000 pairs of shearwaters, along with 8,500 puffins, also nest on nearby Skokholm Island (where you can stay for three–seven nights), while further offshore, Grassholm (boat trips only) appears dusted with summer snow as 36,000 pairs of gannets settle down to nest. Voyages to Grassholm often have the added bonus of porpoise and dolphin sightings, and you might even be lucky enough to glimpse basking sharks, sunfish and minke whales.

Over on the northern edge of St Brides Bay, the focus is on Ramsey Island (just off St Davids Head) where RIB rides combine wildlife watching with high-speed thrills. Although puffins nest on nearby North Bishop Island, you won't see them in anything like the numbers that you find on Skomer. Evening boat trips around Ramsey Island, however, often include the unforgettable sight of Manx shearwaters streaming past at dusk – many will be heading for Skomer and Skokholm to the south, but a small, growing population of around 5,000 pairs also breed on Ramsey.

THE PUFFINS OF SKOMER ISLAND Your puffin pilgrimge begins at Martin's Haven, a rocky cove notched into the very tip of the Dale Peninsula. After boarding the *Dale Princess*, it's only a 15-minute cruise to Skomer – the island's 50m-tall cliffs echoing with the clamour of seabirds as you approach. It may only be a short boat ride, but come prepared with suitable clothing and footwear – there is little shade or shelter on Skomer and you will need to climb 87 steps from the boat landing.

→ Puffin with sandeels (Rudmer Zwerver/S)

There's usually a short briefing from volunteers or the resident warden on keeping a safe distance from cliff edges and minimising disturbance to wildlife. Flushing birds from their nest sites can lead to eggs being accidentally knocked off cliff ledges, or leave chicks vulnerable to gulls and other predators. Head-bobbing may be a sign that birds are agitated, so move slowly away. If they start streaming off the cliffs, you are too close!

A 5.5km circular path loops around Skomer. Walking clockwise from the boat landing at North Haven, you soon reach a dramatic viewpoint across a narrow inlet towards The Wick – a high-rise seabird citadel crammed with fulmars, guillemots, kittiwakes and razorbills. With the noise, smell and great gyrating swarm of airborne birds, it would be utterly mesmerising – were it not for the puffins stealing the show. A large colony lines the footpath and if you sit quietly, one or two might waddle right past you to reach their clifftop burrows.

The bright orange feet and large, flamboyant bills of red, blue and yellow scutes (or horny plates) are just a summer fad designed to impress mates – it all fades away in winter when the puffins have left Skomer and are toughing it out in the

↑ **Clockwise from top left:** Puffin in a burrow on Skomer; Ramsey Island razorbills; Grassholm gannet; Manx shearwater returning to the islands at dusk (William Gray)

North Atlantic. If you're patient, you'll see a puffin flying towards the island, its bill stuffed with sandeels. They catch these slippery fish by propelling themselves underwater using their stubby wings as paddles. Each time they catch one, it's tucked between the tongue and upper mandible, freeing up the lower part of the bill to catch more. Ten sandeels is a normal beakful, but the world record is 80, held by a particularly efficient Norwegian bird.

Short wings are fine for pursuing fish, but they have limitations when it comes to flying. Puffins need to run on water to get aloft, while a fully laden, inbound bird will hold out its webbed feet, like air brakes, when attempting to land.

If you think the adults are comical, you should see the chicks. Hidden away in their burrows, they resemble charcoal-grey powder puffs. Six weeks after hatching, having moulted into smaller, drabber versions of their parents, they emerge into the open, walk to the cliff-edge and take flight. By daybreak, they're out of sight of land and completely on their own. It will be another two or three years before they set eyes on Skomer again.

The island's coast path continues from The Wick to Skomer Head, carpeted in pink thrift and clumps of sea campion during spring. As you walk along this exposed stretch of coast, keep watch for choughs twisting and tumbling above the cliffs. Only a few pairs of these rare, red-billed crows breed on Skomer. Grey seals can often be seen swimming in the surf at Pigstone Bay and there's another seabird cliff at Bull Hole. When you reach the northern tip of the island, look down at the Garland Stone, a small rocky islet where seals often haul out as the tide recedes. The path then turns south, crossing Skomer's interior where you might spot one of the island's short-eared owls drifting over swathes of bluebells on the lookout for wood mice or the indigenous Skomer Island vole. Several pairs of this day-hunting owl nest on the island. After skirting the Old Farm, the path strikes east to North Haven where you have a final chance to enjoy Skomer's seals, puffins and other seabirds before catching the boat back to the mainland.

↑ Walking on water: a puffin struggles to get airborne (William Gray)

GRASSHOLM'S GANNET CITADEL Lying 18km off the Pembrokeshire coast, Grassholm is smothered in a living cloak of gannets. Their guano adds a splash of whitewash to the effect (you'll smell it as you get nearer), while a constant airborne contingent of birds hangs over the island like white flakes of ash rising from a bonfire. Then there's the sound: an incessant cackling, punctuated by the rattling of bills from courting pairs and harsher squawks as fights break out among neighbours. Grassholm requires a bit of a voyage, but that's no bad thing – you can often spot porpoises, dolphins and even the occasional minke whale en route. Seals haul out on rocky outcrops around the island, while the gannets themselves can often be seen feeding out at sea, plunge-diving on fish.

RAMSEY ISLAND BY RIB Strong currents and tricky manouevres require the use of a powerful RIB for trips around Ramsey Island. After boarding the vessel at St Justinian's lifeboat station near St Davids Head, you dash across Ramsey Sound, keeping an eye out for harbour porpoises and gannets feeding in the churned-up waters of the tidal race. It's a more tentative approach to The Bitches – a line of jagged rocks off the island's east coast that have chomped their way through many a doomed ship. Look out for the orange 'carrot noses' of oystercatchers, or shags hanging their wings out to dry. Rounding the southern tip of the island, the RIB feels the swell of the Irish Sea, but your skipper manages to nose the inflatable into giant sea caves or send it skimming through narrow channels. Kittiwakes, guillemots and razorbills crowd cliff-face rookeries, while grey seals loll about on storm coves piled high with shingle. If the sea's not too lumpy, you might make a quick dash to North Bishop to see the puffin colony. It's an exhilarating ride – especially at dusk when tens of thousands of Manx shearwaters return from their daily foraging at sea, rushing past on stiff, straight wings. Most will be heading to Skomer where they nest in burrows. Noisy, nocturnal neighbours for the puffins, they fill the night with their wailing duets.

↑ Aerial view of Skomer Island, looking across The Neck to South Haven and the Mew Stone on the left, and North Haven and the Garland Stone, top right (Stephen Davies/S)

ACTION PLAN

ADVENTURE ESSENTIALS The departure point for boats to Skomer Island, Martins Haven, is 3.5km west of Marloes on the Dale Peninsula. As daily numbers are limited, you need to prebook your boat ticket and landing fee with Pembrokeshire Islands Boat Trips (✆ 01646 603123 ⌂ pembrokeshire-islands.co.uk) and check in at Lockley Lodge Visitor Centre, just above Martin's Haven, an hour before departure. Just up the road, West Hook Farm Camping (⌂ spurted.visitors.verge ✆ 01646 636424 ⌂ westhookfarm-camping.co.uk) has spectacular clifftop views. Overnight stays on Skomer or Skokholm are arranged through the Wildlife Trust of South & West Wales (✆ 01656 724100 ⌂ welshwildlife.org). Pembrokeshire Islands Boat Trips run various cruises in the area, including voyages out to Grassholm. Operating from the lifeboat station at St Justinians, near St Davids, Falcon Boats (✆ 07494 141764 ⌂ falconboats. co.uk), Thousand Islands Expeditions (✆ 01437 721721 ⌂ thousandislands.co.uk) and Voyages of Discovery (✆ 01437 721911 ⌂ ramseyisland.co.uk) offer RIB trips around Ramsey Island, as well as high-speed dashes across St Brides Bay to visit Skomer. Thousand Islands Expeditions also run a ferry to RSPB Ramsey Island Reserve (⌂ rspb.org.uk) from April to the end of October for day visitors who wish to explore the island on foot.

MORE ADVENTURE Based in St Davids, TYF (✆ 01437 721611 ⌂ tyf.com) offers a range of adventure activities in Pembrokeshire, including coasteering and sit-on-top sea kayaking. Coastal Explorer days combine both, with snorkelling thrown in for good measure, while the 2½-hour Rockpool Safaris are ideal for younger children.

ALSO CONSIDER West Cornwall See *Cornish Coast Wildlife Safari*, page 28; **Northumberland** See *Farne Islands Boat Trip*, page 156; **Ceredigion** See *Cardigan Bay Wildlife Safari*, page 176; **Firth of Forth** See *Bass Rock Boat Trip*, page 228; **Shetland Islands** See *Journey to the End of Britain*, page 300.

↑ RIB sea safari to Ramsey Island (Georgina Jeremiah/Falcon Boats)

29 CARDIGAN BAY WILDLIFE SAFARI

FIND OUT WHAT BOTTLENOSE DOLPHINS GET UP TO OFF THE BEAUTIFUL WEST COAST OF WALES

WHERE	New Quay, Ceredigion
WHEN	Year-round, but the best time for dolphin watching is Apr–Nov, while seabirds nest on the cliffs Apr–Aug
HOW LONG	Dolphin-watching boat trips last 1–2hrs
WHO FOR	Any age
ADVENTURE POTENTIAL	Dolphin-watching, boat trips, birdwatching
WILDLIFE WISHLIST	Bottlenose dolphin, harbour porpoise & grey seal are frequently sighted, but you may also see common & Risso's dolphin & minke whale; seabirds include cormorant, gannet, guillemot, kittiwake, Manx shearwater, razorbill & shag; also keep watch for chough, peregrine, basking shark, sunfish & occasional leatherback turtle

↑ Bottlenose dolphins in Cardigan Bay (Dafydd Lewis/New Quay Dolphin Spotting Boat Trips)

J ust imagine… you're standing on the seafront at New Quay, ice cream in one hand, bucket and spade in the other, gazing dreamily across the broad expanse of Cardigan Bay. A splash catches your eye. It was a few hundred metres offshore, but you focus on the spot. Did something roll briefly through the waves? A glistening back? A dorsal fin? It's too far away to be sure. Momentarily forgotten, your ice cream starts to drip down your hand as you stare intently at the sea, hardly daring to blink. Then, as if to dispel any uncertainty, a dolphin suddenly leaps clear of the water, spray fizzing from its tail as it cartwheels through the air. No sooner has it belly flopped back into the sea than another one breaches, spinning like a faulty torpedo before sluicing back into the waves.

Cardigan Bay is one of Britain's strongholds for the bottlenose dolphin (you can also see them in the Moray Firth; page 282), and while sightings are possible from land, the best way to spot them is on a boat trip. Several operators run tours from New Quay, taking you to the offshore reef – a favourite hunting ground for the dolphins – before cruising along the coast in search of harbour porpoises, grey seals, seabirds and perhaps one or two surprises, like a basking shark or sunfish. Before you rush to the quayside, however, be sure to pop into the Cardigan Bay Marine Wildlife Centre (♥ SA45 9PS ✐ 01545 560032 ♂ welshwildlife.org) overlooking the beach. The visitor centre has exhibits on everything from local wildlife and geology to sustainable fishing and marine conservation.

BOTTLENOSE DOLPHIN BAY WATCH For over 30 years, researchers on Dolphin Survey Boat Trips (see *Action plan*, page 179) have been studying Cardigan Bay's population of around 250 bottlenose dolphins. They've not only developed a database of individuals (using photographs to pick out distinguishing features, such as scars or notched dorsal fins), but they've also learnt a great deal about their ecology and behaviour.

These are some of the world's largest bottlenose dolphins, growing up to 4m in length and weighing as much as 650kg. If you're lucky enough to see them bow-riding or breaching near your boat, you'll get a good view of the domed forehead, short beak, sickle-shaped dorsal fin and long, muscular tail – all trademark features of the 'classic' dolphin. But why exactly do they bow-ride or breach? The fixed smile on the face of a dolphin might suggest that they're simply having fun. While that may be true, it's also likely that bow-riding is an efficient way of maintaining speed while locating fish to hunt. As for the acrobatics, that could well be part of the complex social lives of dolphins. Tail-slaps may be used as a warning to other members of the pod, or to express agitation (when a boat gets too close, for example), while tandem leaps may actually be two rival males jousting for dominance. Bottlenose dolphins can be extremely aggressive, not only fighting one another, but also attacking other cetaceans. The most common

cause of death in harbour porpoises found washed up in Cardigan Bay is from injuries sustained by dolphins ramming them.

Researchers have also discovered that the area is an important nursery ground for bottlenose dolphins. Females give birth to a single calf every three years, usually between March and September. Floppy-fluked and creased with foetal folds (after being squished inside its mother's uterus) the baby dolphin is often helped to the surface by another adult 'midwife' to take its first breath. Calves are 'named' soon after birth, their mothers repeating a unique series of signature clicks and whistles until adult and young are well and truly bonded.

As well as a means of communicating with each other, dolphins use clicks, whistles, pulses and sonar to chase down prey. Mullet, sea bass, salmon, mackerel, bottom-dwelling fish and squid are all on the menu in Cardigan Bay. The absence of acoustic pollution from large commercial fishing fleets or oil rigs in the area might explain why there's such a healthy dolphin population here. However, the noise generated by pleasure-boat traffic can still have an impact on their hunting success. The Sea Watch Foundation (⊘ seawatchfoundation.org.uk) publishes a Marine Code of Conduct to help keep disturbance to a minimum.

CARDIGAN BAY'S SUPPORTING CAST Wary of boats and rarely revealing more than a fleeting glimpse of their backs when surfacing, harbour porpoises are usually only found in groups of two or three. About half the size of a large bottlenose dolphin, it's still a thrill to spot them – and you might even double your tally of cetacean species in Cardigan Bay by sighting Risso's dolphins or a minke whale. Occasionally, leatherback turtles drift into these waters, the giant 2m-long reptiles renowned for their trans-oceanic migrations. Plankton-feeding basking sharks are another rare summer visitor, along with sunfish. Grey seals, meanwhile, are common year-round – Cardigan Bay is an important breeding ground, with a population of over 5,000.

↑ Harbour porpoise with young (R Richard/S)

ACTION PLAN

ADVENTURE ESSENTIALS Dolphin Survey Boat Trips (✆ 07796 135490 ⬧ dolphinsurveyboattrips.co.uk) operate hour-long voyages in Cardigan Bay from New Quay aboard the 12-passenger *Anna Lloyd* or *Sulaire* (no minimum age). Researchers gather information on the dolphins (sometimes using a hydrophone to listen to their squeaks and clicks). Other operators include New Quay Boat Trips (✆ 01545 560800 ⬧ newquayboattrips.co.uk) which run cruises lasting one to two hours along the Ceredigion Marine Heritage Coast in search of cetaceans, seals and seabirds. Volunteers from the Sea Watch Foundation often accompany these tours. Elsewhere along the coast, A Bay to Remember (✆ 01239 623558 ⬧ baytoremember.co.uk) offers boat trips from Cardigan aboard a 12-passenger RIB.

MORE ADVENTURE A few miles south of Cardigan, the River Piliau meanders through marsh, reedbed, willow carr and flood pasture – a wetland paradise for wildlife such as otters, kingfishers, waders, warblers, dragonflies and grass snakes. Presiding over this lush landscape, the Welsh Wildlife Centre (📍 SA43 2TB ✆ 01239 621212 ⬧ welshwildlife.org) is a curvaceous creation of wood and glass with panoramic views across the Teifi Marshes Nature Reserve. As well as exploring the reserve's four nature trails, you can go pond dipping, spot the resident herd of water buffalo from the Tree Tops Hide or join a guided canoe tour. Based at the wildlife centre, Heritage Canoes (✆ 01239 613961 ⬧ heritagecanoes.squarespace.com) offer two-hour paddling adventures through the Teifi Gorge between April and September, using Canadian canoes seating two or three people.

ALSO CONSIDER **West Cornwall** See *Cornish Coast Wildlife Safari*, page 28; **Moray Firth** See *Dolphin Beach Watch*, page 282; **Northwest Highlands** See *Wild Camping on the Whale Trail*, page 286.

↑ Guillemot and kittiwake nesting cliffs near New Quay (William Gray)

30 ON THE TRAIL OF THE KITE

SEE HUNDREDS OF RED KITES – ONCE ON THE BRINK OF EXTINCTION – FILL THE SKIES OVER MID-WALES

WHERE	Gigrin Farm, Powys
WHEN	Year-round: kite feeding takes place daily at 14:00 or 15:00 (late Mar–Oct)
HOW LONG	Allow at least two days to explore the area, with an afternoon at Gigrin Farm to watch the kite feeding
WHO FOR	Any age; there's a large field for viewing the kites, as well as several hides for keen photographers
ADVENTURE POTENTIAL	Birdwatching, hiking, cycling, stargazing
WILDLIFE WISHLIST	As well as red kite, you could see buzzard, carrion crow, jackdaw & raven at Gigrin, while the reservoirs, streams, woodlands & uplands of the Elan Valley support a wide range of species, including curlew, dipper, goosander, meadow pipit, merlin, peregrine, pied flycatcher, redstart, stonechat & tawny owl

You've probably put peanuts out for blue tits and greenfinches, and may even have dabbled in mealworms to entice robins and blackbirds to your garden bird table. But just imagine laying on a feast for hundreds of red kites. It happens every day at Gigrin, a family-run sheep farm tucked into the green folds of mid-Wales near the market town of Rhayader. The UK's first official red kite feeding station, it was established in the winter of 1992 to assist the recovery of a bird of prey pushed to the very brink of extinction.

Once a common sight across Britain, the red kite was even found in medieval towns and cities (including Shakespearean London) where it played a useful role scavenging refuse in the streets. In the countryside, however, it was less welcome. Despite carrion forming most of its diet, the red kite was deemed a threat to livestock and relentlessly persecuted. The end of the 19th century saw its final demise as a breeding bird in England and Scotland, with only a few pairs surviving in the remote hills of mid-Wales. In 1989, the RSPB and its partners began an experimental reintroduction project, releasing 186 young red kites (from healthy populations in Spain and Sweden) at secret locations in southern England and northern Scotland. Such was its success that further reintroductions took place across Britain, reversing the fortunes of this beautiful raptor. Today, around 4,600 pairs are thought to breed in the UK, and Gigrin Farm continues to play its part in ensuring a full recovery.

A MAELSTROM OF KITES As feeding time approaches, the skies above Gigrin Farm fill with kites: a gyrating flock of up to 600 or more birds. Usually silent, the prospect of a trailer-load of meaty scraps sends excitement levels soaring and the valley echoes with their insistent, whistling cries. You can't fail to notice their distinctive forked tails – or the extraordinary wingspans, stretching almost 2m.

← Eye contact: red kites have excellent vision (William Gray)

Coupled with a relatively small body weight of around 1kg, it gives this rakish bird the ability to not only soar effortlessly but to twist, dive and tumble with incredible agility. Looking through binoculars, you can admire other features: the hooded, lemon-yellow eyes (razor sharp for scouring the countryside for food) and that hooked bill, wickedly sharp, but not strong enough to tear open a carcass – kites must wait for the more powerful raven or fox to do that.

Then there's the plumage: all the colours of autumn rippling along its flanks; the vividly outlined feathers of chocolate-brown and copper-bronze on the upper wings; the deep russet tail and grey-streaked head. A twist of the tail, and the bird pivots, revealing its underside: white splashes on the wings, black-tipped wingtips and more of that rich ochre.

Kite feeding at Gigrin Farm takes place in the early afternoon, topping up the food that the birds find naturally when they wake, hungry, at dawn. When the tractor trundles into view, and the farmer starts scattering offcuts of meat across the field, the circling flock suddenly disintegrates into a feeding frenzy. Kites swoop on the morsels with breathtaking speed, furling their wings and

↑ **Clockwise from top left:** Red kites often feed in the air, passing food directly from talon to beak; leucistic or 'white kite'; diving for food; grounded buzzard (William Gray)

plummeting towards the ground. They rarely land, but instead snatch at the meat before flying off again. Some come away with nothing more than torn grass clutched in their relatively small, bright yellow talons – but if meat is successfully taken it is quickly eaten on the wing before other kites can engage in airborne piracy. Loitering on the ground, crows, ravens and buzzards hop towards the scraps, fanning their wings and glaring at the dive-bombing kites. There's seldom any interaction between the species – the kites prefer a 'swoop-and-grab', but will occasionally try to cheekily pluck the food from a crow's claws or harass a buzzard into relinquishing its meal.

The viewing field at Gigrin Farm takes in the spectacle of the entire superflock of kites against a backdrop of green hills. For a more intimate encounter, however, several hides overlook the feeding area, offering keen photographers head-spinning views of the kites in action. They're challenging to capture on camera – set a fast shutter speed and try to follow one bird, rather than firing away at random. Don't forget to keep your eyes peeled for the rare 'white kite' – the result of a genetic mutation preventing normal pigmentation developing in the feathers.

↑ Red kite soaring: one of Britain's most arresting natural sights (William Gray)

↑ Aerial ballet of red kites above Gigrin Farm (William Gray)

"As feeding time approaches, the skies above Gigrin Farm fill with kites: a gyrating flock of up to 600 or more birds. Usually silent, the prospect of a trailer-load of meaty scraps sends excitement levels soaring and the valley echoes with their insistent, whistling cries"

THE ELAN VALLEY When the 18th-century poet, William Lisle Bowles, visited the Elan Valley – a few kilometres southwest of Gigrin Farm – he captured its wild spirit in the poem *Coombe-Ellen* (published in 1798) by writing, "No sound is here, save the stream that shrills, and now and then a cry of faint wailing when the kite comes sailing o'er the crags." That was long before the demise, and subsequent revival, of the red kite in Wales, and over a hundred years before the Elan Valley's reservoirs were created to meet Birmingham's growing demand for water. But this 180km² expanse of shimmering lakes, shady woodlands and windswept moors still feels wild and remote.

Claerwen National Nature Reserve lies within the Elan Estate, protecting an upland plateau of acid grassland and blanket bog – a squelchy refuge for no fewer than 18 different kinds of bog moss and an important breeding ground for waders, such as dunlin and golden plover. More accessible, the Elan Valley Trail (⊘ elanvalley.org.uk) offers walkers and cyclists a 13km jaunt, starting in Cwmdauddwr, just west of Rhayader, and finishing at Craig Goch Dam. Along the way, you can look for curlew, meadow pipit, reed bunting and stonechat in upland areas, or glimpse dippers plunging headfirst into the pools of fast-flowing streams to catch aquatic stonefly larvae. Great crested grebe, teal and other wildfowl prefer the open, calmer waters of the reservoirs.

The Elan Valley is also a stronghold for birds of prey. Hen harrier, merlin and peregrine hunt across the moorland, while buzzard, goshawk and red kite nest in the forests. Accessible from the Elan Valley Visitor Centre, RSPB Carngafallt Reserve (♀ LD6 5HP ⌀ 01654 700222 ⊘ rspb.org.uk) includes a rare patch of ancient wood pasture and Celtic rainforest, cloaked in lichens and bryophytes. Stroll through this leafy sanctuary during spring and summer and you might glimpse pied flycatchers flashing black and white through the trees, or redstarts with their quivering orange-red tails. Summer visitors to Britain, both species seek out old trees riddled with holes in which to nest.

↑ **Above left:** Male stonechat; **above right:** male redstart (Paul Tymon; Nick Edge/S)

ACTION PLAN

ADVENTURE ESSENTIALS The Red Kite Feeding & Rehabilitation Centre at Gigrin Farm (♀ LD6 5BL ✆ 01597 810243 ⚲ gigrin.uk) is located near the town of Rhayader at the crossroads of the A44 from the east or the A470 from North or South Wales. Red kite feeding takes place at 14:00 from the last Sunday in October to the last Saturday in March, and at 15:00 from the last Sunday in March to the last Saturday in October. The viewing field is located about 150m from the kite feeding area, while five standard hides are arranged in a curve approximately 30m from where the birds are fed. In addition, there are four specialist photographic hides, offering varying perspectives and viewpoints for more serious photographers with telephoto lenses of 300mm and upwards. As well as a café, picnic area, gift shop and toilets, the farm has a 2.5km walking trail with far-reaching views of the Elan Valley and Cambrian Mountains. To reach the Elan Valley Visitor Centre (♀ LD6 5HP ✆ 01597 810880 ⚲ elanvalley.org.uk), follow the B4518 west from Rhayader for about 5km. As well as bike hire and an information desk for planning walks and cycle rides, the centre has a café, picnic area and an exhibition on the Elan Valley's water scheme, history and wildlife.

MORE ADVENTURE Located 14.5km from Aberystwyth on the A44, Bwlch Nant yr Arian Forest Visitor Centre (♀ SY23 3AB ✆ 01970 890453 ⚲ naturalresources.wales) has trails for walkers and mountain bikers, and also operates a red kite feeding station. Children can borrow discovery backpacks containing binoculars, a magnifying glass, bug pot and nature identification cards. Just off the A487 between Machynlleth and Glandyfi, Dyfi Osprey Project (▦ shifters.geologist.reflected ✆ 01654 645184 ⚲ dyfiospreyproject. com) provides views of nesting ospreys between April and September.

ALSO CONSIDER **Dumfries & Galloway** See *Seeing Red in Galloway*, page 210; **Isle of Mull** See *Eagle Island Adventure*, page 250.

↑ Red kites above the feeding field at Gigrin Farm (William Gray)

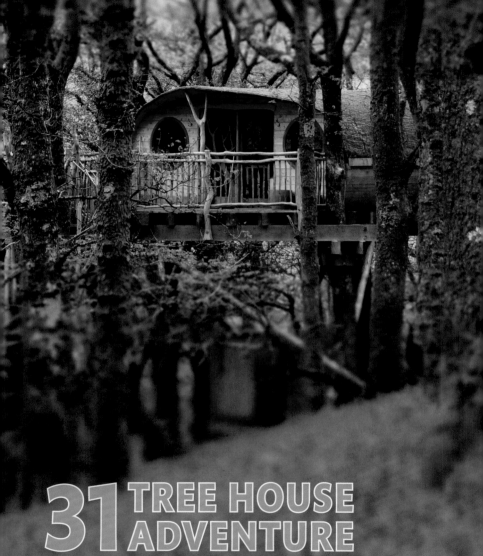

31 TREE HOUSE ADVENTURE

ESCAPE TO A SECLUDED FOREST, SLEEPING HIGH IN THE TREETOPS OF AN ANCIENT OAK WOOD

WHERE	Powys, mid-Wales
WHEN	Year-round
HOW LONG	Stays are generally for two nights
WHO FOR	Families with children aged four & above
ADVENTURE POTENTIAL	Living in the trees, nature watching, den-building
WILDLIFE WISHLIST	Badger, fox, hare, otter, buzzard, red kite, great spotted woodpecker, nuthatch, pied & spotted flycatcher, redstart & other woodland birds

Sharing 99% of our DNA with chimpanzees, we all possess an inner ape, so it's perhaps not surprising that most children (and plenty of adults) have an instinctive urge to climb trees (see page 218 for the ultimate tree climbing adventure). Chimps do it to escape from predators on the ground and to forage for the juiciest fruits and freshest leaves high in the canopy. Even after our ancestors left the primal forest and evolved to walk upright on the plains around four million years ago, they continued to rely on trees for escaping floods and dangerous animals. You're generally safer off the ground where you can gaze across your territory and spot danger coming – so why not sleep in the trees too? Apes build nests in the branches, weaving together leaves and stems to create a rudimentary sleeping platform. The tree house is simply the next evolutionary step – albeit a giant leap in technology and innovation.

THE TREE HOUSE OF YOUR DREAMS Hidden in a wildwood on the slopes of the Dyfi Valley in mid-Wales, six tree houses have been created that take arboreal living to new heights. There's no danger of being chased by bears or lions here; floods aren't a problem either, and you won't need to repel invading hordes. These tree houses have been designed for a different kind of escapism – a wild retreat that entwines you in the leafy embrace of an ancient forest of oak, larch and Scots pine. Designed by Living Room Experiences (see *Action plan*, page 191) these are proper tree houses – not a stilt in sight. Each elaborate structure is suspended in the treetops using an ingenious clamp system that grips the trunk of the host tree without damaging it. As you walk through the forest, carpeted in bluebells during spring, the tree houses are difficult to spot – spaced well-apart and crafted using locally sourced, sustainably harvested wood.

Stepping on to a spiral staircase, you begin your ascent into the trees. Several metres up, a wobbly wooden bridge leads you to the tree house itself. If Tarzan and Bilbo Baggins planned a house-build together, this is what they'd come up with: exciting and epic, yet cosy and homely. Edged with a wonderfully organic and tactile railing of twisted oak 'bonewood' collected from the forest floor, the outside deck offers a flycatcher's view of the forest. Inside, large round windows

← A tree house floats above a tide of bluebells during spring (Living Room Experiences)

allow dappled sunlight to filter through to the open-plan living space. As well as a double bed, fold-down bunk beds and a day bed, there's a sitting area and kitchenette with a fridge and cooker. Well insulated, each tree house has a wood-burning stove to keep it warm and snug year-round.

The attention to detail is remarkable. The stove heats spring water for a ground-level shower; a rope and pulley device can be used to hoist firewood and supplies up to the tree house, while lanterns and tea lights provide a warm, off-grid glow. There's even an en-suite Swedish composting toilet.

It's small wonder that children love it here. When they're not monkeying around in the treetops, there are dens to be built on terra firma, streams to be dammed in the valley and plenty of wildlife to be discovered. Imagine falling asleep to the sound of a tawny owl hooting in the tree next to you, or spying a fox or badger slip past beneath your lofty lookout. Buzzards, woodpeckers and nuthatches become familiar neighbours on a tree house adventure, while 'going ape' also allows you to discover the diverse range of moths, butterflies, weevils and other minibeasts that also call an oak tree home.

↑ **Clockwise from top left:** bouncy bridge leading to one of the tree houses; sitting outside on the deck at night; spiral staircase around a Scots pine; tree house interior (William Gray; Living Room Experiences)

ACTION PLAN

ADVENTURE ESSENTIALS Living Room Experiences (☏ 01650 511900 ◈ living-room.co) have created six tree houses in a remote forest around 13km east of Machynlleth on the A489. Sleeping two adults and two children (plus an extra child on a day bed if required), the tree houses are highly insulated for year-round breaks of two nights. Each one is equipped with a wood-burning stove, kitchenette, spring-fed warm-water shower and composting toilet, while outside decks have a table and chairs for treetop dining. Although there's no minimum age, children under four may struggle with the spiral staircases and wobbly bridges – and require eagle-eyed supervision when up in the tree houses.

MORE ADVENTURE Take the A487 west from Machynlleth and you'll pass the RSPB Ynys-hir Reserve (☏ 01654 700222 ◈ rspb.org.uk) with its species-rich mosaic of oak woodland, wet grassland, saltmarsh and reedbed.

ALSO CONSIDER Scottish Borders See *Tree Climbing Adventure*, page 218.

↑ 'Lofty' the tree house in a group of Scots pines beneath the Milky Way (Living Room Experiences)

32 SNOWDONIA WILDERNESS ADVENTURE

HIKE THE HIGH GROUND, BIKE THE VALLEYS AND FALL UNDER THE SPELL OF THE CELTIC RAINFOREST

WHERE	Snowdonia National Park
WHEN	Year-round, but winter in the mountains is for experienced, well-prepared hikers only
HOW LONG	At least a weekend (but ideally a week or more) to include a range of hiking & cycling trails
WHO FOR	All ages, but choose appropriate trails
ADVENTURE POTENTIAL	Hiking, mountain biking, pack-rafting, sled dog adventures, train rides, climbing
WILDLIFE WISHLIST	Wild goat, peregrine, raven, ring ouzel, rainbow leaf beetle & sub-Arctic plants like Snowdon lily on mountaintops; lesser horseshoe bat, otter, dipper, pied flycatcher, redstart, wood warbler, mosses, lichens & liverworts in Celtic rainforest; pine marten, goshawk & red kite in broadleaf & conifer forest

↑ Cwm Idwal in the Glyderau mountains of Snowdonia National Park (Stephen Bridger/S)

N o fewer than 15 mountains rise to a height of 3,000ft (914.4m) in North Wales. The so-called 'Welsh 3000s' crown the ranges of Carneddau, Glyderau and the Snowdon massif, with Yr Wyddfa (Snowdon) topping them all at 1,085m. A beacon to adventure seekers, Snowdonia's peaks, valleys and cwms were gouged out by glaciers some 2½ million years ago, but the mountains bear the scars of a far more ancient history. Hike to the summit of Snowdon and you can find crushed fragments of fossil shells, laid down in a river delta over 500 million years ago. The story of how they ended up on top of a mountain is one of violent volcanic eruptions and colliding continents – the kind of tectonic mayhem that can warp the seabed and turn mudstone to Welsh slate. Many of the crags and ridges that hikers set their sights on are the stubborn remains of great bubbles of magma – dolerite and granite intrusions – that have held the high ground while softer surrounding rocks have succumbed to aeons of weathering and erosion.

Against the backdrop of this geological blockbuster, ravens twist and tumble through lake-studded cwms; delicate Snowdon lilies quiver in sheltered crevices, while wind-tussled wild goats clatter across loose screes of blue-grey slate. Snowdonia's peaks are harsh and unforgiving – it takes patience to spot its resilient cast of species. But lower down, there are valleys cloaked with verdant woodlands of oak, alder and wych elm – an exuberant contrast to the mountaintops.

SECRETS OF THE CELTIC RAINFOREST Depending on their choice of enchanted wood, children will feel like Harry Potter in the Forbidden Forest or Lady Galadriel in Lothlórien when they set foot in Snowdonia's Celtic rainforest. Also known as Atlantic woodland, this rare habitat is a mysterious mesh of moss-cloaked trees. There are no trolls or giant spiders prowling these forests, but high humidity and low variations in annual temperature have created ideal conditions for one of Britain's most biodiverse hotspots. As well as 200-odd species of bryophyte (mosses and liverworts) and over 100 different lichens, a typical patch of Celtic rainforest is festooned in fungi and home to rare moths and butterflies.

↑ **Clockwise from top left:** life in a Celtic rainforest – dipper; lichens and bryophytes; greater horseshoe bat; angel's bonnet toadstools growing from a mossy stump (William Gray; bat: Ian Redding/S)

During summer, pied flycatchers and redstarts arrive from Africa to nest in old tree holes. Another migrant, the wood warbler builds a dome-shaped nest close to the ground. With zesty, yellow-green plumage, it's difficult to spot, but you might hear its song – a high-pitched trilling with a tempo (and abrupt end) that resembles a coin being spun on a table.

Other secretive inhabitants of Snowdonia's temperate rainforest include hazel dormice, otters and both lesser and greater horseshoe bats. Sit on a moss-covered boulder next to a fast-flowing stream and see if you can spot a dipper. A short-tailed, chocolate-brown bird with a white throat and chest, it can often be seen bobbing up and down at the water's edge, before ducking headfirst into the torrent in seach of aquatic caddisfly and stonefly larvae.

Sadly, much of this enchanted woodland has been lost to conifer plantations, invasive species (like rhododendron and American skunk cabbage) and grazing pressure from sheep and deer. Celtic Rainforests Wales (⊘ celticrainforests.wales) is working to protect the last precious remnants – including the Coed Felenrhyd and Llennyrch woodland (see *Action plan*, page 197).

↑ A mountain stream tumbles through Celtic rainforest in Snowdonia (William Gray)

SNOWDONIA ON TWO WHEELS Although Snowdonia has no shortage of hiking trails, you're more likely to tempt children into the great outdoors on a mountain bike. Coed y Brenin Forest Park (📍 LL40 2HZ 📞 01341 440747 🖥 naturalresources.wales) has eight purpose-built mountain biking trails, but for a ride closer to Snowdon with just as much wildlife potential, head instead to Beddgelert Forest (see *Action plan*, opposite). Three main cycling routes snake through the forest. The 7km Lôn Gwyrfai trail links the villages of Beddgelert and Rhyd Ddu, weaving in and out of a mixed forest of broadleaf and conifer trees, with wonderful views east towards the Snowdon massif.

Slightly more challenging, the 10km Derwen and 6km Bedwen trails delve into the thick of the forest, and include a loop around the tranquil waters of Llyn Llywelyn. Stop here for a break and you might spot fallow deer browsing along the woodland edge. Keep your eyes peeled for birds of prey – red kites and buzzards are frequently seen, but you're in for a treat (albeit a fleeting one) if a goshawk streaks past. Slate-grey above, finely barred below, the phantom of the Welsh forest whips through the trees at high speed, ambushing birds and small mammals. Snowdonia is a stronghold for this ferocious-looking raptor with its penetrating bright-yellow eyes and devlish white eyebrows.

Equally rare and elusive, the pine marten is mainly found in Scotland, but small, fragmented populations are slowly gaining a toehold in the forests of North Wales. Largely nocturnal it spends much of the day tucked up in tree holes or old squirrel dreys, but if you fancy doing a bit of poo detective work, scan the forest trails for scats that have a slight blue or red tinge. Pine martens are partial to bilberries and rowan berries, which can give their droppings a distinctive colour.

↑ Cycling beside Llyn y Gader on the Lôn Gwyrfai trail, with Snowdon in the background (William Gray)

ACTION PLAN

ADVENTURE ESSENTIALS If you've got your sights set on Snowdon, the Llanberis Trail is the longest route to the summit (14.5km there and back), but it's also the easiest way to the top – unless, of course, you take the Snowdon Mountain Railway (☏ 01286 870223 ⌚ snowdonrailway.co.uk). For any mountain hike in Snowdonia, make sure you're properly kitted out with walking boots, waterproof jackets, spare warm clothes, map, compass, whistle, torch, energy snacks and first-aid kit. Camping in Llanberis (☏ 07958 475032 ⌚ campinginllanberis.com) makes an ideal base camp. One of the few remaining patches of Celtic rainforest in Wales, Coed Felenrhyd and Llennyrch (☏ 0330 333 3300 ⌚ woodlandtrust.org.uk) sits above the Vale of Ffestiniog and stretches east from Llyn Trawsfynydd – see website for access details. Forest Holidays (☏ 0333 011 0495 ⌚ forestholidays.co.uk) has a cabin site in Beddgelert Forest, or you could try Beddgelert Campsite (☏ 01766 890288 ⌚ beddgelertcampsite.co.uk). Bike hire is available from 1085 Adventures (☏ 07572 336578 ⌚ 1085adventures.co.uk). Find out more about Snowdonia National Park at ⌚ visitsnowdonia.info.

MORE ADVENTURE Exploring lesser-visited parts of Snowdonia, Tirio (☏ 07450 245561 ⌚ tirio.co.uk) runs pack-rafting adventures where you carry a small, lightweight inflatable dinghy for the walking section of the journey, before getting afloat for the remainder. Day trips and overnight expeditions, wild camping, are available. Based in the South Alwen Forest, east of Snowdonia, Mynydd Sled Dog Adventures (☏ 07931 511217 ⌚ mynyddsleddogadventures.com) offer hiking with sled dogs (June–September, all ages) and husky rides (September–May/June, minimum age six) using their team of racing dogs and special wheeled 'sleds' to grasp the basics of mushing on forest trails.

ALSO CONSIDER Yorkshire See *Yorkshire Moors by Rail and Bike*, page 140; **Scottish Highlands** See *Cairngorms Wilderness Adventure*, page 276.

↑ Mushing and pack-rafting (Mynydd Sleddog Adventures; Tirio)

33 JOURNEY TO THE EDGE OF WALES

FOLLOW THE CURVE OF CARDIGAN BAY TO THE LLŶN PENINSULA AND BIRD-RICH BARDSEY ISLAND

WHERE	Cardigan Bay, Llŷn Peninsula & Bardsey Island
WHEN	Year-round, but summer for wildflowers on the Dyfi dunes & breeding seabirds on Bardsey Island; autumn for seal pups & migrant birds
HOW LONG	Allow a long weekend or a week
WHO FOR	All ages
ADVENTURE POTENTIAL	Boat trips, rockpooling, seal spotting, birdwatching
WILDLIFE WISHLIST	Bottlenose dolphin, grey seal, harbour porpoise, chough, osprey, Manx shearwater & puffin

Reaching like a crab's pincer into the Irish Sea, the 50km-long Llŷn Peninsula curves west from Snowdonia, its coastline crinkle-cut with sandy coves. At its tip lies Bardsey or Ynys Enlli – 'Island of the Currents' – an ancient pilgrimage site that has also become a magnet to wildlife lovers. A journey to this remote outpost takes you from mountain to sea, from the fringes of Snowdonia National Park to the estuaries, bays and offshore reefs of the vast Pen Llŷn a'r Sarnau Special Area of Conservation (SAC). Extending north from the Dyfi Estuary, wrapping around the Llŷn Peninsula and encompassing large swathes of Cardigan Bay, Pen Llŷn a'r Sarnau stretches along 230km of coastline. Boat trips are a great way to witness the area's seabirds and dolphins (page 176), but you only have to peer into a rockpool on the Llŷn Peninsula or go beachcombing on Shell Island to appreciate the wealth of wildlife in these seas.

ESTUARIES OF CARDIGAN BAY A 16km drive north from Aberystwyth on the B4353, the Dyfi National Nature Reserve (🎬 cave.presenter.cupcake 𝄓 01970 872901 🖉 naturalresources.wales) lies alongside the first of three major estuaries in the Pen Llŷn a'r Sarnau SAC. The Ceredigion Coast Path bears south towards Borth where thousands of Manx shearwaters and other seabirds can often be seen feeding close offshore. From the Ynyslas visitor centre, a 2km trail loops through Dyfi's sand dunes. During early summer, look for marsh orchids in the wetter dune slacks, and pyramidal and bee orchids on the drier ridges. Later in the season, lady's bedstraw, thyme and other wildflowers carpet the dunes, attracting common blue, dark green fritillary and gatekeeper butterflies, as well as day-flying moths like the eye-catching scarlet-and-charcoal cinnabar. Look closely and you might spot the vernal mining bee, a solitary species which forages on creeping willow and excavates tunnels in which to raise its young. On a warm, sunny day, walk slowly and keep your eyes peeled for adders and both common and sand lizards basking in the open.

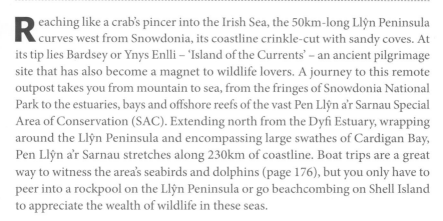

Left: Bardsey Island viewed from the tip of the Llŷn Peninsula; **right:** common blue butterfly (Travel Library/S; William Gray)

The 4km Ynyslas Walk skirts the estuary's saltmarsh, an important feeding ground for waders and wildfowl, including large numbers of wigeon and Greenland white-fronted geese. Try to time your walk to coincide with high tide when curlew, dunlin, oystercatcher and redshank gather to roost above the tideline, waiting for the worm-rich mudflats to be revealed. It's also worth sweeping the estuary with binoculars – you never know when an osprey might make an appearance. A pair of the fish-hunting raptors often nests further inland each summer. Follow the B4543 and A487 towards Machynlleth and, after about 16km, you'll reach the visitor centre of the Dyfi Osprey Project (📖 shifters.geologist.reflected 📞 01654 645184 🌐 dyfiospreyproject.com) where CCTV relays footage of the birds' annual nesting drama. By early April, both adults have usually returned from their West African wintering grounds; chicks start hatching around late May and often fledge by the end of July, before setting off on their migrations a month or so later.

Continue north on the A487, taking the A470 and A496 to reach Barmouth and you'll find yourself at the mouth of the Mawddach Estuary. It's worth spending a day cycling the 14km, traffic-free Mawddach Trail alongside the estuary, all the way to Dolgellau. As well as birdwatching at viewpoints overlooking the sandflats, you can stop at the RSPB Arthog Bog Reserve (📖 distanced.calendars.quantity 📞 01654 700222 🌐 rspb.org.uk) – a good spot for dragonflies and warblers.

From Barmouth, strike north on the A496 for about 13km to reach the low-lying Mochras Peninsula – also known as Shell Island. On a clear day, there are panoramic views of the Llŷn Peninsula, Snowdon and the foothills of Cader Idris, but for beachcombers it's heads down, feasting your eyes on some of the 200 varieties of shell that have been washed ashore here during winter storms.

A short diversion inland, bypassing Portmeirion and Porthmadog on the A4085 and B4410, brings you to the visitor centre at Bywyd Gwyllt Glaslyn Wildlife (📖 washable.shams.takes 📞 07834 575008 🌐 glaslynwildlife.co.uk) – another superb opportunity to observe nesting ospreys during summer. Continue west along the A497 and you reach Criccieth – a Victorian seaside town with a medieval castle perched on a rocky bluff at the threshold of the Llŷn Peninsula.

ALONG THE LLŶN PENINSULA There are dozens of coves and bays nicked into this bony finger of land pointing into the sea. A slow meander to the road's end, zigzagging between the south and north coasts will lead you to Nefyn's 3km-long scimitar of sand, Llanbedrog's sheltered bay and the more feisty surf beaches of Porth Ceiriad and Porth Neigwl. On a calm day, the rocky cleft of Porth Ysgaden is a good spot for snorkelling and rockpooling, while Porth Oer – nestling like azure between pincer headlands – has sand grains of a particular size and texture that resonate when you walk on them, giving the bay its nickname of Whistling Sands.

→ Grey seals hauled out in sheltered Henllwyn Bay on Bardsey Island (William Gray)

When you finally reach land's end – Uwchmynydd – at the tip of the Llŷn Peninsula, you'll find heather-clad slopes and rugged cliffs. Follow the coastal path around this blustery, wave-gnawed headland and you stand a good chance of spotting choughs, the red-billed, red-legged crows making a mockery of the fickle updraughts and ocean breezes as they dive, swoop and pirouette along the cliff edge. Find a rocky outcrop for a spot of sea watching and you might see dolphins or porpoises coursing through the waves below. Your gaze will ultimately be drawn, however, to Bardsey Island lying a few kilometres offshore.

VOYAGE TO BARDSEY ISLAND Boats depart from Traeth Porth Meudwy, just to the south of Aberdaron (see *Action plan*, opposite), crossing the current-strafed sound between the mainland and the legendary Isle of 20,000 Saints. Slipping into the lee of Bardsey Island, the 167m bulk of Mynydd Enlli towers above you before the boat enters Henllwyn bay on the flatter, low-lying southern shore. At low tide, seaweed is drizzled like treacle over the rocks, and grey seals – sometimes up to 300 of them – can be seen hauled out on the exposed shoals.

Since 1953, no fewer than 310 species of birds have been recorded by the Bardsey Bird & Field Observatory (⌀ bbfo.org.uk). Like the devout monks that began visiting Ynys Enlli in the 6th century, when St Cadfan is believed to have started building a monastery on the island, 20,000 pairs of Manx shearwaters make their annual pilgrimage each summer. Other breeding birds include chough, guillemot, kittiwake, puffin and razorbill. Following the track from the landing bay to the crumbling remains of St Mary's Abbey, look for wheatears and rock pipits flitting along the lichen-covered drystone walls. Zealous birdwatchers might even spot one of the season's first rare migrants. Over the years, everything from snowy owl and rose-coloured starling to bee-eater and black-browed albatross has turned up on this captivating island at the very edge of Wales.

↑ Manx shearwaters can be seen feeding off Ynyslas beach, near Borth (William Gray)

ACTION PLAN

ADVENTURE ESSENTIALS Starting in Aberystwyth and travelling north to the tip of the Llŷn Peninsula, plan on driving around 175–200km. After visiting Dyfi National Nature Reserve and the Dyfi Osprey Project, Barmouth is a good option for your first overnight stop. As well as tent pitches, Graig Wen (♥ LL39 1YP ✐ 01341 250482 ⌂ graigwen.co.uk) has yurts and shepherd's huts, plus spectacular views over the Mawddach Estuary and direct access to the Mawddach Trail. Rent bikes from Birmingham Garage Bike Hire (♥ LL42 1EL ✐ 01341 280644 ⌂ birminghamgaragebikehire.com). After a day's cycling, spend your next night camping at Shell Island (♥ LL45 2PJ ✐ 01341 241453 ⌂ shellisland.co.uk) before heading onto the Llŷn Peninsula. Ty Newydd Farm Caravan & Camping Site (♥ LL53 8BY ✐ 01758 760 581 ⌂ tynewyddfarm-site.co.uk) has an enviable location overlooking Bardsey. To reach the island, Bardsey Boat Service (✐ 07971 769895 ⌂ bardseyboattrips.com) operates regular crossings on a fast motor catamaran from Porth Meudwy. Self-catering accommodation can be booked through the Bardsey Island Trust (✐ 07904 265604 ⌂ bardsey.org).

MORE ADVENTURE To the north of Snowdonia, Anglesey is also full of wildlife-watching potential. Highlights of the 225km-long Anglesey Coast Path include the Aberffraw dunes which, like Dyfii on the Cardigan Bay coast, are stippled pink and purple with orchids during early summer. Lapwing and skylark nest in low-lying slacks, while the dunes' prolific invertebrate life offers rich pickings for choughs, which use their long, curved bills to probe the sand. But it's further along the island's west coast that you'll find its most dramatic wildlife spectacle. The RSPB South Stack Reserve (♥ LL65 1YH ✐ 01407 762100 ⌂ rspb.org.uk) offers grandstand views of a seabird-nesting cliff, swirling with a summer blizzard of fulmars, guillemots, puffins and razorbills. Tear yourself away from the cliff-edge drama and there are large swathes of heathland to explore. During spring and early summer, thrift and heath spotted orchids provide puffs of pink among violet patches of spring squill, followed in July by magenta swathes of heather. Silver-studded blue butterflies emerge just before the heather flowers, the males skipping over the heath, eagerly following pheromone trails from the newly emerged females.

ALSO CONSIDER Isle of Wight
See *Island Campervan Safari*, page 70; **Isle of Mull** See *Eagle Island Adventure*, page 250; **Shetland Islands** See *Journey to the End of Britain*, page 300.

→ Grey seal (William Gray)

SCOTLAND

↑ Red deer stag, Galloway Forest Park (William Gray)

34 WILD WINTER GOOSE CHASE

SCAN THE WIDE OPEN SPACES OF THE SOLWAY FIRTH IN SEARCH OF WINTERING FLOCKS OF GEESE

WHERE	This adventure takes you to the Solway Firth, but it's not the only place in Britain for witnessing this spectacle. See *Action plan*, page 209, for other wild goose chases in Britain
WHEN	Mid-Sep–Mar; whooper swans arrive Oct, geese numbers peak mid-Nov
HOW LONG	Allow a full day to visit Caerlaverock NNR, the Wetland Centre & RSPB Mersehead Reserve, or a weekend if you also plan to explore the southern shore
WHO FOR	All ages, but wrap up warm
ADVENTURE POTENTIAL	Mainly birdwatching, but cycling is also possible
WILDLIFE WISHLIST	As well as barnacle, pink-footed & white-fronted goose, other winter visitors include black-tailed godwit, curlew, knot, oystercatcher, pintail, ringed plover & whooper swan. Also look for flocks of linnet, reed bunting & twite, & birds of prey such as hen harrier, marsh harrier, peregrine & short-eared owl

↑ Over the rainbow: barnacle geese fly to their roost (William Gray)

Let's face it, most children (and plenty of adults too) don't like geese. It all stems from those early encounters with nipping, hissing farmyard ganders. Many of us grow up believing all geese are basically evil and should be given as wide a berth as possible. But all that posturing and aggression is mainly due to the fact that domestic geese are large, clumsy birds with nowhere to hide when they feel threatened. A wild goose is completely different. For starters, you give it space. Lots of space. Vast floodplains. Whole estuaries. There's no question of a close encounter. Wild geese are best appreciated en masse, filling an entire landscape – or skyscape – with yelping, babbling, murmuring hordes of a thousand or more birds. To witness such a spectacle, however, you need to know how to plan a proper wild goose chase.

Timing is everything. During summer, the geese nest in the Arctic. It's only when they've raised their goslings on the tundra and the brief window of a polar summer begins to close that they fly south. Several species migrate to Britain, bolstering resident populations of greylag and Canada geese, plus a small breeding contingent of barnacle geese. The numbers are extraordinary. Well over half a million migrant geese hunker down on our mudflats and marshes each winter, including 91,000 'barnies', 102,000 brents, 88,000 greylags, over 500,000 pink-foots and 13,000 white-fronts.

Greenland, Svalbard and Iceland must seem very quiet when they've gone. It's only when you *hear* a superflock of geese flying from their winter roosts out on the saltmarshes of the Solway Firth to grazing pastures further inland that you fully appreciate the scale of these goosey gatherings: the soft thudding of their wings, the honking hubbub. So, woolly hats and gloves on, binoculars at the ready – let the wild goose chase begin.

COAST WITH THE MOST Drive just 13km south of Dumfries along the A725 and you reach goose heaven at Caerlaverock National Nature Reserve (⌗ nature.scot). Stretching 16km along the northern shore of the Solway Firth, this soggy mishmash of mudflats, sandbanks and saltmarsh is the winter refuge for the entire Svalbard population of 33,000 barnacle geese. As you weave through narrow lanes on your way to the small car park at Hollands Farm (♀ DG1 4RS), take a peak through gateways to see if you can spot any geese in the fields beyond. Barnies are grazing birds, moving between estuary and pasture to roost and feed.

At Hollands, put your wellies on and walk south along a hedgerow-lined track. You may see winter thrushes like fieldfare and redwing feeding on hawthorn berries, but soon the path opens out into the big-sky country of the Solway Firth. A boardwalk burrows into a dense swathe of reedbed. Pause for a moment to check for hen harriers wafting over the feathery seedheads, then set off through the rattling stems. Soon, you'll reach the edge of the vast, open saltmarsh (known as *merse*). There's a hide here if you need to shelter from the keen wind; otherwise simply pan your binoculars across the saltmarsh, looking for the distinctive piebald heads of barnacle geese. At any moment, a flock may take flight, but dawn and dusk are the best times to witness long skeins of geese etched across the sky.

After walking back through the reedbed, turn right and follow a footpath that skirts (often waterlogged) fields to reach the Caerlaverock Wetland Centre (♥ DG1 4RS ✆ 01387 770200 ⌗ wwt.org.uk). As well as warming up in the café, you can find out more about the 3,200km migration of the Svalbard barnies. They're joined here by up to 200 whooper swans that have migrated 1,300km from Iceland, travelling in family groups with up to six cygnets. Wardens feed them daily at 2pm at the Whooper Pond outside the Sir Peter Scott Observatory, pointing out other winter visitors, like pink-footed geese.

If you time your visit to coincide with high tide, be sure to also visit the wetland centre's Saltcot Merse Observatory, which offers superb views over the saltmarshes to the Solway Firth and Lake District fells beyond. Thousands of waders are forced off the mudflats by the rising waters – a feathery furore that doesn't go unnoticed by predators like the peregrine falcon.

After leaving the wetland centre, follow the road back to Hollands Farm, checking the fields for barnies as you go. It's a 40-minute drive, via Dumfries, to reach RSPB Mersehead Reserve (♥DG2 8AH ✆ 01387 780579 ⌗ rspb.org.uk) – the next stop on your wild goose chase. Like Caerlaverock, it provides ideal feeding and roosting grounds for migrant geese. As well as a visitor centre and hides, the reserve has two trails – one leading through wetlands and fields (carefully managed to provide winter stubble for finches, larks and sparrows); the other tracing the coast, where you could see rafts of sea duck, like scaup and scoter.

Don't want your wild goose chase to end? Head over to the Cumbrian side of the Solway Firth where the Solway Coast AONB (⌗ solwaycoastaonb.org.uk) includes the RSPB Campfield Reserve and a discovery centre at Silloth.

↑ Green pastures: look for barnacle geese in grazing fields (William Gray)

ACTION PLAN

ADVENTURE ESSENTIALS Dumfries is the gateway town to the north shore of the Solway Firth, with both the B724 and B725 providing access to the Caerlaverock National Nature Reserve. Parking is available at either Castle Corner (♥ DG1 4RU) or Hollands Farm (♥ DG1 4RS). The two sites are linked by the Merse March and Reedbed Ramble footpaths (about 3km one-way). Alternatively, park at the WWT's Caerlaverock Wetland Centre (♥ DG1 4RS). To reach the RSPB Mersehead Reserve (♥ DG2 8AH), take the A710 from Dumfries through the villages of New Abbey, Kirkbean, Prestonmill and Mainsriddle. The reserve is signposted just before the village of Caulkerbush. Remember to dress warmly and take wellies with you. There are cafés and toilets at the wetland centre and RSPB reserve.

Dumfries has plenty of accommodation, or you could stay at Caerlaverock Farmhouse (✆ 0345 268 1269 ⌂ scottish-cottages.co.uk) right in the heart of the WWT reserve. Ideal for families, the five-bedroom property has its own observation tower from where you can spy on geese and swans in the ponds below. There's also a pair of two-bedroom cottages to rent at RSPB Mersehead (✆ 01556 504030 ⌂ discoverscotland.net).

MORE ADVENTURE Don't worry if the Solway Firth is too far-flung for your wild goose chase – the autumn exodus from the Arctic scatters wildfowl right across Britain. At Holkham National Nature Reserve (✆ 01328 713111 ⌂ holkham.co.uk), 3km west of Wells-next-the-Sea, Norfolk, up to 40,000 pink-footed geese, 4,000 brent geese and 13,000 wigeon gather each winter. In Gloucestershire, Slimbridge Wetland Centre (✆ 01453 891900 ⌂ wwt.org.uk) attracts 30,000 overwintering wildfowl, including large numbers of white-fronted geese and Bewick's swans. As well as Mersehead and Campfield on the Solway Firth, other RSPB reserves renowned for large winter flocks of geese include Berney Marshes, Snettisham and Titchwell Marsh in Norfolk. Or you could head north of the Solway Firth to RSPB Scotland reserves such as Insh Marshes and Vane Farm – or try Islay for a Hebridean island adventure in search of barnacle geese (page 246). Also in Scotland, Montrose Basin reserve (✆ 01674 676336 ⌂ scottishwildlifetrust.org.uk) can see over 80,000 pink-footed geese on the Esk Estuary.

ALSO CONSIDER Cambridgeshire and Norfolk See *Witness a Murmuration*, page 106; **Inner Hebrides** See *Isle of Islay Adventure*, page 246.

↑ 'Barnies' in flight (William Gray)

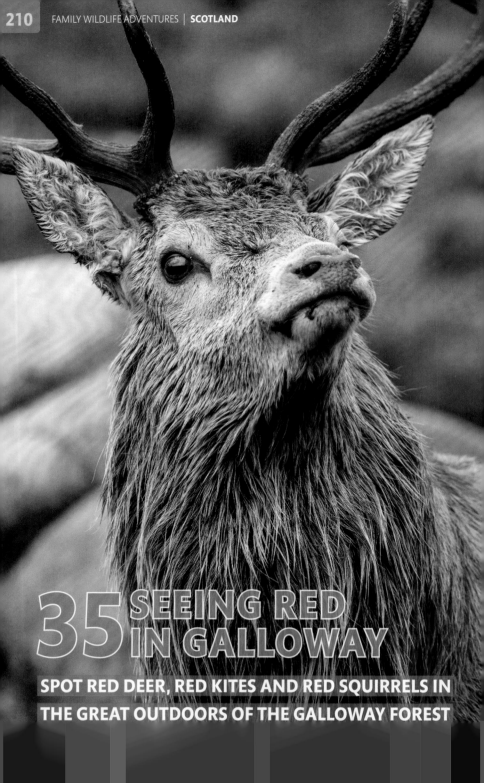

35 SEEING RED IN GALLOWAY

SPOT RED DEER, RED KITES AND RED SQUIRRELS IN THE GREAT OUTDOORS OF THE GALLOWAY FOREST

WHERE	Galloway Forest Park, Dumfries & Galloway
WHEN	Year-round, but autumn coincides with the deer rut
HOW LONG	At least a weekend, but longer if you want to do lots of walking or boost your chances of squirrels
WHO FOR	Any age; young children will love feeding the deer at the Red Deer Range hide
ADVENTURE POTENTIAL	Hiking, mountain biking, stargazing, birdwatching, red deer & squirrel hides, boating
WILDLIFE WISHLIST	As well as the 'red list' (red deer, red squirrel & red kite), you should see wild goat – but otter, pine marten & water vole are secretive & difficult to find. Other birds to spot include black grouse, buzzard, capercaillie, goldcrest, golden eagle, goshawk, great spotted woodpecker, greenland white-fronted goose, hen harrier, raven & willow tit

D riving north on the M6, three things happen as you sail past Junction 22. Firstly, you will have just crossed the border from England to Scotland. Secondly, the M6 will have become the A74(M). And, thirdly, you will have missed the turn-off for the A75 that leads to a wild and wonderful corner of Scotland that's often overlooked on our blinkered pilgrimages to the highlands and islands further north. Delve into Galloway for a few days and you will not only discover a glorious landscape of forest-stubbled mountains, but you're almost guaranteed a riveting encounter with red deer and red kites – and if you're lucky, you might spot red squirrels too. As well as tracking down the 'red list', children will also get a buzz from the wide range of activities available, from mountain biking to stargazing. So let's assume you didn't miss Junction 22. Where do you head next...?

OFF TO A FLYING START Thirty minutes after leaving the M6, the A75 bypasses Dumfries before looping southwest for another half an hour to reach Castle Douglas. Stock up on supplies (the 18th-century market town is renowned for its local produce) before heading to nearby Carlingwark Loch for a picnic. You can hire rowing boats here, nosing around the willow- and reed-fringed shore looking for great crested grebes and tufted ducks – a gentle prelude to the avian drama that lies ahead.

Around 10km west of Castle Douglas (following the A713 and A795), Bellymack Hill Farm (♥ DG7 2PJ ⊘ bellymackhillfarm.co.uk) becomes centre-stage each day for a gripping aerial ballet of red kites. There's no need to book in advance for this feathered extravaganza – just get there before 2pm when the curtain rises (or rather the meaty scraps go down) and the skies above the farm fill with the rakish silhouettes of up to 200 kites.

← All fired up: Galloway red deer stag during the autumn rut (William Gray)

A large outdoor viewing deck provides front-row seats on the feeding frenzy as the raptors pirouette, swoop and snatch in quick succession. You can hear the air rushing through their finger-tipped wings as they swirl overhead. Their soft whistling cries drift across the grassy slope below you, while the hills of Galloway roll away in the distance.

Persecuted by gamekeepers and egg collectors, red kites became extinct in Scotland in 1879, but following a successful reintroduction programme by the RSPB and Scottish Natural Heritage during the early 2000s, numbers have soared. There are now an estimated 4,600 pairs nesting in the UK.

A 10-minute drive north from the red kite feeding station, via the A762, the RSPB Ken Dee Marshes Reserve (♥ DG7 2LY ✆ 01988 402130 ⌖ rspb.org.uk) is edged with woodland. It's another good location for seeing red kites, particularly during autumn when juveniles (with their russet-streaked bellies) can often be seen drifting lazily above the treetops. As you follow the nature trail into the woods, keep your eyes peeled for red squirrels harvesting acorns. Out on the reserve's wet meadows, look for the winter's first arrivals of Greenland white-fronted geese and greylag geese. They'll be here until early April, when Ken Dee's spring shift takes over – lapwing, curlew and oystercatcher nesting in the open fields, while redstart and pied flycatcher take up residence in the bluebell-carpeted woodland.

HIDDEN TRAILS AND DISTANT GALAXIES You will have plenty of other opportunities to spot red squirrels as you gallivant around Galloway. The eastern border of the 774km² Galloway Forest Park (Britain's largest) is barely 15km from Castle Douglas. As you drive north on the A762, you can either head to

New Galloway before following the Queen's Way (A712) into the heart of the park or, for a dusty, more adventurous short-cut, turn left shortly after the village of Mossdale to join the Raider's Road Forest Drive. Open April–October, the 16km gravel track is popular with walkers, cyclists and horseriders, so drive slowly and take time to enjoy the leafy route as it winds alongside the Blackwater of Dee. Halfway along, stop at Otter Pool, a peaceful picnic spot overlooking a series of shallow rapids. Dippers are often

↑ Red squirrel (Liz Miller/S)

seen here, the white-bibbed birds rummaging underwater for aquatic insects, but you'd have to pick a very quiet day to stand any chance of seeing otters.

The forest drive meets the Queen's Way near Clatteringshaws (♀ DG7 3SQ ✆ 0300 067 6000 ⌂ forestryandland.gov.scot) – one of three visitor centres in Galloway Forest Park. Gaze across Clatteringshaws Loch and you should be able to see 843m-tall Merrick, the highest point in the Southern Uplands.

Linger after nightfall and, if it's clear, you can see considerably further... Galloway was declared Britain's first Dark Sky Park in 2009 and its lack of artificial light pollution can bring the cosmos into sharp relief. Wander from the visitor centre along the loch shore to a granite stone where Robert the Bruce is said to have rested, then turn off your torches and wait 20 minutes for your eyes to adjust to the darkness. On a moonless night in summer, the Milky Way will form a glittering arch in the south and you may be able to make out its closest neighbour – the Andromeda Galaxy, over 2½ million light years from Earth. In autumn, the Draconid and Orionid meteor showers can be seen. There are several other mesmerising spots for stargazing in Galloway Forest Park, including Knockman Wood, near Newton Stewart. To wise up on your planets and constellations, visit the Scottish Dark Sky Observatory (✆ 01292 551118 ⌂ scottishdarkskyobservatory.co.uk) near Dalmellington, off the A713.

AN AUDIENCE WITH ROYALTY Britain's largest land mammal struts its stuff in Galloway each autumn as the red deer rut reaches fever pitch. Weighing up to 240kg, adult stags swagger back to the home range to compete for hinds

↑ Juvenile red kite (William Gray)

↑ RSPB Wood of Cree Reserve (William Gray)

"As this rare patch of Scottish temperate rainforest – or Atlantic oak woodland – envelops you, it almost feels like you've stepped into Narnia or Middle Earth"

by engaging in testosterone-charged displays. Roaring and bellowing, they size up rival males by parallel walking. This is usually sufficient to deter a smaller individual from escalating matters, but similar-sized stags may lock antlers in order to assess dominance and claim exclusive mating rights with the hinds.

Although Galloway Forest Park is one of the best places in Britain to witness the mighty clash of rutting deer, the Red Deer Range (5km west of Clatteringshaws Visitor Centre on the Queen's Way) also shows a more peaceful side to these impressive creatures. A hide overlooks a bracken-cloaked hillside that's home to around 25 red deer. Bales of hay entice them to within a few metres of where you're sat – close enough to see your reflection in a stag's eyes and the thick growth of grizzled fur on its muscular neck. But that's not all. An adjacent wooden screen has several slots just wide enough for posting carrots into the velvety muzzles of hungry deer – a popular activity for children, and a rare opportunity for such an intimate encounter with the Monarch of the Glen.

INTO THE ENCHANTED FOREST Continue west for a few kilometres along the Queen's Way and you reach the Wild Goat Park. It's worth a brief stop to spy the shaggy boulder-hoppers, but if red squirrels are still on your must-see list, push on to Kirroughtree Visitor Centre (signposted off the A75 at Palnure). An easy 500m-long trail leads to the Wild Watch Hide where feeders often attract squirrels and a variety of woodland birds. If that doesn't work, try for a squirrel sighting at the RSPB Wood of Cree Reserve (𝒫 01988 402130 𝒶 rspb.org.uk). You'll find this beautiful ancient woodland by backtracking to Newton Stewart and following the narrow C50 beyond Minnigaff.

From the car park, a trail threads between moss-fuzzed oaks, tracing an exuberant stream that sluices through fern-strewn gullies. As this rare patch of Scottish temperate rainforest – or Atlantic oak woodland – envelops you, it almost feels like you've stepped into Narnia or Middle Earth. Red squirrels might prove as difficult to spot as nymphs or elves... but find a spot to just sit and watch. In spring, when bluebells seep through the wood, you might glimpse a pied flycatcher or redstart perched near its nest hole, while summer sees purple hairstreak butterflies flickering high in the canopy where they feed on honeydew. Late autumn and winter, however, are the best times for spotting red squirrels. Not only is there a glut of acorns, but the trees have shed their leaves, making it far easier to detect the sudden flurry of red fur as a squirrel bounds for cover.

Not far to the north, Glentrool Visitor Centre (▥timeless.view.nips) offers more opportunities for exploring ancient oak woodland. As well as short walks, like the Goldcrest Trail, the Loch Trool Loop offers a more challenging 10km circuit with views towards Merrick and a chance to spot red squirrel, roe deer and crossbill.

ACTION PLAN

ADVENTURE ESSENTIALS Galloway Forest Park is managed by Forestry and Land Scotland (☏ 0300 067 6000 ⊘ forestryandland.gov.scot). Three visitor centres – Clatteringshaws, Glentrool and Kirroughtree – offer access to the park's hills, forests and lochs through a wide network of hiking and cycling trails. Mountain bike hire is available at Kirroughtree from the The Break Pad (☏ 01671 401303 ⊘ thebreakpad.com). For a weekend exploring the region, you could spend one day in the east, combining the 14:00 red kite feeding at Bellymack Hill Farm with a visit to the RSPB Ken Dee Marshes Reserve or a dawdle along the Raider's Road Forest Drive to Clatteringshaws Visitor Centre (for walks and stargazing). And then on your second day, head further west, taking in the Red Deer Range and Wild Goat Park before exploring the forests at Kirroughtree, Glentrool and the RSPB Wood of Cree Reserve.

WHERE TO CAMP Located near the hamlet of Shawhead, around 15km west of Dumfries, Barnsoul (♥ DG2 9SQ ☏ 01387 730533 ⊘ barnsoulcaravanpark.co.uk) offers camping pitches and glamping pods in 32 hectares of unspoilt countryside – you may even spot deer and red squirrels in the site's wooded areas. Glamping pods, wigwams and bothies – some with wood-fired hot tubs – are available at Gorsebank (♥ DG5 4QT ☏ 01556 610174 ⊘ gorsebankglamping.co.uk) 16km southeast of Castle Douglas. Pitched right on the edge of Galloway Forest Park, Glentrool Camping & Caravan Site (♥ DG8 6RN ☏ 01671 840280 ⊘ glentroolcampingandcaravansite.co.uk) is a good choice if you're serious about hiking or mountain biking.

MORE ADVENTURE A 480km road trip around Dumfries and Galloway, the Southwest Coastal 300 (⊘ visitsouthwestscotland.com/swc300) skirts the Solway Firth before reaching the hammerhead peninsula known as the Rhins. Kids will love climbing to the top of the Mull of Galloway Lighthouse, while top beaches include Sandyhills (near Dalbeattie), Sandhead (near Stranraer) and Greenan (near Ayr).

ALSO CONSIDER London See *A Day in the Urban Jungle*, page 86; **Yorkshire** See *On the Trail of the Red Squirrel*, page 134; **Northumberland** See *Dark Sky Adventure*, page 150; **Powys** See *On the Trail of the Kite*, page 180; **Isle of Mull** See *Eagle Island Adventure*, page 250.

↑ Dinner time: a red kite at Bellymack Hill Farm feeding station (William Gray)

36 TREE CLIMBING ADVENTURE

SCALE THE CANOPY OF OAKS AND OTHER MIGHTY TREES IN THE COMPANY OF AN EXPERT CLIMBER

WHERE	Scottish Borders & throughout Scotland
WHEN	Year-round, but Apr–Oct is best
HOW LONG	Sessions lasts an hour, but can be tailor-made
WHO FOR	Minimum age is six
ADVENTURE POTENTIAL	Tree climbing, birdwatching, art sessions
WILDLIFE WISHLIST	Birds to look & listen out for include blackcap, blue, coal & great tit, buzzard, chaffinch, chiffchaff, goldcrest, goldfinch, great spotted woodpecker, jay, mistle thrush, nuthatch, redstart & treecreeper

↑ Trunk calling: a young climber rises to the challenge of scaling a turkey oak (William Gray)

W e're primates. We came from the trees. Evolution may have led us out on
to the plains on all-twos, but there's a little bit in us that still craves the
canopy – to clamber back into the branches of our primeval forest kingdom. Not
that there's anything primitive about professional climber Tim Chamberlain.
His Wild Tree Adventures will transport you (and your little monkeys) into the
head-spinning world of some of Scotland's mighty trees using only the safest,
most high-tech climbing gear. Our arboreal adventure took place in a 200-year-
old oak growing in the grounds of Paxton House (a grand Georgian residence
with landscaped grounds sweeping down to the River Tweed), but climbs are
possible in a variety of trees at locations across Scotland.

Tim and his team spend hours scoping out potential trees. By the time you
arrive on the scene, a suitable specimen will have been rigged with ropes, carefully
secured to ensure that they not only provide safe, interesting climbing routes,
but also cause no harm to the tree itself. Tim's background is in zoology and
conservation – his passion for tree climbing stems from ringing the chicks of
goshawks and other birds of prey in their lofty nests. His ethos is to leave each
tree just as he found it, full of leaves and full of life.

THE TREE OF LIFE When it comes to oaks, the abundance and diversity of life
supported by a single tree is quite astonishing. Standing at the base of a mature,
30m-tall oak, its boughs spreading in a dense mesh above your head, you might
hear the whistle and chatter of thrushes, tits and finches, and glimpse one or two
birds flitting through the emerald shroud of leaves. However, some 2,300 other
species can also be found hidden among its bark and foliage – and over 320 of
them rely on oaks for their survival.

Conspicuous butterflies include purple hairstreak and speckled wood, but it's
the motley multitude of moths – over 200 species – that cause the biggest flutter
in an oak tree. Geometrid moths, like the brindled beauty, have camouflaged
wings that blend seamlessly with lichen-covered bark; tiny micro moths (with
wingspans of less than 25mm) include the green oak tortrix, renowned for its
ravenous caterpillars, capable of defoliating entire trees, while the macro moths
include the intriguing buff-tip which resembles the tip of a dead twig when at rest.

Then there's the beetles – cockchafers, ladybirds, nut weevils, longhorn, soldier
and stag beetles – boring through bark or preying on other invertebrates. From
sap-sucking leafhoppers and aphid-munching lacewings to long-legged harvest
spiders and lime-green bush-crickets, an oak tree carries the weight of an entire
ecosystem in its branches.

Despite this teeming biodiversity, it takes a trained eye to spot these minibeasts.
What are conspicuous, however, are the round nodules – or galls – clustered
around some of the leaf stems. These strange growths are produced by the tree

→ **Overpage:** Brave new world: the vast spreading canopy of an oak tree (William Gray)

in response to the larvae of tiny oak gall wasps. Over 70 species are found in Britain, each one stimulating the tree to create a particular size and shape of gall that swells around the developing grub, protecting it from predators.

UP, UP AND AWAY At first, the subtleties of birdsong and insect lifecycles might be swamped by adrenaline as children begin their ascent. Wild Tree Adventures are on a completely different scale to the tree houses they may be used to. It's a slow, relaxed process, however, with Tim meticulously fitting climbing harnesses and safety helmets before demonstrating the straightforward technique of using the special rope system. After choosing one of the installed climbing lines, you're attached with a locking karabiner and then it's simply a case of 'step-sliding' up the line, flexing your legs against a foot loop to push yourself upwards. Whenever you feel like a rest, or a moment to study the particularly striking specimen of forest shield bug that's just landed on a nearby leaf, you simply sit back in your harness.

Some of the climbing lines take you to the top of the tree, while others reach swing seats or hammocks that Tim has preinstalled in the canopy. He climbs alongside you, offering encouragement and nuggets of tree lore. The oak looked big from the ground, but when you're high in its branches, suspended in an all-encompassing tree hug, it feels like you've entered a new world. After the exhilaration of reaching the hammock or the top of your line, Tim takes a moment to chat quietly to each climber: a few seconds to study the intricate, coral-like growths of an *Usnea* lichen, or filter the high-pitched trilling of a treecreeper from the background churring of blue tits.

No matter how confidently you took to the treetops, or how high you chose to climb, children and adults return to earth with a massive sense of achievement and a rekindled respect for our majestic trees and the life they support.

↑ **Above left:** Wild Tree Adventures' Tim Chamberlain; **above right:** hammock hang-out (William Gray)

ACTION PLAN

ADVENTURE ESSENTIALS Suitable for anyone aged six and above, Wild Tree Adventures (☏ 0800 622 6465 ☞ wildtreeadventures.com) offer one-hour tree climbing sessions in locations across Scotland, including Paxton House near Berwick-upon-Tweed (♥ TD15 1SZ) and Traquair House near Innerleithen (♥ EH44 6PW). Two highly trained and experienced tree climbing instructors lead each session, fitting participants with safety harnesses and helmets before demonstrating how to climb high into the tree on pre-rigged ropes. No previous experience is required, but you will need a moderate level of fitness and an adventurous spirit. A special harness is available for those with impaired mobility. You need to wear comfortable-fitting clothing (no strappy tops or bare midriffs) and walking shoes or trainers. As you're starting from ground level and slowly making your way upwards, at your own pace, people with a fear of heights often overcome their phobia on a Wild Tree Adventure.

MORE ADVENTURE Contact Wild Tree Adventures for other locations in Britain where 'pop-up' tree climbing events are held.

ALSO CONSIDER London
See *A Day in the Urban Jungle*, page 86; **Yorkshire Dales** See *On the Trail of the Red Squirrel*, page 134; **Powys** See *Tree House Adventure*, page 188.

→ Great spotted woodpecker (Piotr Krzeslak/S)

37 ON THE TRAIL OF LEAPING SALMON

RAGING RAPIDS AND FLYING FISH... WITNESS THE EPIC MIGRATION OF THE ATLANTIC SALMON

WHERE	Ettrick Weir, Philiphaugh Estate, Scottish Borders
WHEN	May–Jun or Sep–Nov
HOW LONG	A few hours to visit the Philiphaugh Salmon Viewing Centre and Ettrick Weir; a full day to include a walk in the estate's woodland, & a weekend or more to visit some of Scotland's other wild rivers in search of leaping salmon
WHO FOR	School-age children will enjoy the interactive displays & live camera feeds at the Salmon Viewing Centre; remember to be extra vigilant when taking young children near deep or fast-flowing water
ADVENTURE POTENTIAL	Riverside & woodland walks, birdwatching
WILDLIFE WISHLIST	Atlantic salmon is the star of the show, with a supporting cast of brown trout, eel, grayling, lamprey & perch. Birds include dipper, goosander, grey heron, grey wagtail & kingfisher; visit early for a chance to spot otter or red squirrel

↑ Onwards and upwards: nothing gets in the way of Atlantic salmon (Chanonry/S)

A wildlife adventure in search of salmon? If you're wondering whether this fishy quest might be a hard sell to children, don't worry. Forget boring fish paste sandwiches – you're about to experience a feast of wild scenery, tingling suspense and bursts of action – along with a blockbuster narrative that rivals anything in the animal kingdom. If the Atlantic salmon was a Marvel character its superpowers would include body morphing and mind-bending memory skills. Its athleticism is equivalent to Olympian Tom Daley propelling himself from the swimming pool back on to the high diving platform.

CURRENT AFFAIRS Following spring or autumn rains, Scotland's wild rivers swell and the salmon migration gets underway, the fish swimming, squirming and leaping upriver to reach spawning beds in the highlands. It's one of the most fascinating and dramatic events in Britain's nature calendar.

One of the best spots is the Philiphaugh Salmon Viewing Centre (♥ TD7 5LX ☎ 01750 21766 ⊘ salmonviewingcentre.com) on the Philiphaugh Estate, near Selkirk. As well as watching fish leap the weir on Ettrick Water, live video feeds from underwater cameras provide a glimpse of the epic struggle taking place beneath the churning surface.

Salmon have been known to leap over 3m in their determination to scale weirs and waterfalls, such is their instinctive urge to return to native headwaters to spawn. Stake out a prime spot, like Ettrick Weir, and your patience can be rewarded by the spectacle of these silvery-pink fish erupting from foaming torrents and hurling themselves up seemingly unassailable chutes and rapids. You hold your breath for a few short seconds as an airborne salmon beats its powerful tail from side to side, pectoral fins tucked in as it drives itself forwards and upwards through the spray. But just when you think it will make it, the fish loses momentum and falls back into the turbulent pool at the base of the weir. Almost immediately, another salmon takes up the challenge. Your emotions rise and fall with every leaping, flailing, struggling fish. You become deeply invested in their ordeal. When one fish jumps high and slices like an arrow into the smooth water above the weir, you instinctively cheer. It deserves your applause. This is just one part of a gruelling journey that began years earlier.

TO THE SEA AND BACK AGAIN Baby salmon hatch in early spring, the alevin still attached to yolk sacs as they hide among the gravel beds of spawning sites in the upper reaches of rivers like the Tweed and Tay. Around April or May, the fry disperse, but they will remain in their birthing rivers for two or three years. At about 10cm in length, the young fish, known as parr, undergo physiological changes to equip them for life at sea. Before they take the leap of faith from fresh to salt water, however, the ocean-bound fish (now called smolt) are thought to memorise the distinctive chemical signature of the river in which they were born.

After entering the Atlantic, the salmon swim to rich feeding grounds off southwest Greenland or around the Faroe Islands, gorging on herring, sand eels and krill – while trying to avoid falling prey to orca, seal and shark. They remain at sea for between one and four years, growing rapidly before hormones trigger the homeward migration. The vast majority return to their spawning rivers, but how they do this is still largely a mystery. Out in the open Atlantic, the salmon are thought to navigate using ocean currents and the Earth's magnetic field. Then, as they approach the Scottish coastline, the chemical memories of their youth take over and they are somehow able to 'sniff out' their natal rivers. The more they sense the smell of their birthplace, the greater their urge to swim upstream. If the smell fades, they know they're swimming up the wrong river and they turn around. But if it grows stronger, they surge onwards and nothing – not even a 4m-high weir – will stop them trying to reach their spawning grounds. Of the 5,000 or so eggs shed by each female, only five are destined to complete this epic life cycle. You truly are witnessing the superheroes of the fish world.

ACTION PLAN

ADVENTURE ESSENTIALS The Philiphaugh Salmon Viewing Centre is located 3km from Selkirk on the A708 Selkirk to Moffat Road. From Selkirk you can also follow the 5km Salmon Leap Walk. Start at the riverside car park, taking the path up to a bridge that leads to Ettrickhaugh Road. Follow this for a few hundred metres before crossing a footbridge that leads back to the main riverbank, then continue upstream to reach the weir. The most reliable sightings of leaping salmon tend to be from October–November, particularly after heavy rain. The fish are more active in the early morning and evening, which is also the best time for observing otters, herons and other wildlife. Find a good vantage point near a weir or waterfall, but take care near slippery banks. With luck you may be able to distinguish the blue-black females, swollen with eggs, from the more coppery coloured males. Wild salmon have declined by 70% in the last 25 years – find out more from the Atlantic Salmon Trust (⌀ atlanticsalmontrust.org).

MORE ADVENTURE As well as Ettrick Weir, other good locations to witness the salmon migration in Scotland include the Falls of Feugh, Kincardineshire, where a viewing platform and footbridge provide a good vantage of the foaming torrents. The Falls of Shin in Sutherland also has viewpoints over spectacular waterfalls, while Pitlochry Dam in Perthshire has a salmon ladder, which allows thousands of fish to migrate upstream to Loch Faskally every year. Buchanty Spout on the River Almond, Cargill's Leap on the River Ericht and The Hermitage at the Falls of Braan are also good locations in Perthshire to witness leaping Atlantic salmon.

ALSO CONSIDER South Cornwall See *River Fowey Adventure*, page 36; **Herefordshire** See *A Paddle along the River Wye*, page 102.

↑ Calmer waters: Atlantic salmon resting before the next jump (Marek Rybar/S)

38 BASS ROCK BOAT TRIP

VISIT THE FIRTH OF FORTH'S RAUCOUS SEABIRD CITY WHERE 150,000 GANNETS RULE THE ROOST

WHERE	Firth of Forth, near North Berwick
WHEN	Gannets usually start returning to Bass Rock in late Feb, the nesting season is at its peak Apr–Aug, while the birds start to leave in Sep–Oct
HOW LONG	Bass Rock boat trips last 1hr; landing trips include around 3hrs on the island
WHO FOR	Boat trips are for all ages, but the minimum age for Bass Rock landings is 16
ADVENTURE POTENTIAL	Birdwatching, boat trips, dolphin spotting
WILDLIFE WISHLIST	As well as northern gannet, you should see cormorant, fulmar, guillemot, kittiwake, puffin, razorbill & shag, with dolphins, harbour porpoise & seals also possible

As you drive along the East Lothian coast towards North Berwick, you can't miss the strange island lying offshore. Even when it's overcast, Bass Rock appears to glow. The white shroud draped over its precipitous, 100m-tall cliffs has nothing to do with the unmanned lighthouse nestled on the three-hectare island. Nor is the curious gleam caused by flecks of feldspar that crystallised when Bass Rock's tough, igneous phonolite was being forged deep in the neck of an active volcano, 350 million years ago.

It's birds that turn Bass Rock white – over 150,000 of them. A short boat ride from the mainland, 5km away, the world's largest colony of northern gannets is the setting for one of Britain's most spectacular wildlife spectacles. You can see other gannetries at Bempton Cliffs in Yorkshire, Grassholm off the coast of Pembrokeshire and at Noss in the Shetland Islands, but Bass Rock offers the most intense experience. Such is its significance that the northern gannet's scientific name – *Morus bassanus* – gives a nod to the island. For any budding ornithologist, Bass Rock is an unrivalled avian treat. You have to wait until you're 16 before you can land on the island, but until then, a boat trip offers a head-spinning ride into the kingdom of Britain's largest seabird.

A RENDEZVOUS WITH ROCK STARS Lying just off the coast of North Berwick, Craigleith is the warm-up act for boat trips to Bass Rock. You'll spend a few minutes pottering around the island's craggy shoreline – a nesting site for guillemots, razorbills, puffins and shags, but not a single gannet.

As you turn northeast and head towards Bass Rock, you might wonder why so many gannets crowd on to this one island each spring to nest, flying up to 6,000km from their wintering grounds off the African coast. There's certainly safety in numbers from predators, while the island's gently undulating summit offers plenty of good nesting sites. Permits for landing on the island are also

Left: Approaching the 'white rock'; **overpage:** a closer view of the gannetry (William Gray)

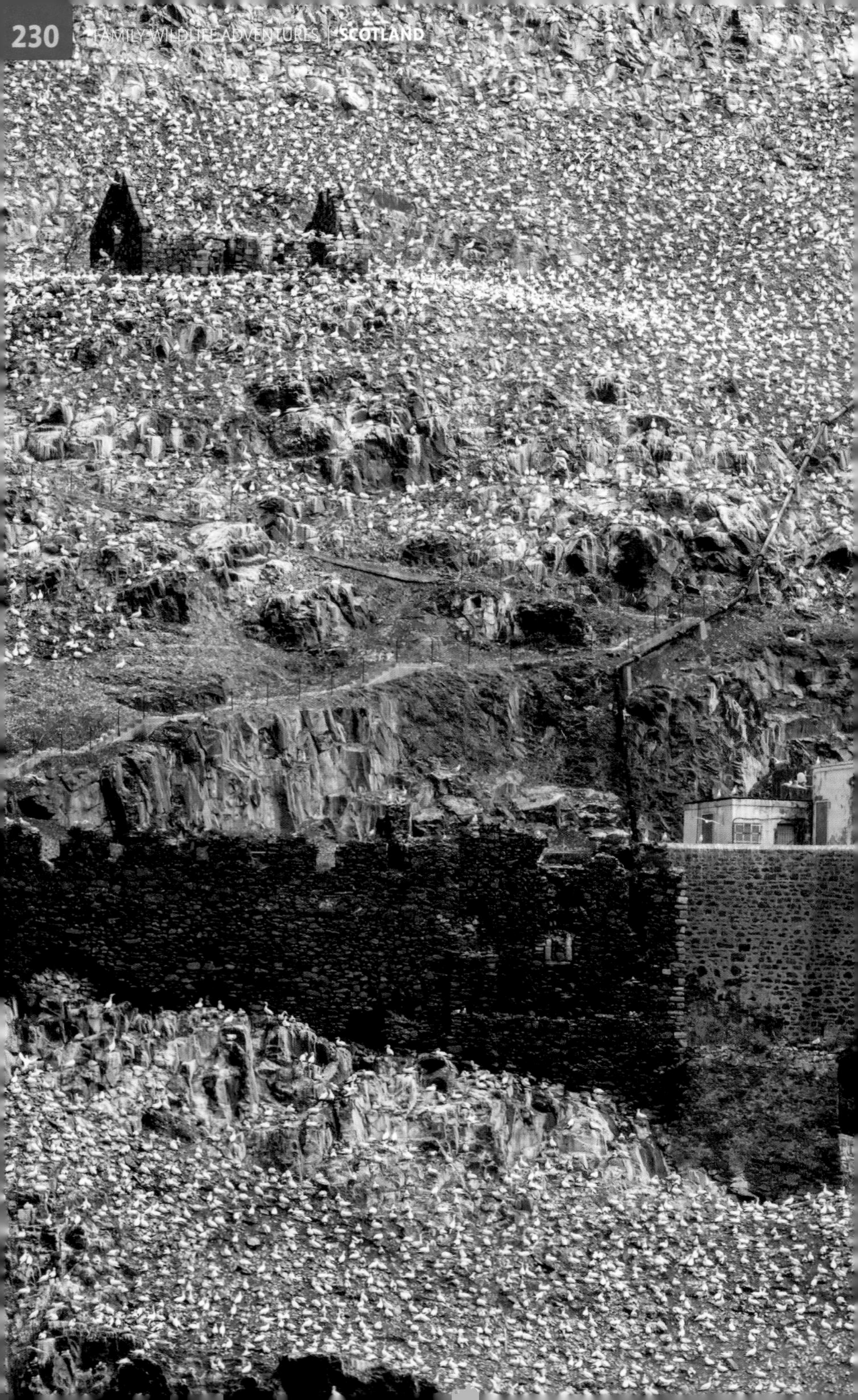

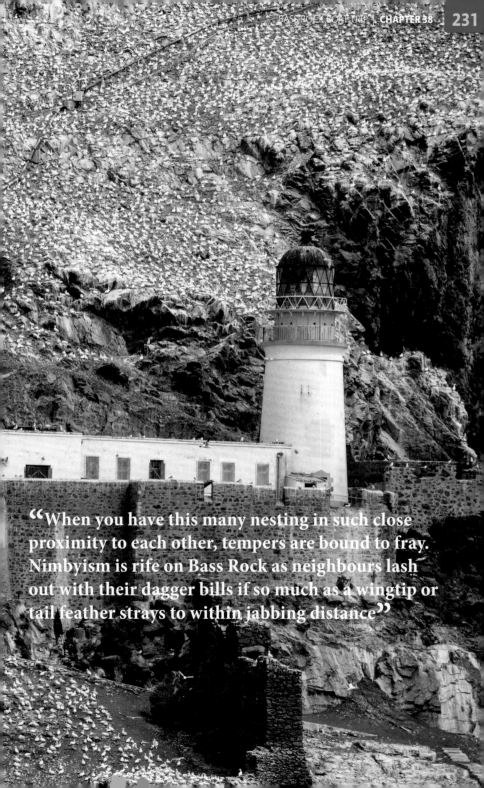

"When you have this many nesting in such close proximity to each other, tempers are bound to fray. Nimbyism is rife on Bass Rock as neighbours lash out with their dagger bills if so much as a wingtip or tail feather strays to within jabbing distance"

carefully controlled, so human disturbance is kept to a minimum. And because gannets are such accomplished travellers, soaring over vast distances on their 2m wingspans, they can easily find enough food to sustain the breeding colony.

It's the sight of birds flying that you begin to notice as the boat approaches the Rock... a gannet confetti swirling over the island. You might see some fishing in the surrounding waters, diving from heights of 30m, wings folded back, hitting the water at speeds of nearly 90km/h. Muscles lock their neck vertebrae in place before entry, while air sacs help cushion the impact. When one gannet starts diving, numerous others often join in, dropping like fluted arrows into the sea, churning the surface and disorientating the fish so they're easier to catch.

But the commotion out at sea is nothing compared to the throng of birds on Bass Rock itself. As the boat sidles into the lee of the island, the sound and smell of 150,000 gannets engulfs you. These are birds with attitude (check out the risqué shade of turquoise eye shadow) and when you have this many nesting in such close proximity to each other, tempers are bound to fray. Nimbyism is rife on Bass Rock as neighbours lash out with their dagger bills if so much as a wingtip or tail feather strays to within jabbing distance.

There's also a gentler side to these magnificent birds. Pairs mate for life, reavowing their bond by standing face to face, bowing and rattling bills. The male is the homebuilder, constructing a nest of seaweed, feathers and dirt, cemented together by droppings – the copious amounts of guano deposited on Bass Rock not only contribute to its white glow, but also lend the island its heady aroma of ammonia and fish. A single egg is laid, hatching into a blue-black, almost featherless chick. Young gannets – or gugas – rapidly acquire a fuzz of white fluff, followed by brown feathers when they fledge after 90 days. During late September and October, they spend a few weeks swimming on the surface, so chubby and buoyant that they're unable to fly properly or dive for food. By November, the Rock is almost deserted.

↑ **Above left:** gannet eyes are positioned forward for binocular vision to enable them to judge distances when diving; **above right:** neighbourly love on a crowded island (Mark Cane/S; William Gray)

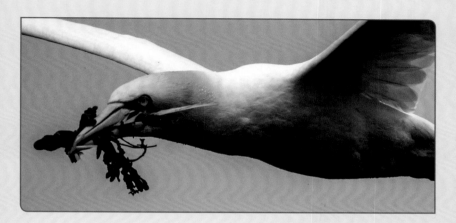

ACTION PLAN

ADVENTURE ESSENTIALS Located in North Berwick, the Scottish Seabird Centre (📍 EH39 4SS 📞 01620 890202 🔗 seabird.org) runs boat trips to Bass Rock and other islands in the Firth of Forth from April to September. The Seabird Catamaran Cruise is the most family-friendly option, combining Bass Rock and the island of Craigleath in an hour-long cruise aboard the stable, 55-seater *Seafari Explorer*. Slightly longer, the Three Islands Seabird Seafari (minimum age seven) uses a high-speed RIB to include the island of Lamb where some 680 pairs of puffins breed. Landing trips on Bass Rock (minimum age 16) allow around three hours on the island in the company of an experienced guide. Getting ashore can sometimes be challenging if the sea is rough, there are no toilets on the island and the terrain can be slippery and exposed – but you will experience the thrill of sitting close to nesting gannets, surrounded by the noise, smell and activity of the colony. Two-hour Gannet Diving Photography boat trips (also for ages 16 and above) provide another superb photographic opportunity. Back on the mainland, don't miss the seabird centre's excellent Discovery Experience where CCTV cameras relay live footage from Bass Rock. Also operating out of North Berwick, Sula Boat Trips (📞 01620 849289 🔗 sulaboattrips.co.uk) offer 90-minute cruises to Bass Rock and Craigleath.

MORE ADVENTURE Both of the above operators also run boat trips to the Isle of May, a nature reserve around 17km from North Berwick. As well as heaving with puffins and other seabirds during summer, it's an important stop-over for migrant birds during spring and autumn, while October–January is pupping season for the island's large colony of grey seals – about 2,000 young are born each season.

ALSO CONSIDER **West Cornwall** See *Cornish Coast Wildlife Safari*, page 28; **Northumberland** See *Farne Islands Boat Trip*, page 156; **Pembrokeshire** See *On the Trail of the Puffin*, page 170; **Shetland Islands** See *Journey to the End of Britain*, page 300.

↑ Male gannet carrying seaweed and feathers for its nest (William Gray)

39 LOCH LOMOND FARM ADVENTURE

GO GLAMPING AT PORTNELLAN FOR SPECTACULAR VIEWS, WATERSPORTS AND ABUNDANT WILDLIFE

WHERE	Portnellan Farm, Loch Lomond
WHEN	Year-round
HOW LONG	Glamping is available from two nights
WHO FOR	Any age, but minimum of 12 for paddleboarding
ADVENTURE POTENTIAL	Kayaking, paddleboarding, farm walks, boat trips
WILDLIFE WISHLIST	Badger, brown hare, pine marten, red squirrel, roe deer, barn & tawny owl, goldeneye, great crested grebe, grey heron, kingfisher, osprey, skylark, swallow

Speedboats, banana boats, jet skis, yachts, seaplanes, pleasure cruisers… if it floats, you'll find it on Loch Lomond. But for wildlife watchers, the best way to explore Britain's largest expanse of freshwater is by kayak or paddleboard. Both can be hired from the small marina at Portnellan Farm on the loch's southeastern shore – and by staying here, you also get an opportunity to discover the diverse wildlife that flourishes on the 93-hectare organic beef farm.

WILDLIFE ON THE FARM Intensive agriculture leaves little room for wildlife and has led to declines of more than 80% in farmland species such as corn bunting, grey partridge, tree sparrow and turtle dove. The moment you arrive at Portnellan Farm, however, it becomes abundantly clear that wildlife and farming can thrive side by side.

Stretching along 2km of Loch Lomond shoreline, Portnellan converted from dairy to an organic beef suckler herd in 2010. During summer, swallows dip and swoop among the grazing cattle like restless paper darts. The owners, David and Freda Scott-Park, ask you to leave the old milking shed doors open so the birds can reach their nests – intricate cups of dried mud, lined with grass and feathers, tucked into the rafters. If you're glamping at Portnellan (staying in the cosy bell tent with its candle lanterns and wood-burning stove), the swallows become familiar neighbours, flitting over your head each time you enter the shed with its toilet, shower and simple kitchen.

Glowing with buttercups and clover, lush meadows cloak the hillsides above the farm. In mid-summer, they will be cut for silage, but not before the skylarks have nested, lining small hollows in the ground with grass, leaves and hair. Keep your eyes peeled for a pair of black-tipped ears protruding above the vegetation – brown hares are common on the farm and, during spring and early summer, you might see them boxing or chasing each other, zigzagging across the fields at speeds of up to 70km/h.

Left: the view from the farm; **right:** swallow (William Gray)

At dusk, barn owls patrol the meadows at a more leisurely pace – wafting silently on pale wings, hovering briefly, then dropping on hapless rodents. Another beautiful cream-and-brown raptor, the osprey also nests at Portnellan Farm. Follow the hedgerows to the skyline, where grassland meets forest, and you may well find a pair soaring above the hills, surveying the vast fishing grounds of Loch Lomond stretching away to the north.

TAKING TO THE WATER It's always worth keeping watch for an osprey while you are out on Loch Lomond. Train your binoculars on this summer visitor and you can't miss its hooked bill and large talons – ideal for snatching trout, pike and other fish from the water. White-tailed eagles are also a possibility as the species looks set to recolonise the area after an absence of more than a century.

Paddling a sit-on kayak or SUP (stand-up paddleboard) from the wooden jetty at Portnellan Farm, you're more likely, at first, to see common waterbirds, such as mallards and cormorants. Just offshore, you can explore woody islets where alder trees rise above the surface – on a hot, still summer's day, it feels like you're entering a tropical mangrove swamp. Listen for the gruff croak as a grey heron takes flight, or the high-pitched whistle of a hidden kingfisher.

Great crested grebes sometimes nest among the stands of flooded alder, building rafts of reed stems and sticks. Adorned with chestnut head plumes and orange ruffs, the flamboyant birds engage in elaborate courtship dances. Ruffs puffed up and heads held high, a pair face each other, head shaking, bowing and 'bob-preening' (a quick ruffling of back feathers). If that goes to plan, the birds then spontaneously dive, reappearing with little gifts of waterweed which are presented with much excitement as they rear up in front of one another, furiously treading water or skittering across the surface in a frenzied 'aquatic tango'. Eggs are laid as early as February and, although the chicks can swim soon after hatching, they often ride on a parent's back, snug between its wings.

↑ **Left to right:** fur and feathers – brown hare and osprey at Portnellan Farm (William Gray)

ACTION PLAN

ADVENTURE ESSENTIALS Located on the southern shores of Loch Lomond, Portnellan Farm (♥ G83 8NL ☏ 01389 830487 ⊘ portnellanfarm.co.uk) is around 9km north of Balloch – 45 minutes by car or train from Glasgow. As well as a three-bedroom farmhouse to rent, the farm offers glamping in a 5m-wide bell tent with double bed and two single futons, a small wood-burning stove and candle lanterns. It's pitched next to the Old Byre, a former milking barn, that now has a toilet, shower and kitchen, equipped with fridge, freezer, microwave oven and hob. Outside the tent there's a fire pit and barbecue with panoramic views across Loch Lomond towards Ben Lomond, Scotland's most southerly munro. A track leads down to the shore where paddleboards and kayaks can be rented. With a full day to explore, the islands of Inchmurrin, Creinch, Torrinch and Inchcailloch are all within striking distance of Portnellan. The farm also offers speedboat tours and guided walks where you can learn about organic farming and enjoy some home baking. Cruise Loch Lomond (☏ 01301 702356 ⊘ cruiselochlomond.co.uk) and Sweeney's Cruise Company (☏ 01389 752376 ⊘ sweeneyscruiseco.com) offer boat trips from several locations, including Balloch, Balmaha, Inversnaid, Luss and Talbert. To find out more about Loch Lomond and the Trossachs National Park, head to the visitor centre at Balmaha (♥ G63 0JQ ☏ 01389 722600 ⊘ lochlomond-trossachs.org).

MORE ADVENTURE There are numerous hiking and cycling routes in the national park. The 48km Great Trossachs Path runs between Callander and Inversnaid, weaving through the Great Trossachs Forest, an ambitious woodland restoration project covering 160km², while the 28km West Loch Lomond Cycle Path links Balloch and Tarbert, with plenty of opportunities for loch-side picnics.

ALSO CONSIDER **West Sussex** See *Rewilding Safari at Knepp*, page 76; **Cumbria** See *Farm and Fell Safari*, page 146; **Ceredigion** See *On the Trail of the Kite*, page 180.

↑ Glamping at Portnellan (William Gray)

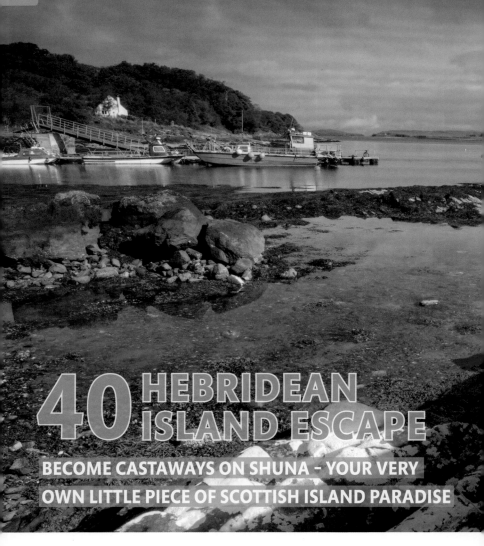

40 HEBRIDEAN ISLAND ESCAPE

BECOME CASTAWAYS ON SHUNA - YOUR VERY OWN LITTLE PIECE OF SCOTTISH ISLAND PARADISE

WHERE	Isle of Shuna, Argyll & Bute
WHEN	Year-round, but Apr–Oct is best for wildlife
HOW LONG	Holiday cottages are available for weekly rental
WHO FOR	All ages; just watch young children around water
ADVENTURE POTENTIAL	Boat trips, sea kayaking, rockpooling, beachcombing, animal tracking, pond dipping
WILDLIFE WISHLIST	Common dolphin, harbour porpoise, harbour seal & otter; fallow, red & roe deer; eider, gannet; golden & white-tailed eagle; oystercatcher, peregrine & woodcock

↑ The harbour and Birchwood - one of the holiday cottages on the Isle of Shuna (William Gray)

We were standing barefoot on the deck of our cottage, soon after breakfast, when the otter swam into Castle Bay. The sea was as smooth as taut satin; we could clearly make out its head (flat-topped, low in the water) and a long arrow-shaped wake, glinting silver in the morning sunlight. Just as we reached for binoculars, the otter dived, flicking sparkling droplets from its tail, before surfacing a hundred metres or so further along the shore. It was clearly heading for a gently sloping rocky headland. Our first day on Shuna – we hadn't even started exploring the island – and we were watching an otter gambol ashore, shake itself vigorously, then slip back into the sea again.

For the next week, our time on Shuna would reset to island life – the ebb and flow of the tides gurgling and popping through the seaweed-smothered rocks a few steps from our door; fallow deer tiptoeing outside our kitchen window at dawn and dusk, and the constant wildlife vigil – scanning 'our' patch of sea from the deck, waiting for the next otter, a harbour seal, or maybe even a porpoise.

PLAYING THE CASTAWAY A week on the Isle of Shuna is like a cottage holiday, mini-expedition and wildlife adventure rolled into one. You need to take all your food and supplies with you. There's no WiFi, shop, pub or roads... just a handful of cottages – some clustered around the rudimentary harbour, others dotted through the birch, oak and rhododendron forest that cloaks much of the island.

To get around, you either walk (a track known as the M1 links one end of the 5km-long island with the other), launch a sea kayak or hop into the small aluminium skiff, with small outboard engine, that comes with your cottage.

The adventure begins before you even set foot on the island. Reaching Shuna requires a carefully timed rendezvous at Arduaine's lonely pier, half an hour's drive south of Oban (the best place to stock up on supplies before casting yourself adrift from the mainland). A bright orange landing craft arrives to collect you and your gear for the 20-minute crossing.

As you approach Shuna, you can't fail to notice a small castle poking above the island's low, wooded hills. Now abandoned and derelict, the mock-Edwardian pile was built by the adventurer and philanthopist George Alexander McLean Buckley in the early 1900s. A Stone Age burial mound near the southern tip of the island suggests Shuna may have been settled some 9,000 years earlier. Bronze Age swords dating from around AD800 have also been discovered, while the ruins of 18th-century lime kilns point to an industrial past before the island eventually

↑ South End House has views along the Sound of Jura (William Gray)

passed to its current owners. The Gully family live on nearby Seil, running Shuna as a low-impact holiday business, alongside sheep grazing and fish farming. On arrival, you're met by the island's resident caretakers, Rob and Kathryn James. A full briefing on island life, including how to operate your boat, is given the following morning.

MESSING ABOUT IN BOATS This is a holiday that actively encourages children to get back to nature. As well as rockpooling, crabbing and otter spotting, you'll need to collect firewood, refine your stone-skimming skills, synchronise with the tides and become an avid weather watcher. After checking the daily forecast posted in the boathouse, you can plan your own boat trips, exploring the seas around Shuna and neighbouring islands.

Pottering past the rocky shoreline, the water is often so clear you can see kelp swirling several metres below you. Compass, lion's mane and moon jellyfish gently pulse through the calm shallows of sheltered bays – and you may also spot the closely related comb jelly. Look carefully at this cylindrical, almost transparent ctenophore and you may notice multicoloured ripples of bioluminescence flickering along the sides of its body. Tie up on a skerry at low tide and you'll find rockpools twitching with hermit crabs and scattered with beadlet anemones, like rubies burst from a treasure chest.

Oystercatchers, sandpipers, gulls, jackdaws and hooded crows are commonly seen foraging along the coast, but keep casting your gaze skywards for a chance to spot a white-tailed eagle soaring over the island.

Boat excursions can sometimes become impromptu whale-watching trips. Heading south along the Sound of Shuna, we encountered a pod of five harbour porpoises, their backs arching briefly above the surface. If you're lucky enough

↑ Picnic on the rocks: exploring Shuna's rocky islets in your own boat (William Gray)

"In Lime Kiln Bay, the wreck of the *Maid of Luing* lies high and dry, the timbers of the 1950s turntable car ferry split and flaking; rusty nails studding her wooden beams and deck boards"

↑ Kayaking to the shipwreck in Lime Kiln Bay (William Gray)

to spot cetaceans, always remember to slow down, maintain a constant speed and observe them from a distance of at least 100m. Never steer straight towards them or attempt to follow a pod. Don't get carried away either... the seas beyond the southern tip of Shuna's neighbouring island of Luing are a submarine training zone and strictly out-of-bounds to Shuna boats.

KAYAKING AND HIKING Paddling one of Shuna's sit-on kayaks north from the harbour takes you to a series of beautiful coves: black rocks daubed with rust-coloured *Xanthoria* lichen and a pink fuzz of thrift. Drift silently and you might encounter fallow deer browsing along the edge of the island's wild wood of twisted birches and moss-draped oaks. In Lime Kiln Bay, the wreck of the *Maid of Luing* lies high and dry, the timbers of the 1950s turntable car ferry split and flaking; rusty nails studding her wooden beams and deck boards.

You can also hike to the shipwreck, bushwacking through bracken and bog myrtle, before coasteering along the shoreline back to the harbour. A less challenging option is to follow Shuna's M1 walking trail – a 5km return hike between the harbour and South Bay.

The track climbs through woodland before straddling the island's grassy interior, where skylark song fills the air and large red damselflies flash like sparks above peaty pools. After passing Stone Age and Bronze Age burial mounds, you reach South Bay, a lone cottage facing Jura and the Atlantic beyond. The path fizzles out, but follow the shoreline a little further south and you'll find damp grassland stippled with ragged robin, its pink, frayed petals tusselled by the ocean breeze. Quivering spikes of northern marsh orchid add darker splashes of magenta, contrasting with the yellow slipper-shaped flowers of bird's-foot trefoil – a riot of summer colour matched by Shuna's equally mesmerising rockpools.

↑ Fallow deer on the Isle of Shuna (William Gray)

ACTION PLAN

ADVENTURE ESSENTIALS Located between the island of Luing and the mainland settlement of Craobh Haven, the 400-hectare Isle of Shuna (☎ 01852 314244 ⌖ islandofshuna.co.uk) is accessed by boat from Arduaine Pier (▥ piled.mingles.dogs), 30km south of Oban on the A816. Shuna has seven holiday cottages, including Boat House (a luxury apartment for six with views of the harbour), Birchwood (an idyllic two-bedroom cottage with a deck overlooking a rocky cove), Garden Cottage (located next to the old walled gardens of the castle), Oakwood Cottage (sleeping ten and with its own track leading to a sheltered bay) and South End House (a secluded five-bedroom property with stunning views towards Jura). All have electricity (from the island's solar panels and small wind turbine), wood-burning stove, gas-powered fridge-freezer and filtered spring water. A 5m-long assault craft with outboard engine is provided with each cottage – no previous boating experience is required and you are given a full briefing on reefs, safe routes etc. Sea kayaks are also available. You need to bring all your food and supplies with you (the nearest supermarket is in Oban) and be ready for collection at Arduaine on changeover days. Cars can be parked nearby while you are on Shuna.

MORE ADVENTURE Offering wildlife-watching boat trips to the northern end of Jura, Scarba and the Corryvreckan whirlpool, Farsain Cruises (☎ 07880 714165 ⌖ farsain-cruises.business.site) can arrange pick-ups from the Isle of Shuna.

ALSO CONSIDER North Devon See *Lundy Island Adventure*, page 44; **Shetland Islands** See *Journey to the End of Britain*, page 300.

Above: Shuna Castle; **right:** northern marsh orchid (William Gray)

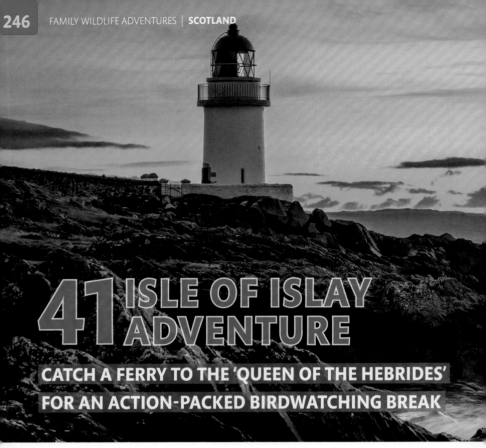

41 ISLE OF ISLAY ADVENTURE

CATCH A FERRY TO THE 'QUEEN OF THE HEBRIDES' FOR AN ACTION-PACKED BIRDWATCHING BREAK

WHERE	Isle of Islay, Inner Hebrides
WHEN	Year-round; Oct half-term is ideal for witnessing the arrival of migrant geese, but summer promises fairer weather for boat trips and beaches
HOW LONG	At least a long weekend – ideally 4–5 days
WHO FOR	With its range of beaches and activities, an Islay adventure can be adapted for all ages (min age 8 for sea kayaking trips, 12 for fat-biking tours)
ADVENTURE POTENTIAL	Hiking, boat trips, sea kayaking, cycling & birdwatching
WILDLIFE WISHLIST	Common dolphin, grey seal, otter, red deer, barnacle and white-fronted goose, chough, corncrake, plus various waders & birds of prey (including golden eagle & hen harrier)

The Isle of Islay (pronounced 'eye-lah') is renowned for its peaty single malt whiskies (there are nine distilleries on the island), but wildlife connoisseurs will be just as keen to sample its vintage wildlife. A heady treat for birdwatchers,

↑ Sunrise at Port Charlotte, looking northeast towards the Paps of Jura (KevinStandage/S)

each autumn sees the mass arrival of migrant geese from Greenland, while Islay's resident critters – including otters and golden eagles – offer exhilarating wildlife encounters throughout the year. For families, there's the added appeal of the island's stunning beaches – particularly Machir, Saligo and Sanaigmore on the west coast. Simply tracking down these Atlantic-raked bays, and discovering you have them all to yourself, is a rewarding adventure in itself. Islay is also home to two RSPB reserves, while activities such as boat trips, sea kayaking and fat biking add a splash of adrenaline to your wildlife-spotting forays.

ISLAY BOUND As the ferry leaves Kennacraig on Scotland's Kintyre Peninsula and bears west across the Sound of Jura, keep your binoculars handy. Gannets are a common sight, scything the whitecaps; pods of common dolphins course through the swells and you may even glimpse a minke whale – its arched back glinting briefly above the surface like a pebble of polished basalt. The triple peaks you can see to the right are the Paps of Jura, rising to 785m, but look ahead to Islay and you'll find a less forbidding island – perfect for hiking and cycling.

EXPLORING THE OA PENINSULA Islay is laced with paths, tracks and quiet country roads. Base yourself in Port Ellen, where the ferry docks, and you can hire bikes and set off on a ride in search of elusive otters, or hike the coastal path into the wilds of The Oa peninsula. Wind-tossed crows, tumbling and swirling along the cliff edge, might well be choughs – look for their distinctive scarlet legs and a matching bill that's slender and slightly curved; ideal for plucking invertebrates from soil, dung or strandline. Around 9km southwest of Port Ellen, the fields at RSPB The Oa Reserve (✆ 01496 300118 ⌂ rspb.org.uk) are managed to provide food for these charismatic corvids, as well as large, over-wintering flocks of twite. Spare a thought for these diminutive cinnamon-tinged finches – they're completely upstaged by The Oa's golden eagles. Scan each and every rocky outcrop for a sighting of this magnificent raptor, scowling from its moorland roost, or catch your breath as one stoops on a hare or wild goose. Peregrines and hen harriers also patrol this lonely corner of Islay, but remarkably there's another reserve on the island that's just as good, if not better, for birds.

A GANDER AT LOCH GRUINART Having flown over 3,200km from nesting sites in Greenland, the wet grasslands of the RSPB Loch Gruinart Reserve (✆ 01496 850505 ⌂ rspb.org.uk), 27km north of Port Ellen, make an ideal winter feeding ground for up to 25,000 barnacle and white-fronted geese. Dense flocks of black-and-white 'barnies' pepper the skies over Islay, their yappy cries and thudding wingbeats reverberating across the brooding landscape of saltmarsh, moorland and sea loch. Early morning and late afternoon are the best times to witness 'wall-to-wall feathers'. Intersperse your geese-ogling with a picnic at nearby Sanaigmore, or a walk to Killinallan Point where seals often haul out on sandbanks. If you're visiting in spring or summer, focus instead on corncrake – a rare visitor from Africa, skulking through Loch Gruinart's flower-filled grassland, its rasping call like a fingernail drawn across a comb.

KAYAKING AND BOAT TRIPS After allocating a couple of days to exploring Loch Gruinart and The Oa, a sea kayak or boat trip offers a contrasting perspective of the island. A few hours paddling a kayak along a sheltered stretch of shore is one of the best ways to spot grey seals, as well as seabirds such as black guillemot and Arctic tern. Gliding silently in and out of rocky inlets, you might spot an otter. They're superbly camouflaged when resting on kelp-covered rocks, so look for movement. Hooded crows sometimes scavenge around feeding otters, or you could see one in open water, swimming with just its broad muzzle and flattish head above the surface. Boat trips depart from the marina in Port Ellen, skirting the southeast coast of Islay where you might see both golden and white-tailed eagles, grey seals, common and bottlenose dolphins and basking sharks.

ACTION PLAN

ADVENTURE ESSENTIALS Caledonian MacBrayne (℘ 0800 066 5000 ⊘ calmac.co.uk) operates a vehicle/passenger ferry between Kennacraig and either Port Ellen or Port Askaig on Islay. The crossing takes 2–2½ hours. You can travel to the Kennacraig Ferry Terminal by bus from Glasgow using Scottish CityLink (⊘ citylink.co.uk), while Logan Air (℘ 0344 800 2855 ⊘ loganair.co.uk) offers flights to Islay from Glasgow and Edinburgh. Accommodation on Islay ranges from hotels and guesthouses to self-catering cottages and campsites – for an online directory, see Islay Info (⊘ islayinfo.com). You don't have to bring your car to Islay. Help reduce local traffic by hiring electric bikes from Islay E-Wheels (℘ 07497 090716 ⊘ islayewheels.co.uk) in Port Ellen.

Islay Sea Adventures (℘ 01496 300129 ⊘ islay-sea-adventures.co.uk) operates several boat trips from Port Ellen, including a 2–2½-hour wildlife tour suitable for all ages. Other options range from fishing trips and seafood cruises to a high-speed RIB ride (from Port Askaig) along the coast of Jura to witness the maelstroms and standing waves of the Corryvreckan whirlpool. As well as half- and full-day sea kayaking tours suitable for families with children aged from eight and 12 respectively, Kayak Wild Islay (℘ 07973 725456 ⊘ kayakwildislay.co.uk) offers fat biking tours (minimum age 12) exploring beaches and inland tracks on mountain bikes with super-sized tyres. If you want to boost your chances of seeing rare species, such as otter, golden eagle or hen harrier, local guide Donald James MacPhee from Islay Outdoors (℘ 01496 850643 ⊘ islayoutdoors. com) knows all the best spots. For a wet-weather bolthole, head to the Nature Centre of The Islay Natural History Trust (♀ PA48 7TX ℘ 01496 850288 ⊘ islaynaturalhistory.org) in Port Charlotte where you'll find aquariums, exhibits and activities for children.

MORE ADVENTURE Home to 200 people, 5,000 deer and one whisky distillery, the Isle of Jura lies across a narrow strait from Islay and is easily reached on the 5-minute ferry crossing between Port Askaig and Feolin. Wild and untamed, it's a wonderful island for hiking, cycling and wildlife watching. Take your bikes with you on the ferry or explore using the local bus service. The quartzite peaks of the Paps of Jura might be tempting, but they require a challenging 10-hour hike. Shorter walks include the 1½-hour island crossing at Tarbert.

ALSO CONSIDER Gwynedd See *Journey to the Edge of Wales*, page 198; **Isle of Mull** See *Eagle Island Adventure*, page 250; **Isle of Skye** See *Hike and Kayak on Skye*, page 270.

→ Chough (KB Photography/S)

42 EAGLE ISLAND ADVENTURE

SAIL TO MULL IN SEARCH OF GOLDEN AND WHITE-TAILED EAGLES, PLUS OTTERS, SEALS AND WHALES

WHERE	Isle of Mull, Inner Hebrides
WHEN	Year-round; the Mull Eagle Watch viewing project runs Apr–Oct; summer is the best time to see marine wildlife; visit in autumn for the red deer rut
HOW LONG	At least 2–3 days, but a week would be better
WHO FOR	All ages – although eagle spotting can require patience & persistence, & views can be fleeting
ADVENTURE POTENTIAL	Wildlife safaris, boat trips, birdwatching, whale watching, wild camping
WILDLIFE WISHLIST	In addition to golden and white-tailed eagle, you could see buzzard, hen harrier, merlin & short-eared owl; seabirds include gannet, guillemot, puffin & razorbill, while keen birders can seek out crossbill, golden plover, red-throated diver, ring ouzel & rock pipit; resident mammals include grey & harbour seal, otter & red deer; bottlenose dolphin & harbour porpoise are joined by summer-visiting basking shark, common dolphin & minke whale

↑ White-tailed eagle soaring over Mull (Mark Caun/S)

Your wildlife adventure starts as soon as you board the ferry in Oban for the 45-minute crossing to Craignure on Mull's southeast coast. Harbour porpoises are frequently seen and, during summer, you might also glimpse the dark triangular dorsal fin of a basking shark as it tacks back and forth through tidal currents. But it's eagles that steal the limelight on this wildlife-rich isle...

SPYING ON SEA EAGLES Larger than golden eagles, with wingspans up to 2.4m, white-tailed eagles (sometimes called sea eagles) nest in forests along the shores of Mull's kelp-fringed coast. You might be lucky enough to see them soaring overhead, or even hunting offshore, but your best hope of a sighting is from the hide operated by Mull Eagle Watch (✆ 01680 812556 ✆ mulleaglewatch.com). Its location can change from year to year depending on where a suitable nest has been established – you'll receive details for your rendezvous with the 'eagle rangers' when you book the 90-minute experience.

Peering through binoculars or a telescope as one of the adults appears, swooping towards the nest, its huge, yellow bill jutting forwards and that distinctive white tail fanned to break its dive, is an unforgettable – and privileged – experience.

White-tailed eagles once bred throughout Britain with at least 100 eyries recorded in the early 19th century. Shooting and poisoning, however, decimated the population and in 1916 the last two birds were killed on Skye. In 1975, a reintroduction programme helped these regal raptors reclaim their former Scottish haunts. Mull has become a stronghold, and eagles are now being released on the Isle of Wight (page 74) in the hope of further restoring their range.

Depending on when you visit the hide at Mull Eagle Watch, you might see one of the adults brooding her precious clutch. You'll have no difficulty spotting the nest – a great tangle of branches and twigs that is used on and off for several years, with both parents adding fresh material each spring. On average, white-tailed eagles live for 21 years, forming lifelong bonds with their mates. Two or three eggs are laid in March or April, with the first chick hatching after 38 days. Over the next ten weeks or so, you can watch the parents flying in with fish, as well as the odd puffin or mountain hare. The chicks grow rapidly, morphing from floppy bundles of pale grey down to scruffy, brown-and-white-flecked juveniles, flexing their wings, eager to fledge. Even when they do leave the nest, the young remain close-by, dependent on their parents, for another month or two.

SEARCHING FOR GOLD After the exhilaration of Mull Eagle Watch, you now face a bigger challenge. Whereas white-tailed eagles often nest in relatively accessible shoreline forests, golden eagles are wilder spirits, drifting over Mull's remote glens, mountains and moorland. But while your chances of a sighting are slimmer, the opportunities for adventure are enormous. Instead of staking out a nest from a hide, you will need to embark on a wildlife safari across Mull to stand any chance of spotting Britain's second largest bird of prey.

↑ White-tailed eagle (Jamie Harwood/S)

Local wildlife experts lead regular tours (see *Action plan*, page 255), or you can set off on your own. From Craignure, the A849 loops south through forest before ascending rugged Glen More. Just before you climb into the mountains, a left turn tempts you south to Lochbuie and the remote sweep of Laggan Sands where you can visit Moy Castle and an ancient stone circle.

Back on the main road, weaving beneath 966m Ben More, pull over in one of the parking spaces to scan the ridges of Beinn Talaidh and Ben Buie for the telltale silhouettes of soaring eagles. With wingspans a good 20cm shorter than white-tailed eagles, 'goldies' are smaller, but that's not much help when you're squinting at a distant, lone bird. Instead look closely at the wings. Golden eagles hold them in a shallow V-shape and the wings narrow where they meet the body, compared to the uniformly broad and 'rigid' set of a sea eagle's wings. In good light, you might be able to make out large white patches on the underside of a golden eagle's wings, or its longer, more wedge-shaped tail and darker head. Just don't fall for a buzzard. They're common on Mull and, beautiful as they are, they're only half the size of their big cousins.

As you continue west along the Ross of Mull, following the southern shore of Loch Scridain, keep your eyes peeled for seals. At Pennyghael, there's a small shop for picnic snacks. Then, after another 11km, a track branches south from Bunessan to the white-sand beauties of Uisken and Ardalanish. Both beaches have views to Colonsay and Jura, and are good spots for seal and dolphin watching.

From Bunessan, it's around 9km to Fionnphort and the road's end – or rather the slipway for the ferry to Iona and boat trips to Staffa and Treshnish. South of the village, Fidden Beach is pimpled with pink granite outcrops and pockets of pebbles, speckled like birds' eggs – a paradise for beachcombing and rockpooling.

↑ Golden eagle (Ian Duffield/S)

Returning to Craignure at the end of the day, try to stop by a quiet stretch of shore on a rising tide. Sit and watch, keeping a low profile, as each swell chuckles through heaped piles of kelp, massaging them to life until they're twitching, swirling and cavorting with the sea. It could be just the right place, time and conditions for otters to be out hunting for crabs and butterfish.

MULLING OVER MINKE WHALES If the eagles and otters have given you the slip, splash out on a boat trip with Tobermory's Sea Life Surveys (✆ 01688 302916 ⏾ sealifesurveys.com). You'll get four hours at sea in the company of an experienced skipper and professional wildlife guide, exploring the waters between Mull, Ardnamurchan and the Isle of Coll. It's the perfect opportunity to spot white-tailed and golden eagles, as well as a wide variety of seabirds. It's all eyes on deck for marine mammals too. Working with the Hebridean Whale and Dolphin Trust (⏾ hwdt.org), Sea Life Surveys have been conducting a photo-identification study of minke whales since 1990. Lured to the rich feeding grounds around Mull each summer, over 100 individual whales have been identified and catalogued.

Keep watch for gannets plunge-diving into the sea – it could be a feeding frenzy: minke whales chasing fish to the surface and attracting the attention of hungry seabirds. Common and bottlenose dolphins sometimes join in. You will almost certainly see grey seals hauled out on rocky skerries or surfacing nearby. And as for the ever-elusive otter, keep alert as you sidle back into the harbour at Tobermory – you might just spot one playing with the mooring buoy of a yacht.

↑ Thar she blows! Whale watching off the coast of Mull (William Gray)

ACTION PLAN

ADVENTURE ESSENTIALS Caledonian MacBrayne (☎ 0800 066 5000 ⬦ calmac.co.uk) operates a 45-minute vehicle/passenger ferry service between Oban and Craignure on Mull. You can also catch a ferry from Lochaline to Fishnish or Kilchoan to Tobermory. Self-drive offers the most flexibility for a wildlife-watching dawdle through Glen More and along the Ross of Mull. For a guided safari, Mull Wildlife Tours (☎ 01680 812440 ⬦ mullwildlifetours.co.uk) takes groups of up to four on full-day trips. In addition to Sea Life Surveys (see opposite), boat trips are operated by Turus Mara (☎ 01688 400242 ⬦ turusmara.com) from Ulva Ferry (📍 PA73 6LY) to the puffin colony on Lunga in the Treshnish Isles (May–July), as well as Fingal's Cave on Staffa. A short stroll from the ferry pier at Craignure, Sheiling Holidays (☎ 01680 812496 ⬦ shielingholidays. co.uk) has pitches overlooking the Sound of Mull, as well as sheilings – traditional tents with carpets, beds, wood-burning stoves, ensuite facilities and basic kitchens. Other options include Tobermory Campsite (☎ 01688 302615 ⬦ tobermory-campsite.co.uk) and Fidden Farm Camping (☎ 01681 700427) – basic, but with a great location at Fidden Beach in the far southwest. For self-catering cottages, try Isle of Mull Holidays (☎ 01681 700260 ⬦ isleofmullholidays.com).

MORE ADVENTURE Peak time for seeing basking sharks in Hebridean waters is July–September. Basking Shark Scotland (☎ 07975 723140 ⬦ baskingsharkscotland. co.uk) runs full-day tours (minimum age 8) in search of the world's second-largest fish, including a chance to snorkel with them. You need to catch an early ferry from Oban to the Isle of Coll where the tour begins. Wetsuits and snorkelling gear are available to hire.

ALSO CONSIDER Gwynedd See *Journey to the Edge of Wales*, page 198; **Isle of Shuna** See *Hebridean Island Escape*, page 238; **Isle of Skye** See *Hike and Kayak on Skye*, page 270.

↑ Crunch time: an otter brings ashore a large crab (Nick Edge/S)

43 ON THE TRAIL OF THE OTTER

JOIN AN EXPERT GUIDE, TRACKING OTTERS AND LEARNING BUSHCRAFT IN THE WILDS OF MOIDART

WHERE	Moidart, West Highlands
WHEN	Year-round, but summer is best for family trips
HOW LONG	Full-day & overnight sessions are available
WHO FOR	Minimum age is usually eight, but bushcraft days can be tailor-made. No prior experience required.
ADVENTURE POTENTIAL	Otter tracking, bushcraft, canoeing, foraging
WILDLIFE WISHLIST	As well as otter, look out for harbour porpoise, pine marten & red squirrel, plus birds such as golden & white-tailed eagle, various gulls, terns & waders.

Turn left at the Lochailort Inn, midway between Fort William and Mallaig, and meet me in the layby a few miles down the road. Leon Durbin – wildlife biologist, bushcraft expert and otter tracker – was easy to find: his car was the one with the big green canoes on the roof.

It was low tide – tangled seaweed strewn along the shore; an amber tidemark sandwiched between the placid blue waters of Loch Ailort and the steely mountains of the Ardnish Peninsula. Apart from one or two lobster pot marker buoys and a small, floating mussel farm, there was no sign of human habitation. Leon pointed out a lone golden eagle corkscrewing over a distant, treeless ridge, flecked with outcrops of purple-grey psammite – the 800-million-year-old metamorphic sandstone that forms the rugged spine of this remote, timeless tract of the West Highlands coast.

We launched the canoes and paddled towards the nearest island. The only sound was the trickle of water beneath our hulls and the occasional splash of a common tern diving nearby. Skimming across sandy shallows, we beached the canoes in a tiny cove. Leon wanted to show us how to forage for seaweed and other tidal morsels. But something else caught his eye: paw prints, clearly stamped in the soft wet sand just below the strandline. Seaweed foraging would have to wait. We crouched around the tracks while Leon deciphered the spoor. The 6cm-wide prints were pristine – some clearly showed five toes, claw marks and the soft impression of a large rear pad. A quick process of elimination ruled out dogs (with their four-toed prints), American mink (with their much smaller feet) and pine marten (also smaller, and extremely unlikely to leave tracks on a beach). Clearly we were on the trail of otters.

Bent double, we moved slowly up the beach. In the drier sand above the high-tide mark, Leon found several narrow grooves where the otters had briefly swished their tails. A few metres further and he focused our gaze on a patch of grass encrusted with sugary grains of sand. We were entranced as he conjured an image of a pair of otters emerging from the sea sometime after high tide, running up the beach, their low-slung bellies brushing through the grass.

← Guiding star: Leon Durbin of Wildwood Bushcraft (William Gray)

Just behind the beach, we found a dark brown, brackish pool of water – exactly the kind of spot where otters like to rinse the salt from their fur to maintain its insulating properties. Then we picked up a narrow, trampelled path weaving through the dense birch wood that crowded the rocky shore. At one or two points along the 'otter highway', we came across spraints or otter droppings: some old, white and crumbly, others fresh, black and slimy. Leon teased out a few scales and bones – evidence of the otters' fishy diet – and encouraged us to have a sniff. Otter spraints are said to have a sweet odour reminiscent of hay or jasmine tea...

Highly territorial, they use spraints to scent-mark their home ranges, which can extend along several kilometres of shoreline. At least half of Scotland's population of around 8,000 Eurasian otters inhabit coastal areas. The wild peninsulas and islands of the west coast remained a stronghold for the species during the 1950s, 60s and 70s when otters were lost from many of Britain's rivers and lakes due to pesticide pollution. Still shy and elusive, they are notoriously difficult to spot and it is only with the expert tracking skills and local knowledge of people like Leon that you stand much of a chance – and even then, there's no guarantee of a sighting.

Pigeon-stepping along the otter trail, fearful of snapping twigs, we eventually found a holt. Otters use these shelters for sleeping and raising their young. In Scotland, litters of two or three kittens are born, usually in summer. We held back while Leon crept towards the burrow. After a moment or two, he beckoned us over. The muddy ground outside the holt was smooth and trackless, and there were spiders' webs strung, intact, across the entrance. Nobody was at home. We took a long, lingering look at the sea, peering through the lichen-fuzzed branches of the birches, but nothing broke the surface. No otters yet – but the thrill of tracking them had been electric.

↑ Otter country: the wildwood-lined shores of the Ardnish Peninsula (William Gray)

↑ Traffic sign: otter prints on the beach (William Gray)

FEAST ON THE BEACH Back at the cove, we plucked sprigs of channel wrack and stringy, green gutweed. Leon showed us how to find edible periwinkles on the slippery fronds of spiral wrack; we prised a few limpets off the rocks and tried (unsuccessfully) to scoop shrimps from a rockpool. On a low spring tide, we could have harvested razor clams buried in the sand – but we already had plenty. Bushcraft, according to Leon, was taking only what you needed, and leaving as little sign of your passing as possible.

Bagging our seashore ingredients, we paddled north to another wild beach. We needed to make a fire, so Leon took us foraging for tinder and kindling in the elfin forest of birch and oak that stood behind the beach. He demonstrated how to gently tease paper-thin curls of loose bark from the birch trees and collect dead wood from clumps of gorse. Then, back among the seaweed-covered boulders, away from the precious woodland, we learnt how to strike sparks from a handheld fire steel. Soon there was smoke, a lick of flame, and within minutes we were boiling a billycan of bramble tea. Leon diced the seaweed we had collected earlier into a batter of flour and water to make a simple Scottish bannoch, or flatbread, to bake on the fire. We saved some of the tea to poach the periwinkles and (after deftly dispatching them with a knife) popped the limpets upside down in the embers, to cook in their own little pots. They tasted like smoky bacon, and the bannoch was crisp and salty with a seaweed tang.

We were almost too preoccupied with eating to notice the thin silver-blue wake spreading across the surface of the loch at the far end of the bay. Leon clapped his binoculars on it and, seconds later, we were crabbing along the beach, hunkered down to keep our profiles low. The otter surfaced, upwind, less than 20m away. We froze, clamped like limpets to a low bluff, but the otter seemed oblivious to our presence. Whiskered muzzle held aloft, tail beating slowly side to side, it cruised through the shallows, dived twice, then clambered on to a rocky shoal before slipping away on the far side.

↑ Seaweed bannock cooked over a fire on the beach (William Gray)

ACTION PLAN

ADVENTURE ESSENTIALS Accredited with a NCFE Certificate in Bushcraft Leadership, biologist Leon Durbin founded Wildwood Bushcraft (☏ 01687 470415 ⊘ wildwoodbushcraft.com) in 2005. He offers a variety of wilderness experiences in Moidart and the Trossachs, including survival weekends, coastal foraging days and canoe journeys, but his Private Bushcraft Days are probably the best option for families. These can be tailor-made to suit your children (minimum age is usually eight), but will typically feature an island survival adventure where you learn how to build a campfire, forage for shellfish and seaweed, track wildlife and find out about trees, herbs and fungi and their safe uses in bushcraft. Depending on how much time you have, other activities can include leaf shelter building, water collection and purification, knifework, spoon carving and navigation. Prior experience is not necessary – you just need to come prepared for a day in the outdoors, with wellies or walking boots, full waterproofs and a water bottle. For west coast adventures, you can either meet at Wildwood Bushcraft's base in Roshven, Moidart, or arrange a pick-up from the nearest railway station at Lochailort.

MORE ADVENTURE Just south of Moidart, rugged and remote Ardnamurchan is Britain's most westerly peninsula – a single-lane track extending from Salen along much of its length. The Ardnamurchan Natural History Visitor Centre (♀ PH36 4JG ☏ 01972 500209 ⊘ ardnamurchannaturalhistorycentre.com) has a Living Building designed to encourage birds, bumblebees, voles and pine martens, while the RSPB Glenborrodale Reserve (♀ PH36 4JP ☏ 01463 715000 ⊘ rspb.org.uk) protects oak woodland on the shores of Loch Sunart that's home to redstarts and wood warblers. Head to the Garbh Eilean Wildlife Hide (⧉ downhill.sandbags.upsetting) to spot otters, seals and sea eagles.

ALSO CONSIDER **South Devon** See *Foraging along the Devon Coast*, page 40; **Kent** See *Wildlife Tracking and Bushcraft*, page 80; **Shetland Islands** See *Journey to the End of Britain*, page 300.

↑ Close encounter: a dog otter slips past in Loch Ailort (William Gray)

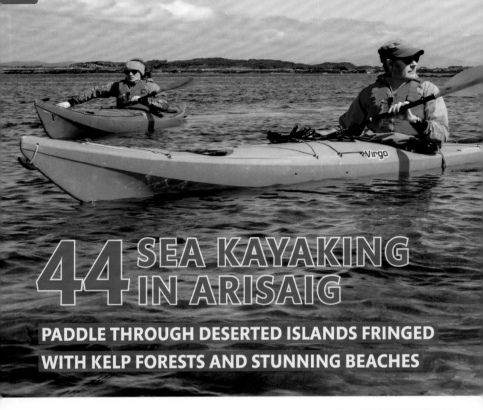

44 SEA KAYAKING IN ARISAIG

PADDLE THROUGH DESERTED ISLANDS FRINGED WITH KELP FORESTS AND STUNNING BEACHES

WHERE	Arisaig, Lochaber, west coast of the Scottish Highlands
WHEN	Easter–September for the most settled conditions
HOW LONG	Choose from day trips or overnight mini-expeditions, wild camping on remote islands
WHO FOR	Minimum age 15; no experience is required
ADVENTURE POTENTIAL	Sea kayaking, beachcombing, seal spotting
WILDLIFE WISHLIST	Common dolphin, harbour porpoise, harbour seal, otter, cormorant, grey heron, little ringed plover, oystercatcher, shag, white-tailed eagle, basking shark

Riven by sea lochs and scattered with countless skerries and islands, the northwest coast of Scotland is a paddler's paradise. Trace your finger across a map, west from Fort William until you meet the sea, just below the toe of Skye, and you will find the coastal village of Arisaig. To the south lies the broad Sound of Arisaig and the remote, rocky finger of the Ardnamurchan Peninsula; the Small Isles (Eigg, Muck, Rum and Canna) dimple the western horizon, while Knoydart – a virtually roadless wilderness – looms in the north.

↑ Sea kayaking in the sheltered waters of Loch nan Ceall (William Gray)

Launch a sea kayak at Arisaig and you will find yourself right at the heart of this wild, magical place. Irrresistible to paddlers, it's one of the best spots for kayaking in Britain, if not the world. Not only is the location rugged and far-flung, but the entrance to the inlet of Loch nan Ceall, on which Arisaig sits, is liberally sprinkled with hundreds of tiny islands – a magnet to free-spirited kayakers. At low tide, the miniature archipelago is wreathed in sandy coves, lapped by the kind of turquoise waters that wouldn't seem out of place in the South Pacific. Writhing meadows of kelp grow in sheltered inlets; harbour seals and seabirds breed on the islands, while all around you there are views of distant mountains, from the saw-toothed Cuillins of Skye to pyramid-shaped Askival on Rum.

The geography of the area – particularly the Small Isles in the west – help to protect this paddling haven from rough seas. There are no strong tidal races or challenging currents. Not that this is a place for messing about in boats. The weather can be fickle and you need to be well prepared. Book with one of the local operators and your guides will not only know the area intimately, safely navigating the maze of channels and leading you to spectacular beaches, but they will also enhance your experience with insights into the local ecology and wildlife.

KELP FORESTS AND MAERL BEDS Our day trip with Arisaig Sea Kayak Centre began – as all kayaking trips do – with some serious kitting out. We were each given a waterproof paddling jacket and trousers, buoyancy aid, spraydeck and paddle (see *Action plan*, page 269, for a full list of what you need to bring). As it was a calm, almost windless day, we were each allocated a single kayak – doubles are sometimes used for extra stability if it's rough, or if younger children need to pair up with an adult. After squirming into our paddling garb, we loaded the kayaks with spare clothing, water bottles and food, stowing everything in compartments sealed with watertight hatches. Then, still with the kayaks on dry land, we clambered into the snug cockpits, adjusting seatbacks and foot pedals to ensure our knees were comfortably braced against the hull. We practised fitting the spraydeck around the rim of the cockpit, and warmed up with some 'air paddling'. Only then did we carry the kayaks down to the water's edge and get afloat.

It was low tide; seaweed draped across the shore in amber dreadlocks, a lone grey heron hunched, motionless, rooted to its reflection. Our guide spent a few minutes teaching us simple paddling techniques and how to steer the kayaks, then we pointed our bows out to sea and made for the skerries.

Soon we were gliding through narrow channels in the labyrinth of islets, the kayaks skimming effortlessly across shallow areas covered with tangled rafts of bladderwrack. We paused often to stare into the limpid waters: a mesmerising world of writhing kelp and gently pulsing moon jellyfish.

Kelp can grow from depths of 40m or more (especially on Scotland's outer west coast around islands like St Kilda), their fronds reaching towards the sunlit surface layers like the canopy of a great underwater jungle. And just like any great forest, the kelp supports a rich and diverse community of species, from sponges, sea squirts and sea anemones to bryozoans, brittle stars and bivalves.

But there's another type of seaweed in the waters around Arisaig that is actually the architect of its famous white-sand beaches. Maerl is a purple-pink 'coralline' seaweed that carpets the seabed. As it grows, lime is deposited in its cell walls, creating a hard, brittle skeleton which, like the spent shells of molluscs and crustaceans, can eventually be washed ashore. With maerl, however, the wave-ground remains of the algae actually build the beaches. Paddling our kayaks to the first in a series of dazzling white coves, we stepped ashore not on shelly sand or crushed coral, but a seaweed graveyard. Our feet sank ankle-deep into the strange matrix of calcified tubes and nodules. On closer inspection, it was dotted with periwinkle shells, scallop shards and fragments of urchins – Arisaig's maerl beds are an important habitat for a host of burrowing bivalves, worms and other seabed critters, and are protected not only for their rich biodiversity, but for the important role they perform as a marine carbon store.

← Tideline treasure: razor clam, periwinkles, topshells, whelks and a lone Arctic cowrie shell (William Gray)

"What Arisaig's maerl beaches lack in sandcastle potential, a sea kayaking expedition more than makes up for with the satisfaction of exploring deserted islands under your own power"

↑ Playing the castaway on a deserted island off the Arisaig coast (William Gray)

PADDLING WITH HARBOUR SEALS What Arisaig's maerl beaches lack in sandcastle potential, a sea kayaking expedition more than makes up for with the satisfaction of exploring deserted islands under your own power. It also brings you closer to nature – the salt spray on your face, the briny aroma of sun-baked seaweed and the intimate, sea-level perspective you get from the cockpit of a sea kayak.

This is an adventure that's more to do with the journey than the wildlife, but as we paddled deeper into the rash of islands, we began to encounter dozens of harbour seals. Our guide told us that the archipelago is a pupping ground, so we kept our distance, careful not to disturb them. Hauled-out seals are often resting, conserving their energy after ten-minute feeding dives, so we gave them as wide a berth as possible to avoid startling them into the sea. For many, however, curiosity got the better of them. A splash and a snort and we'd spin our heads to find the glistening, domed head of a seal a few metres behind us.

Many had young, the pups braying for their mothers whenever they surfaced. Unlike grey seals, which nurse their offspring on land for several weeks before venturing into the sea, harbour seals have well-developed young that can swim within a few hours of being born. It allows them to breed on remote, predator-free shoals and sandbars that are only uncovered by the tide for a short period of time. Harbour seals usually give birth in June or July, the single pup doubling its weight on a diet of rich milk during the first three or four weeks.

As the tide turned, the character of the islands slowly changed as beaches, and even entire islands, disappeared beneath the waves. Shallow, turquoise waters deepened and darkened. A fishing party of cormorants worked an inundated passage that had been clogged with kelp at low tide. Oystercatchers scurried along the shoreline, their high-pitched cries gradually fading behind us as we paddled back towards the mainland. It would be another 12 hours or so before Arisaig revealed its tidal secrets – emerging from the sea like a Scottish Atlantis.

↑ **Above left:** approaching a beach of maerl; **above right:** close-up of the coral-like sand (William Gray)

ACTION PLAN

ADVENTURE ESSENTIALS Located around an hour's drive west of Fort William on the A830, Arisaig Sea Kayak Centre (**e** arisaigseakayakcentre@gmail.com ⊘ arisaigseakayakcentre.co.uk) offers guided sea kayaking day trips around the Arisaig coastline. Although there's a minimum age of 15, younger children may be accommodated on request. No sea kayaking experience is required, but you do need to have a reasonable level of fitness and be able to help carry kayaks to and from the shore. Where you paddle depends on sea conditions. As well as Loch nan Ceall and the skerries, options include Loch Ailort and the Ardnish Peninsula or Loch Moidart and Castle Tioram. The kayaks are easy to paddle (doubles are available for extra stability), and all tuition and paddling gear is provided. Wear synthetic leggings or shorts and a long-sleeved top under the waterproof paddling jacket, trousers, spraydeck and buoyancy aid. You'll need to wade into the sea when launching and landing, so bring neoprene booties or trainers that you don't mind getting wet. Other essentials include hat, sunglasses, sun cream, water bottle, lunch and snacks. Capsizing is unlikely, but you should still bring a change of clothes. Nature Scot (⊘ nature.scot) has guidelines on watching marine wildlife from sea kayaks.

MORE ADVENTURE Arisaig Sea Kayak Centre also runs overnight sea kayaking tours, wild camping on remote islands. Slow-paced, expedition-style trips, you will need to pack your kayak with everything you need, including a tent, sleeping bag, food and freshwater. Rockhopper (✆ 07739 837344 ⊘ rockhopperscotland.co.uk) also offers full-day and overnight sea kayaking adventures in the Arisaig area.

ALSO CONSIDER **South Cornwall** See *River Fowey Adventure*, page 36; **Herefordshire** See *A Paddle along the River Wye*, page 102; **Norfolk** See *Canoeing on the Broads*, page 110; **Hebrides** See *Hike and Kayak on Skye*, page 270.

↑ Harbour seals hauled out on a skerry near Arisaig (William Gray)

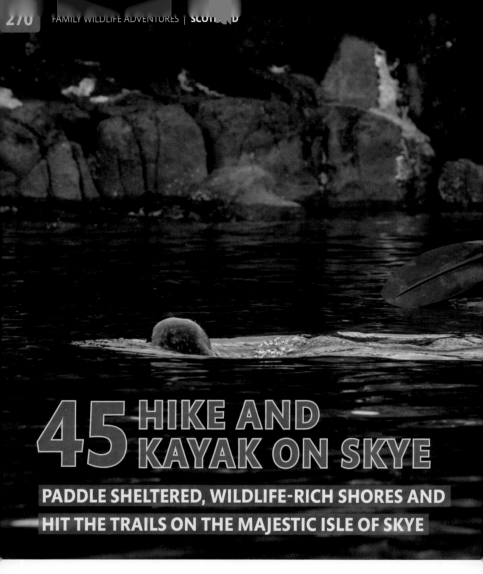

45 HIKE AND KAYAK ON SKYE

PADDLE SHELTERED, WILDLIFE-RICH SHORES AND HIT THE TRAILS ON THE MAJESTIC ISLE OF SKYE

WHERE	Isle of Skye, Inner Hebrides
WHEN	Easter holidays to Oct half-term
HOW LONG	Allow a week to try a good range of hikes
WHO FOR	All ages; there are hikes for a range of abilities
ADVENTURE POTENTIAL	Hiking, sea kayaking, dinosaur tracking, boat trips, rockpooling, otter watching, minibus safaris
WILDLIFE WISHLIST	Common dolphin, minke whale, grey & harbour seal, otter, red deer, gannet, golden & white-tailed eagle, hen harrier, merlin, peregrine, raven & short-eared owl

↑ Kayaking with a harbour seal in Staffin Bay (William Gray)

S taffin Bay was glassy-smooth when we launched our sea kayaks from a small slipway tucked down a single-lane track on the Trotternish Peninsula. It was so calm that we actually heard the moment when the tide turned, gurgling and popping as the sea began to creep back into the cracks and crevices of the kelp-covered shore. A soft puff of breath and we spun our heads to find a lone harbour seal staring at us with large solemn eyes that concealed its mischievous mood. For the next hour or so, as we kayaked around Staffin Island, the playful pinniped followed us, occasionally leaping acoss our bows or porpoising alongside. It was only when we paused to admire a lion's mane jellyfish, glowing like an orb of

liquid amber in the early evening sunshine, that the seal lost interest and slipped away. Paddling into the lee of the island we nuzzled into thick, leathery straps of kelp and peered through limpid water at the seabed daubed with limpets and anemones. Looking south, sheer cliffs, ribbed with basalt columns, marched along Skye's 'dinosaur coast', while to the west – the brooding massif of the Quiraing rose above sun-spangled Staffin Bay.

HIKING IN THE FOOTSTEPS OF DINOSAURS Even in summer, Hebridean weather can be notoriously fickle. Brisk winds and a succession of storms over the next few days shredded our plans to launch the kayaks again. But the Isle of Skye is a paradise for walkers as well as paddlers, so we swapped boats for boots and set out to sample some of the island's wildlife-rich hikes.

One of the best (but least well-known) walks for families is the 3km jaunt to Brother's Point. Drive around 20km north from Portree along the A855 and park in the layby on the left, just past the Glenview Hotel (♀ IV51 9JH). After crossing the road, follow the path to Rubha nam Braithrean, snaking past the remains of a 19th-century crofter's dwelling before reaching the coast. If it's low tide, walk out on to the wave-cut platforms. As well as shallow rockpools encrusted with pink coralline algae and flickering with gobies, you might find dinosaur footprints. The rocks beneath your feet were laid down in a tropical lagoon 170 million years ago when menacing megalosaurs stalked herds of browsing hadrosaurs along the Jurassic shoreline. The entire Staffin Bay area on the east coast of Skye's Trotternish Peninsula is one of Scotland's most important dinosaur sites. If Brother's Point fires your imagination, try dino-hunting at An Corran beach near Staffin Harbour (♀ IV51 9JT) – and for expert advice, pop into Ellishadder's Staffin Dinosaur Museum (♀ IV51 9JE ✆ 01470 562321 ⌂ staffindinosaurmuseum.com).

↑ Dinosaur coast: Brother's Point on the Trotternish Peninsula (William Gray)

CLASSIC HIKES ON SKYE Most visitors to Skye are unaware of the Brother's Point hike, but there are two other nearby trails that everyone makes a beeline for. A 50m-tall pinnacle of rock jutting from the Trotternish escarpment, the Old Man of Storr is clearly visible from the A855, 10km north of Portree (you can't miss the large car park). Allow around an hour to hike to its base, then push on uphill for the best views of the Old Man, rising like a wonky canine above smaller crags,

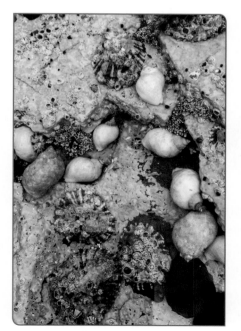

with panoramic views of the Cuillin Hills, Raasay Island and Applecross Peninsula in the distance.

Equally popular, the 6.8km Quiraing circuit can be accessed from the car park at Maoladh Mor on the single-track road linking Staffin and Uig. A gigantic landslip, edging a centimetre or two towards the sea every year, the hidden valleys of the Quiraing were once used by locals to hide their cattle when Viking ships appeared on the horizon. Hike the circuit clockwise, taking the steep uphill path on to a plateau before descending into the Quiraing's rucks and folds, cowering beneath rocky spires and sheer cliffs echoing with the brusque, rasping cries of ravens.

↑ **Top:** the Quiraing and Staffin Bay; **above:** rockpool at Brother's Point (William Gray)

OTTER WATCHING AT KYLERHEA About 5km after crossing the bridge to Skye (or 58km if driving south from Portree), a turning off the A87 leads to Kylerhea (📍 IV42 8NH ☎ 0300 067 6100 🔗 forestryandland.gov.scot) – a prime otter-watching spot overlooking the narrow straits between the southeastern corner of Skye and the mainland. From the car park, follow the 2km Marine Mammal Trail to a hide where (with binoculars) you can scan the waters below for otters feeding in the rich, current-churned waters. It's one of the best places in Britain to spot them – just don't expect close-up views as the hide is set quite high above the shore. Seals are attracted here as well, particularly on an incoming tide, and you might glimpse dolphins, porpoises or even a minke whale. Back at the car park, there's another hide manned by the RSPB where you can find out if any white-tailed eagles have been sighted in the area.

SKYE'S WILD WEST Take the A87 south from Portree to Sligachan (admiring the dragonback peaks of the Black Cuillins if it's clear), then continue west on the A863/B8009 to Talisker Bay. Walking along the farm track towards this wave-lashed beach, you'll pass wedges of Atlantic hazel wood – remnants of ancient Celtic rainforest clinging to misty, rain-swept coasts, their limbs cloaked with mosses, liverworts and lichens. Reaching the beach, be prepared for a bracing walk, sidestepping marooned jellyfish and watching sandpipers and oystercatchers scuttle along the strandline.

A 50-minute drive north brings you to Dunvegan. Continue north to Claigan for the gentle walk to Coral Beach (created by the crushed remains of coralline algae, or maerl, rather than coral), or head west to Neist Point where basalt columns form stepping stones down to the ocean, reminiscent of the Giant's Causeway. Walk to the lighthouse or out on to the clifftops – there are few places in Britain more exhilarating for sea watching. You'll almost certainly see gannets and seals, but linger for one of Neist Point's renowned sunsets and you might just be rewarded with a swimpast from a pod of common dolphins stampeding through the surf.

↑ Cliffhanger: Neist Point Lighthouse (William Gray)

ACTION PLAN

ADVENTURE ESSENTIALS Most visitors drive over Skye Bridge, but you can also reach the Isle of Skye by ferry from Armadale (☏ 0800 066 5000 ⌖ calmac.co.uk) or Glenelg (☏ 01599 522700 ⌖ skyeferry.co.uk). If taking your own sea kayaks to Skye, always seek local advice, and check weather and sea conditions before setting off. You should have open-water paddling experience and stick to very sheltered locations – especially if you are using inflatable kayaks. Organised kayaking tours are available with South Sea Kayak (⌖ southskyeseakayak.co.uk) and Whitewave (☏ 01470 542414 ⌖ white-wave.co.uk). Skye has hundreds of walks, varying in terrain and difficulty. If you have young children, try easy walks, like Coral Beach, Kylerhea and Talisker Bay. Older children, that you can trust near cliff edges, will love the challenge of more demanding hikes like the Quiraing. For guided walking adventures, contact Sky Hikers (☏ 01478 611861 ⌖ skyehikers.com) or Skye Wilderness Safaris (☏ 01470 542229 ⌖ skye-wilderness-safaris.com). Whales, dolphins, porpoises, seals, basking sharks and white-tailed eagles are all possibilities on boat trips from Portree with Stardust (☏ 07795 385581 ⌖ skyeboat-trips.co.uk).

MORE ADVENTURE With around 30 pairs of golden eagle, Skye has one of the densest populations in Scotland. An expert-led minibus safari with Isle of Skye Wildlife Tours (☏ 07972 260249 ⌖ skyewildlife.com) dramatically increases your chances of a sighting. Their record for white-tailed eagles is 13 different birds in a single day, while hen harrier, otter and red deer are also regularly seen.

ALSO CONSIDER East Devon and Dorset See *Jurassic Coast Adventure*, page 60; **Gwynedd** See *Snowdonia Wilderness Adventure*, page 192; **Dumfries & Galloway** See *Seeing Red in Galloway*, page 210; **Moidart** See *Sea Kayaking in Arisaig*, page 262.

↑ Staffin Bay's friendliest harbour seal (William Gray)

CAIRNGORMS
46 WILDERNESS ADVENTURE

EXPLORE THE MOUNTAINS AND CALEDONIAN FOREST OF BRITAIN'S LARGEST NATIONAL PARK

WHERE	Cairngorms National Park, Scottish Highlands
WHEN	Year-round, but Jun–Jul is the best (& safest) time for exploring the high mountain regions; ospreys nest at Loch Garten Apr–late Aug; capercaillies are active at their courtship leks Mar–Apr
HOW LONG	At least a long weekend, ideally 3–5 days
WHO FOR	All ages, but 6–8+ for hiking and mountain biking
ADVENTURE POTENTIAL	Hiking, mountain biking, canoeing, SUP, reindeer walks, squirrel & birdwatching hides, camping, stargazing
WILDLIFE WISHLIST	Mammals include mountain hare, pine marten, red deer, red squirrel, reindeer & extremely rare wildcat; birds range from mountain-dwelling dotterel, golden eagle, ptarmigan & snow bunting to forest species like capercaillie, crested tit & crossbill; osprey nest near lochs where you can also see goldeneye & red-breasted merganser; look for insects such as wood ant & common hawker dragonfly; mountain flowers include moss campion & purple saxifrage

↑ Reindeer herd on the summit of Cairn Gorm (William Gray)

A t 4,528km² in area, the Cairngorms National Park could comfortably swallow Hampshire or Somerset. Twice the size of the Lake District, this vast, rucked-up cloak of mountain and moorland is home to around a quarter of Britain's threatened species. Golden eagles spiral over remote glens, while ospreys snatch fish from its lochs. Wildcats and pine martens prowl ancient stands of Caledonian pine forest, red deer roam the open moors, and herds of reindeer stream like smoke across the mountain tops.

Many of these animals are difficult to spot – secretive, rare or simply consumed by the sheer scale of the landscape – but that's what makes the Cairngorms so special. Hike or bike into this lofty wilderness and you'll feel the tingle of excitement that comes from exploring somewhere raw and remote. This is a place to connect with primeval Britain. Pack a picnic, midge repellent and weatherproof clothing, and keep walking or cycling until you leave the crowded tourist centres behind. Find yourself a quiet patch of forest, a deserted stretch of loch shore or mountain viewpoint, then take a moment to pause and tune into your surroundings: a landscape that emerged after the last ice age 10,000 years ago and has remained largely unchanged to this day.

A RENDEZVOUS WITH RUDOLF Currently numbering around 150 individuals, there's been a free-roaming herd of reindeer in the Cairngorms since 1952 when two bulls and five cows were brought over from Sweden. It's not just that reindeer feel at home in this 'ice age' national park – they actually belong here. According to the medieval *Orkneyinga* saga, reindeer were hunted in Caithness by the Earls of Orkney around 800 years ago. They were wiped out soon after, but the sub-arctic Cairngorms remained an ideal habitat, offering reindeer both the space to roam and an abundant supply of lichens on which to feed.

At the Cairngorm Reindeer Centre (🖳 grabs.noodle.nutty 🖉 01479 861228 🖯 cairngormreindeer.co.uk) in Glenmore, you can hand-feed a group of paddock reindeer and stroke their velvety muzzles. Calves are born in May and June, rapidly growing to run with the herd and adapt to life on the move. During summer, reindeer moult their thick, pale-coloured fur for dark, summer coats and migrate to higher slopes. The reindeer centre's guided hill walks provide an insight into their free-spirited lives – or you could drive up to the Cairngorm Mountain car park and hike to the summit for a chance to see a herd in the wild.

REACHING NEW HEIGHTS Swarming with skiers during winter, the 1,245m munro of Cairn Gorm (🖉 01479 861261 🖯 cairngormmountain.co.uk) is a completely different world in mid-summer. Hike the well-marked trail to the summit of Britain's sixth-highest peak and, two hours after setting off, you'll emerge on a seemingly barren, rock-strewn plateau. It's only when you look closely that small clumps and cushions of moss campion, purple saxifrage, alpine lady's-mantle and other arctic flowers catch your eye. Find a sheltered spot to sit and you may glimpse movement: a perfectly camouflaged ptarmigan twitching among lichen-spattered scree or a snow bunting – the males with striking black-and-white plumage – flying back and forth to its nest in a rocky crevice.

Cairn Gorm is the crowning glory of many family hiking trips in the national park, but there are other quieter, more remote mountain trails where you might glimpse elusive species, such as dotterel – a handsome plover with a distinctive chestnut belly and white eye-stripes that nests on a few Scottish mountaintops. And, of course, whenever you hike the high ground of the Cairngorms, it's always worth keeping an eye to the sky (like any self-preserving ptarmigan or mountain hare) for the distinctive silhouette of a golden eagle. There's no particular hotspot for seeing these magnificent birds in the Cairngorms – they could crest a distant ridge or soar into view on a thermal at any moment.

← Male snow bunting (William Gray)

INTO THE WILD WOODS Brown bear, wolf, lynx and elk have long vanished from the Caledonian forest of the Cairngorms, but this ancient woodland – directly descended from the first pines to colonise post-glacial Scotland – still exudes a timeless, untouched quality. One of the best places to fall under its spell is Rothiemurchus (✆ 01479 812345 ⊕ rothiemurchus.net), just south of Aviemore on the B970. The level, 5km trail around Loch an Eilein delves into heather-lined avenues of Scots pine. Listen for the soft trilling of crested tits as they forage in the treetops and see if you can spot one dangling from a pinecone or probing for insects in the pink, scaly bark. Keep an eye out, too, for red squirrels dashing helter-skelter around the tree trunks.

You can often give both species a tick by visiting the Loch Garten Nature Centre (▦ slide.bells.cuddled ✆ 01479 831476 ⊕ rspb.org.uk). Located in Abernethy National Nature Reserve – another glorious swathe of Caledonian forest – the centre's feeders attract great spotted woodpeckers and siskins, as well as crested tits and red squirrels. Signposted off the A95 from Aviemore and Grantown-on-Spey, the centre is best known for its nest cam footage of ospreys on Loch Garten.

↑ Hiking beneath Caledonian pines in Rothiemurchus Forest (William Gray)

The fish-eating birds of prey have used the site since the mid-1950s, returning each spring from wintering grounds in West Africa. In late March, the pair are hopefully back at the nest and incubating eggs by mid-April. The CCTV drama becomes more gripping during early June when the chicks hatch and both parents are busy catching trout from the freshwater loch to feed their hungry offspring. The chicks prepare to fledge in July and early August, bringing Loch Garten's avian blockbuster to a climax. By late August, most if not all of the ospreys have migrated south.

Making a song and dance (but never quite managing to upstage the ospreys), capercaillies strut their stuff in Abernethy Forest during courtship rituals in spring. The turkey-sized males (glossy black with scarlet eye shadow) attempt to woo females in communal courting grounds known as leks. Tails fanned and heads pointed skyward, the puffed-up males launch into an extraordinary serenade of frantic chirps and chattering, followed by a series of staccato clicks that always end with an emphatic 'pop'. Sadly, these charismatic birds are in serious decline, but check at the nature centre for any organised 'caper watches'.

↑ **Clockwise from top left:** osprey, mountain hare, crested tit, red squirrel (Mark Medcalf, Carl Day, L Galbraith, Piotr Krzeslak/S)

ACTION PLAN

ADVENTURE ESSENTIALS Two major roads access the Cairngorms National Park (⊘ cairngorms.co.uk). The A93 between Perth and Aberdeen loops through the southeast, while the A9 Pitlochry–Inverness road follows the River Spey to Aviemore – a popular base for exploring the region. The B970 leads west from Aviemore to Rothiemurchus Estate, Loch Morlich and Glenmore Forest. Aviemore is also the western terminus of the Strathspey Steam Railway (⊘ 01479 810725 ⊘ strathspeyrailway.co.uk) which runs to Boat of Garten and Broomhill. Two of the best options for pitching a tent in the heart of the Cairngorms National Park are Glenmore Campsite (🖳 strictly.emulated.vibrating ⊘ 0247 642 3008 ⊘ campingintheforest.co.uk) and Rothiemurchus Camp and Caravan Park (🖳 eyelashes.kingdom.eggplants ⊘ 01479 812800 ⊘ rothiemurchus.net). Visitor centres at Glenmore Forest and Rothiemurchus have details of ranger-led activities, guided walks and talks. You can hire mountain bikes at Bothy Bikes (⊘ 01479 810111 ⊘ bothybikes.co.uk) in Aviemore, while both Loch Insh and Loch Morlich have watersports centres offering canoe rental. Speyside Wildlife (⊘ 01479 812498 ⊘ speysidewildlife.co.uk) runs three-hour wildlife watching evenings (minimum age 8) at a hide near Aviemore where, in addition to badgers, you might see pine martens, roe deer and tawny owls. Glenlivet Wildlife (⊘ 01807 590241 ⊘ glenlivet-wildlife.co.uk) offers Land Rover safaris on the Glenlivet Crown Estate.

Always take warm clothing, wet-weather gear, drinking water, snacks and sun protection on mountain hikes. Midges can be a nuisance during summer months – locals recommend Smidge repellent (⊘ smidgeup.com).

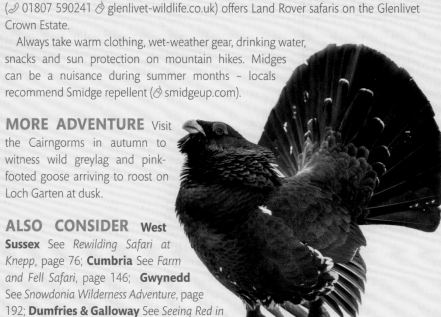

MORE ADVENTURE Visit the Cairngorms in autumn to witness wild greylag and pink-footed goose arriving to roost on Loch Garten at dusk.

ALSO CONSIDER West Sussex See *Rewilding Safari at Knepp*, page 76; **Cumbria** See *Farm and Fell Safari*, page 146; **Gwynedd** See *Snowdonia Wilderness Adventure*, page 192; **Dumfries & Galloway** See *Seeing Red in Galloway*, page 210.

→ Capercaillie (Rudmer Zwerver/S)

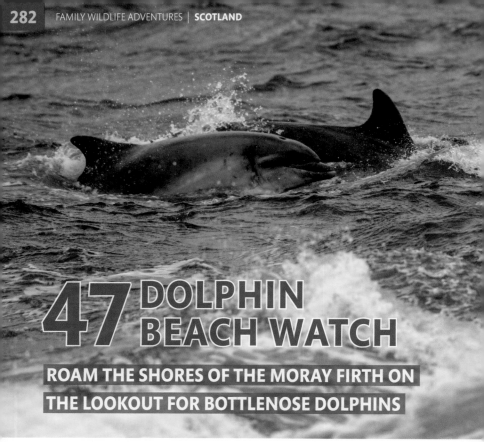

47 DOLPHIN BEACH WATCH

ROAM THE SHORES OF THE MORAY FIRTH ON THE LOOKOUT FOR BOTTLENOSE DOLPHINS

WHERE	Moray Firth, Northeast Scotland
WHEN	Bottlenose dolphins are resident all year
HOW LONG	You could be lucky & see them at Chanonry Point five minutes after arriving, but it's more rewarding to incorporate this dolphin hotspot into a few days exploring the Moray Firth
WHO FOR	All ages
ADVENTURE POTENTIAL	Land-based dolphin watching, boat trips, birdwatching
WILDLIFE WISHLIST	Bottlenose dolphin, grey & harbour seal, harbour porpoise, minke whale, long-finned pilot whale & orca; shorebirds include curlew & oystercatcher during summer, and autumn migrants such as black-tailed godwit, dunlin, knot, ringed plover & sanderling; search dunes and coastal heaths for stonechat & wheatear; birds of prey include osprey, red kite & short-eared owl; cliff-nesting seabirds include fulmar, gannet, guillemot, kittiwake, razorbill & puffin

↑ A shore thing: bottlenose dolphins feeding off Chanonry Point (William Gray)

The tide has turned and you can sense the anticipation. A dozen or so people have gathered at the tip of Rosemarkie beach beneath Chanonry Lighthouse – all eyes on the turbulent sea just off the point. Common terns beat against a stiff breeze, their shrill cries rising above the hiss of waves through the pebbles. A lone gannet wheels offshore, its dagger-bill aimed at the seething waters, while half a dozen sanderling skitter along the strandline, dashing to pluck morsels deposited by the incoming tide.

Suddenly, a dark sickle-shape appears among the whitecaps. Steely grey. Fleeting. Unmistakable. The spectators on the beach fling out their arms, pointing, as a second, then a third dorsal fin rolls through the waves. Moments later, a dolphin erupts from the sea, corkscrewing mid-air before bellyflopping back into the Moray Firth. Another lunges from a wave crest, its smooth, domed head glinting in the weak morning sunshine and, for a fraction of a second, you can make out the stubby beak and unmistakable 'smile' of a bottlenose dolphin.

Jutting from the northern shore of the Moray Firth, the pebble spit at Chanonry Point snags the tides. It's a favourite spot for the dolphins to corral fish – especially on a rising spring tide – while the beach allows human admirers to get within a dozen or so metres of the feeding spectacle. It's almost as if the dolphins know they're being watched (and applauded) as they somersault and cavort in the current-strafed waters. For the price of a £1 ticket at Chanonry Lighthouse car park it is, without doubt, Britain's best land-based dolphin watching.

Armed with a tide table, you could cut to the chase and head straight there. But, although Chanonry Point – just 30 minutes' drive north of Inverness – is the most reliable place for dolphin sightings in the Moray Firth, there's no guarantee you will see them. Numbering around 200 individuals, the world's most northerly population of bottlenose dolphins is wide ranging. You could spot them anywhere along the 800km coastline of the triangular-shaped inlet. If you have two or three days to spare, combine Chanonry Point on the north shore with the Moray Firth's south coast, touring the 160km between Inverness and Troup Head.

CITY LIFE Occasionally, bottlenose dolphins swim beyond Chanonry Point, passing under Kessock Bridge, just to the north of Inverness. For your best chance of sighting them this close to the city, head out to Merkinch Local Nature Reserve or Carnac Point. Alternatively, join a boat trip with Dolphin Spirit (✆ 07544 800620 ⅋ dolphinspirit.co.uk) which operates 75-minute cruises from the marina.

→ Sanderling (William Gray)

DOLPHINS FOR LANDLUBBERS Leaving Inverness, drive 20km east along the A96 and B9039 to Fort George (✆ 01667 460232 ⊘ historicenvironment.scot). Built following the 1746 Jacobite uprising at nearby Culloden, the fortification's battlements offer excellent views of the Moray Firth at its pinch point with Chanonry, barely a kilometre across the water on the north shore's Black Isle.

Around 13km further east, you reach Nairn – worth a quick scan from the pier perhaps, but otherwise push on to Findhorn. The almost enclosed estuary of Findhorn Bay is nationally important for birds. Rising tides nudge flocks of waders from the mudflats – oystercatchers and curlews during summer; dunlin, knot, godwits and plovers during autumn and winter – forcing them to roost around the fringes of the bay. A birdwatching hide, accessed from a small car park off the B9011 just south of Findhorn, provides the best views.

Continue through the small town to the beach car park and you reach the spectacular scimitar-sweep of Burghead Bay: over 17km of rippled sand, pockmarked with wormcasts and scattered with cockle shells. Drag your kids from the beach and you can walk part of the Moray Coast Trail through sand dunes and coastal heath twitching with butterflies, stonechats and yellowhammers.

Burghead itself is a prime lookout for dolphins. There are regular sightings from Burghead Visitor Centre (✆ 01343 835518 ⊘ burghead.com), perched on the cliffs between the harbour and the remains of a Pictish fort sacked by Vikings in the 9th century. On the southern outskirts of Burghead, Roseisle Forest is home to red squirrels and pine-loving birds like the crested tit and crossbill.

A few kilometres east of Burghead, Hopeman often rewards dolphin spotters, especially those that stake out the coast from East Beach Car Park. From Hopeman, head inland, returning to the A96 and driving 26km to Fochabers where the B9104 follows the River Spey on its final stretch to the Moray Firth.

Located in an 18th-century salmon fishing station at Spey Bay, the WDC Scottish Dolphin Centre (📍IV32 7PJ ✆ 01343 820339 ⊘ dolphincentre.whales.org) delves into the lives of the region's celebrated cetaceans. You'll learn how individual bottlenose dolphins can be identified by nicks and notches on their dorsal fins and how the charity campaigned to get the Moray Firth designated as a Special Area of Conservation (SAC) for cetaceans in 2005. As well as scanning the sea for dolphins (lured here by the juicy prospect of salmon migrating up the Spey), you can walk alongside the river, spotting seals, ospreys and even otters. The centre also has a large collection of whale bones from the area, as well as an exhibit on life below the waves of the Moray Firth.

An hour's drive from Spey Bay, the RSPB Troup Head Reserve (✆ 01346 532017 ⊘ rspb.org.uk) is a fitting finale to your dolphin watch. The 90m-high cliffs not only provide a lofty vantage from which to spot cetaceans, but they also host 38,000 nesting seabirds in summer, including puffins and 2,000 pairs of gannets.

ACTION PLAN

ADVENTURE ESSENTIALS The Moray Firth's prime dolphin-watching location, Chanonry Point (♥ IV10 8SD) lies between Fortrose and Rosemarkie on the Black Isle. Although there's a small car park at the point itself, it is often full. Park in Rosemarkie instead and walk the 'dolphin mile' along the beach to the lighthouse. Alternatively, catch a bus from Inverness to Fortrose and walk approximately 1.5km from there. Try to plan your cetacean vigil at Chanonry Point to coincide with a rising tide when dolphins often gather to hunt fish attracted by the strong currents. Walk out on to the small shingle spit and focus on the narrow channel separating Chanonry Point from Fort George on the southern shore. Boat trip operators offering dolphin-spotting cruises in the Moray Firth include Dolphin Spirit (page 283), Dolphin Trips Avoch (𝒥 01381 622383 𝄐 dolphintripsavoch.co.uk), Ecoventures (𝒥 01381 600323 𝄐 ecoventures.co.uk) in Cromarty, North 58 Sea Adventures (𝒥 01309 690099 𝄐 north58.co.uk) in Findhorn and Lossiemouth, and Scottish Marine Safari (𝒥 07939 487518 𝄐 scottishmarinesafari. com) in Buckie.

MORE ADVENTURE Around 25km southwest of Inverness, the Loch Ness Centre & Exhibition (♥ IV63 6TU 𝒥 01456 450573 𝄐 lochness.com) has all the information you need to plan a Nessie-spotting expedition. Cruises are available from Drumnadrochit.

ALSO CONSIDER **West Cornwall** See *Cornish Coast Wildlife Safari*, page 28; **Ceredigion** See *Cardigan Bay Wildlife Safari*, page 176; **Northwest Highlands** See *Wild Camping on the Whale Trail*, page 286.

↑ Bottlenose dolphins leaping past the battlements of Fort George (Grafxart/S)

WILD CAMPING
48 ON THE WHALE TRAIL

PITCH YOUR TENT WITH A VIEW OF BRITAIN'S RICHEST WHALE AND DOLPHIN SEAS

WHERE	Northwest Highlands
WHEN	Late spring to early autumn; ideal as part of a summer holiday adventure in Scotland
HOW LONG	One night minimum, but longer if you don't mind basic, no-frills camping
WHO FOR	Adventurous children of any age, but perhaps take them 'normal camping' first
ADVENTURE POTENTIAL	Wilderness camping, beachcombing, snorkelling, boat trips
WILDLIFE WISHLIST	Minke whale, orca, common & bottlenose dolphin, harbour porpoise, grey & harbour seal, otter, basking shark, white-tailed eagle

↑ Bay watch: camping in the remote Northwest Highlands (William Gray)

Imagine adapting your life, for just a few days, to the natural rhythms of tide and daylight –waking with the dawn and unzipping your tent to breathe in the briny tang of the sea; sprinting across pristine, rippled sands at low tide; rockpooling, shell seeking, paddling, snorkelling... but always with a keen eye on the sea, waiting for that telltale puff of breath, or a black dorsal fin rolling through the waves. Wild camping along the Hebridean Whale Trail combines two elemental pleasures that every child should experience: the buzz of sleeping out in an untamed wilderness and the thrill of trying to spot a whale or dolphin surfacing offshore.

Extending north from the Isle of Arran, to Mull, Skye and the Outer Hebrides, this ultimate pilgrimage to Britain's cetaceans also includes a breathtaking section along the coast of the Northwest Highlands between Applecross and Cape Wrath. Deeply notched by sea lochs and crinkle-cut with rocky coves and turquoise-fringed beaches, this rugged shore faces the Minch – the most cetacean-rich sea to be found anywhere around Britain. No fewer than 23 species of whale, dolphin and porpoise have been recorded in these waters, ranging from summer visitors like minke and fin whales, gorging on the fishy spoils of plankton blooms, to resident orca, bottlenose dolphin and harbour porpoise.

You can boost your chances of a sighting by joining a boat trip from the harbour at Gairloch. Definitely do that – perhaps as a treat at the end of your holiday – but try not to let anything intrude on your wild camping experience.

We spent the best part of a day dawdling along the coast between Ullapool and Torridon, exploring single-track lanes that fizzled out in lonely hamlets or kelp-wrapped coves. Eventually, we chanced upon a deserted sandy bay and pitched our tents facing a broad sweep of mountains, sea and islands, burnished gold by the setting sun. The exact spot will remain nameless. Wild camping relies on the lightest footprint. Promoting choice pitches can lead to overuse and potential damage to the fragile ecology of coastal habitats like sand dunes. You must simply look until you find your own quiet spot, away from others, and then ensure you follow the Wild Camping Code (page 13) to minimise your environmental impact.

This is a wildlife adventure that requires a bit of planning. You need to be totally self-sufficient, bringing everything you need, including fresh water, food, camping and cooking gear. But once your tent is pitched and there's a kettle brewing on the camp stove, you quickly relax into wilderness mode, tuning into the natural world around you.

It was late August and the sand dunes behind 'our' beach were speckled with purple tufts of scabious. The strandline was equally colourful – a swirl of pink, green and amber seaweed, punctuated by blue jellyfish beached by the ebbing

↑ Common dolphin (Niall Dunne/S)

tide. Small groups of waders – sanderling, turnstone and ringed plover – scurried along the beach, following ribbons of foam left by spent waves. Cormorants arrowed across the sea close offshore, low and purposeful, while gannets plunge-dived; white fluted arrows dropping into the lumpy grey hide of deeper water. A buzzard hovered over a nearby headland, more carefree, embracing the breeze. We double-checked its size. Not a white-tailed eagle. Not this time. But when you're wild camping on the remote shores of the Northwest Highlands you never know when one of these majestic birds of prey – large hooked bills and 2.5m wingspans – might soar into view.

Whales and dolphins are just as unpredictable. During our three-day sojourn, we spent countless hours scouring the sea. Occasionally a seal would surface and meet our gaze with large, apologetic eyes. But it didn't matter that cetaceans eluded us. Just to know that they were out there – that orca patrol these waters; that super-pods of several hundred common dolphin are sometimes sighted – was more than enough to keep us alert and ever watchful.

There is never a dull moment when you're wild camping on a deserted beach in this part of Scotland. Teeming with gobies, hermit crabs, shrimps and anemones, the rockpools will keep children of all ages captivated for hours. Bring wetsuits and snorkelling gear and there are sheltered bays where you can peer into swaying kelp forests, searching for cuttlefish, dogfish and ballan wrasse. Older children can forage for mussels to cook over an open fire; the stargazing (miles from artificial light pollution) is superb and, of course, nothing could be more exciting than burrowing into a tent, snuggling into a sleeping bag and listening to the distant roar of surf – knowing that somewhere just beyond the breakers there are whales and dolphins swimming past your wild campsite.

↑ Cetacean-rich seas off the coast of Red Point, with the Isle of Skye in the distance (William Gray)

"Deeply notched by sea lochs and crinkle-cut with rocky coves and turquoise-fringed beaches, this rugged shore faces the Minch – the most cetacean-rich sea to be found anywhere around Britain"

↑ Gold coast: evening sunlight gilds the shores of Loch Ewe (William Gray)

SPOT WHALES
Launched in June 2019 by the Hebridean Whale & Dolphin Trust (☏ 01688 302620 ⊘ hwdt.org), the Hebridean Whale Trail (⊘ whaletrail.org) connects over 30 locations for low-impact, land-based whale and dolphin watching, and includes routes, transport options and opportunities for volunteers to record marine wildlife.

JOIN A BOAT TRIP There are several wildlife boat trip operators along the coast of the Northwest Highlands. Gairloch Marine Wildlife Centre and Cruises (☏ 01445 712636 ⊘ porpoise-gairloch.co.uk) has an excellent information centre on the quayside and operates two-hour wildlife survey cruises in search of otters, seals, basking sharks, eagles and cetaceans. In Ullapool, Seascape Expeditions (☏ 07511 290081 ⊘ sea-scape.co.uk) and Shearwater Cruises (☏ 0771 325 7219 ⊘ summerqueen.co.uk) offer boat trips in the Summer Isles, visiting seal and seabird colonies, while searching for whales and dolphins.

GO SNORKELLING Established by the Scottish Wildlife Trust (☏ 0131 312 7765 ⊘ scottishwildlifetrust.org.uk), several Living Seas Snorkel Trails can be found along the coast of the Northwest Highlands (as well as Berwickshire and the Isle of Harris – see page 298), including sheltered locations like Ardmair and Achmelvic Bay that are ideal for beginners. Download the guide from the website for detailed maps, a responsible snorkelling code and a spotter's guide to everything from butterfish to moon jellyfish. You will need a wetsuit, mask, snorkel and fins. Remember: never snorkel alone or in rough weather, do not touch wildlife and always tell people where you are going.

↑ **Top:** gannet in flight; **above:** natural isolation at a wild campsite on Loch Ewe (William Gray)

ACTION PLAN

ADVENTURE ESSENTIALS To reach the Northwest Highlands coast, follow the A835 from Inverness towards Ullapool, or the A87 from Invergarry to Auchtertyre and then north on the A890/A896. Either route provides access to coastal roads like the A832, A837 and B869, which offer the best opportunities for wild camping. Allow plenty of time to explore single-lane tracks leading to promising locations in areas such as Achmelvic Bay, Loch Ewe and Loch Torridon. You may need to investigate several options before settling on a spot that's not already occupied. Large family tents are inappropriate – take smaller, lightweight tents instead. Even in summer, you'll be thankful for three-season-rated sleeping bags. Other essentials include a single-burner gas stove and spare cylinder, head torch, dry wash gel or baby wipes, warm clothing and all the water and food you need. It's important that you have a method of dealing with waste and toileting while wild camping. Be sure to pack a pocket trowel and dog poop bags, or similar. Ticks can be an issue – avoid walking in long grass or bracken, wear long sleeves, tuck trousers into your socks and take fine tweezers and antiseptic cream to deal with any bites. Although midges are worse during summer, sea breezes usually keep them at bay in coastal areas – but best to be prepared with Smidge repellent (⊘ smidgeup.com), head nets and long-sleeved clothing.

FOLLOW THE WILD CAMPING CODE
The Scottish Outdoor Access Code (⊘ outdooraccess-scotland.scot) has guidelines for responsible wild camping. You should only camp in any one area for up to two or three nights, ensuring you avoid causing access problems for local people. Use a camping stove (don't light a fire in dry conditions), remove all traces of your tent pitch and leave nothing behind. See page 13 for more details.

MORE ADVENTURE
If you don't fancy pitching a tent, consider catching the train to Inverness and renting a campervan. Inverness Campervans (✆ 01667 258080 ⊘ inverness-campervans.co.uk) has a range of VW campervans sleeping up to four.

CONSERVATION HEROES
Established by a group of schoolchildren, Ullapool Sea Savers (✆ 0770 279 2596 ⊘ ullapoolseasavers.com) will inspire any child passionate about the environment. Campaigning on issues such as plastic straw use and kelp bed dredging, the group raises awareness of the threats facing marine life. Each member is an ambassador for a key species in the area, from flame shell to white-tailed eagle.

ALSO CONSIDER
South Devon See *Foraging along the Devon Coast*, page 40; **East Devon & Dorset** See *Jurassic Coast Adventure*, page 60; **Gwynedd** See *Journey to the Edge of Wales*, page 198.

49 WESTERN ISLES WILDLIFE SAFARI

ISLAND HOP THROUGH THE OUTER HEBRIDES ON THE TRAIL OF WHALES, DOLPHINS AND EAGLES

WHERE	Outer Hebrides
WHEN	The machair flowers May–Aug when it's home to breeding waders and corncrake; summer is also the best time to spot cetaceans & seabirds, while autumn is best for otters & birds of prey
HOW LONG	Allow a week or more for an island-hopping adventure covering Lewis, Harris and the Uists
WHO FOR	All ages; the west coast has spectacular beaches
ADVENTURE POTENTIAL	Island hopping, boat trips, birdwatching, whale watching, sea kayaking, surfing, snorkelling, coasteering
WILDLIFE WISHLIST	Cetaceans, such as bottlenose, common & Risso's dolphin, minke whale & orca; otter & red deer are widespread; birds of prey include buzzard, golden eagle, hen harrier, kestrel, long-eared owl, merlin, short-eared owl & white-tailed eagle; machair supports breeding corncrake, dunlin, golden plover, lapwing, ringed plover, oystercatcher & snipe, while Arctic skua, divers & red grouse can be found on moors & lochs

↑ Mealastadh on the west coast of Lewis (William Gray)

D rive or hike through the Hebridean island of Harris and you will find yourself surrounded by rocky hills of gneiss, some of them striped black and white like giant, half-chewed humbugs. Sea lochs glint like sapphires embedded in folds of wind-ruffled heather; cotton grass speckles the peat bogs and sheep fix you with vacant stares. It looks and feels like a wild and remote corner of Scotland. Imagine your surprise, then, as you crest a mountain pass and gaze west towards the Atlantic coast to find a broad sandy bay, nuzzled by turquoise waters – a slice of the Bahamas slipped into a Scottish sandwich (or *piece* as they call it here).

The Outer Hebrides not only boast some of Europe's most breathtaking beaches, they're also rich in wildlife, culture and history. It's the kind of place where children could look up from their sandcastles to find a white-tailed eagle flying offshore, or a pod of dolphins cruising past. Island-hop through the 210km-long archipelago and you'll discover its strong Celtic heritage pulsing through Gaelic music and traditional arts and crafts. The history of the Western Isles, meanwhile, goes back three billion years to when Lewisian gneiss – the oldest rock in Britain – was forged. The Calanais Standing Stones on the west coast of Lewis, were hewn from these archaic metamorphic rocks some 5,000 years ago.

Ferries from several ports on the Scottish mainland tack back and forth across the Minch – the stretch of sea separating the Northwest Highlands from the Outer Hebrides. Coupled with inter-island ferry services, they not only make touring a breeze (you can arrive in the north of the archipelago and leave from the south, or vice versa), but the sailings offer excellent opportunities for spotting seabirds and cetaceans. Keep watch for minke whales, harbour porpoises and both common and bottlenose dolphins. Fulmars and gannets should be fairly easy to spot, but you'll need binoculars to decipher Manx, sooty and great shearwater, storm and Leach's petrel and great, Arctic, pomarine and long-tailed skua.

ON THE LOOKOUT FOR WHALES AND DOLPHINS Once you've made landfall in the Outer Hebrides, there are several themed wildlife trails you can follow through the islands. The Hebridean Whale Trail (⊗ whaletrail.org, see also page 286) connects several sites, starting with the Butt of Lewis at the northernmost tip of the Western Isles. Stand beneath the red-brick lighthouse and scan a near-360° panorama of wild, churning Atlantic. You might just glimpse a pod of Risso's dolphins rolling past the cliffs. Sometimes they mingle with bottlenose dolphins, but you can tell them apart by their more rounded heads, blunter snouts and grey-and-white colouration. Follow the coastal path west from the lighthouse to combine dolphin and otter spotting from the clifftops with a picnic on the golden sands of Eoropie Beach.

At the tip of the Eye Peninsula on Lewis, Tiumpan Head looks out across the Minch and is regarded as one of the best places in Europe for land-based whale watching. Volunteers from WDC Shorewatch (⊘ 07918 739636 ⊗ uk.whales. org) will be able to tell you about the latest sightings. Back on the west coast, both Gallan Head (near Aird Uig) and Huisinis (near Amhuinnsuidhe Castle) are good locations for spotting basking sharks, porpoises and seals.

↑ Arctic tern, short-eared owl ↗ dunlin, northern marsh orchid (William Gray; Sandra Standbridge, Björn Kruspig/S)

SECRETS OF THE MACHAIR As if the dazzling white sandy bays of the west coast weren't a revelation in themselves, they've also led to the creation of a rare wildflower habitat known as machair. Windblown sand and crushed shells provide a calcium-rich substrate for swathes of buttercup, clover, cranesbill and vetch; damper areas are ablaze with marsh marigold, ragged robin and yellow iris, while orchids rise from the petalled plains like pink exclamation marks.

You can witness the colourful displays during summer all along the Atlantic coast of the Western Isles, but the best place for combining flowers and birds is on North Uist at the RSPB Balranald Reserve (♀ HS6 5DL 𝒫 01876 560422 𝒪 rspb.org.uk). Start by just sitting and listening. The first birds you're likely to hear are Arctic terns, their shrill, grating calls carrying across the bay where they dive on small fish to feed their young. A small, brown-streaked bird singing its heart out from a fence post could well be a corn bunting – a Red List species that's suffered a 90% decline since the 1970s. But it's the corncrake – another endangered farmland bird – that Balranald is most well-known for. The reserve offers a lifeline to this secretive, skulking relative of the moorhen and coot. Its scientific name, *Crex crex*, is onomatopoeic, succinctly capturing its terse, rasping call.

Balranald's machair also supports breeding waders, including dunlin, red-necked phalarope, redshank, ringed plover and snipe. Look for lapwing chicks (speckled fluff-balls with oversize feet) taking their first wobbly forays through the flowers. And don't forget to keep an eye on the sea. You don't want to miss the moment when a white-tailed eagle decides to make a fly-past.

→ Corncrake (Rosa Jay/S)

RAPTOR SPOTTING The Outer Hebrides are a stronghold for ten species of birds of prey, including golden and white-tailed eagle, hen harrier, merlin and short-eared owl. Joining the dots between 11 locations and two ferry crossings, the Birds of Prey Trail stretches the entire length of the island chain, with interpretation panels at each site to improve your chances of sightings (download a trail leaflet at ⊘ visitouterhebrides.co.uk).

Choice locations on Lewis include Loch Stiapabhat (⌑ ironclad.splinters. flattered), where flocks of wildfowl and waders are frequently strafed by hunting peregrine and merlin, and Ravenspoint (⌑ full.diverged.radio) – a good base for exploring white-tailed eagle territory at Loch Erisort and the Pairc peninsula.

On Harris, a track from the car park at Bogha Glas (⌑ glimmers.blushes.fuzz) leads into a rugged glen where you could spot either species of eagle soaring above the ridgelines. Your best chance of a golden eagle sighting, however, is at the North Harris Eagle Observatory (⌑ gobblers.waxes.president) where you can spy on one of the island's 20 resident pairs. Tucked into Glen Meavaig, the turf-roofed lookout can be reached by following the A859 north from Tarbert, before turning left on the B887 towards Huisinis. You'll need to walk the 2km from the car park.

On North Uist, Committee Road (⌑ user.trek.majors) straddles moorland south of the crofting village of Malacleit – perfect vole-hunting grounds for hen harrier and short-eared owl. At nearby Beinn Langais, a wild tapestry of mountain, moorland, peat bog and loch could turn up anything from kestrels and buzzards to golden eagles. Two of South Uist's best locations for birds of prey are Loch Druidibeag (⌑ shun.reinstate.best) and Loch Sgioport (⌑ gold.highlighted.tree), while a ferry trip across the Sound of Barra can often be rewarded by sightings of peregrine falcons and white-tailed eagles.

NORTH HARRIS SNORKEL TRAIL A partnership between the North Harris Trust (✆ 01859 502222 ⊘ north-harris.org) and Scottish Wildlife Trust (✆ 0131 312 7765 ⊘ scottishwildlifetrust.org.uk), this chain of snorkelling sites offers a fascinating glimpse into the marine life of kelp forests, seagrass meadows and rocky reefs in the Outer Hebrides (see also page 292). This is a self-guided trail, so you will need your own wetsuits, masks, snorkels and fins. With children in tow, stick to the more sheltered sites, don't swim out too far and be sure to let someone know your plans. The small inlet at Rhenigidale (⌑ ratio.chipper. escapes) is ideal for beginners. You should see a variety of species, such as ballan wrasse, moon jellyfish and sunstar – a bright splash of orange, with 10–12 arms. Buoyed with confidence, head next to Carragraich Bay (⌑ confined.albums. nature) where kelp beds conceal lesser-spotted dogfish, sea urchins, lobsters, brittlestars and maybe a curious seal or two.

ACTION PLAN

ADVENTURE ESSENTIALS Ferry services between the Scottish mainland and Outer Hebrides are operated by Caledonian MacBrayne (📞 0800 066 5000 💻 calmac.co.uk). Popular routes include Ullapool–Stornoway (Lewis), Uig–Tarbert (Harris), Uig–Lochmaddy (North Uist), Mallaig/ Oban–Lochboisdale (South Uist) and Oban– Castlebay (Barra). Hopscotch tickets allow you to combine different outbound and return ports, and include inter-island ferries. Logan Air (📞 0344 800 2855 💻 loganair.co.uk) flies to the Western Isles, including Barra's famous cockle-strand airstrip at Traigh Mhor beach. The islands are connected by causeway, bridge, road or ferry, so getting around is easy. Car rental is widely available, but if you're planning a motorhome holiday, be sure to book ferries and campsites well in advance. Bikes can be hired in Stornoway from Bike Hebrides (📞 07775 943355 💻 bikehebrides.com). As well as camping, accommodation in the Outer Hebrides includes a wide choice of hotels, B&Bs, holiday cottages and glamping pods (💻 visitouterhebrides.co.uk). Operating from Miavaig Pier on the west coast of Lewis, Seatrek (📞 01851 672469 💻 seatrek.co.uk) runs two- to three-hour RIB tours in Loch Roag, searching for dolphins, eagles, otters and seabirds. Boat trips to see dolphins in the Sound of Barra and puffins on Mingulay, an abandoned island near the southern tip of the Outer Hebrides, are offered by Uist Sea Tours (📞 07833 690693 💻 uistseatours.co.uk) from Lochboisdale. Roam Outer Hebrides (📞 07845 136867 💻 roamouterhebrides.co.uk) run half- and full-day sea kayaking tours in the glorious white-sand bays and rocky inlets of Harris (suitable for children aged 12 and above).

MORE ADVENTURE Visiting St Kilda is expensive and involves several hours at sea – but you'll never be closer to the legendary, far-flung archipelago than the Outer Hebrides. Home to over a million seabirds, the World Heritage Site also boasts the tallest seacliffs in the British Isles, including the towering 196m-tall Stac an Armin. Boat trips with Hebridean Sea Tours (📞 01871 817803 💻 hebrideanseatours.co.uk) and Sea Harris (📞 01859 502007 💻 seaharris.com) traverse 60km of open ocean and allow up to five hours ashore, visiting the deserted settlement of Village Bay.

ALSO CONSIDER Isles of Scilly See *Island-Hopping Adventure*, page 20; **Gwynedd** See *Journey to the Edge of Wales*, page 198; **Shetland Islands** See *Journey to the End of Britain*, page 300.

↑ Fulmar (William Gray)

50 JOURNEY TO THE END OF BRITAIN

SAIL NORTH TO WITNESS THE SEABIRD CITIES AND MARINE LIFE OF THE FAR-FLUNG SHETLAND ISLES

WHERE	Shetland Islands
WHEN	Boat trips operate early Apr–Oct; prime months for seabirds and cetaceans are May–Aug
HOW LONG	If you're going all that way, make it a week or two
WHO FOR	All ages — just take care near cliff edges
ADVENTURE POTENTIAL	Island hopping, boat trips, hiking, birdwatching, whale watching, otter spotting, Viking history
WILDLIFE WISHLIST	Grey & harbour seal, harbour porpoise & otter are the most commonly seen mammals, but you may be lucky and spot orca & minke whale (23 species of cetacean have been recorded in Shetland waters, including humpback whale, common, Risso's & white-sided dolphin); sea cliffs host huge colonies of fulmar, gannet, guillemot, kittiwake, puffin, razorbill & shag; other birds range from Arctic tern, great skua & red-throated diver to golden plover, red-necked phalarope & snipe

History pulses through the Shetland Islands. Everywhere you look in this remote archipelago there are clues to the past – from Neolithic burial chambers and Iron Age brochs (circular stone towers) to traces of Viking longhouses. Over 5,000 years of human settlement have left their mark on Britain's most northerly outpost, 150km off the Scottish mainland and just six degrees south of the Arctic Circle. Little is known of the first Shetlanders, but one thing is certain – they arrived by sea.

Clouds slouched over the horizon when we first laid eyes on the islands. During the overnight voyage from Aberdeen, the ferry's windows had frosted over with salt grime, so we ventured out on deck to watch Fair Isle, the most southerly of the Shetland Isles, slipping past on our port side. It was mid-July – height of the seabird breeding season – and a swirling procession of gannets and fulmars followed in our wake as we continued north towards Mainland, largest of the archipelago's hundred or so islands. Soon, we were passing the cliffs of Sumburgh Head, just one of the lofty seabird citadels scheduled for our wildlife odyssey. Disembarking at Lerwick, we drove inland to the village of Tingwall, a central base for exploring both the wildlife and archaeological treasures of Shetland.

ON THE TRAIL OF VIKINGS It's not surprising that Vikings once lived here. Straddled between Norway and Scotland, almost equidistant between Aberdeen and Bergen, Shetland not only made a convenient base for raiding Britain, but also offered sheltered bays, fertile valleys and grazing for livestock.

Located near Sumburgh, the remarkable prehistoric and Norse settlement of Jarlshof (♀ ZE3 9JN ✆ 01856 841815 ⬙ historicenvironment.scot) was clearly a

← Gannet riding the ocean breeze at Eshaness (Philippe Clement/S)

desirable residence. Withstanding four millennia of Atlantic storms, the headland, perched above the natural harbour of West Voe, is riddled with ruins, including a Bronze Age smithy, Iron Age broch, Norse longhouses and – literally topping it all – the remains of a 17th-century laird's mansion. Archeologists have found middens suggesting that around 2000BC, some of Shetland's earliest inhabitants harvested the sea, hunting seals and collecting eggs from nearby Sumburgh Head.

THE SEABIRD CITY OF SUMBURGH HEAD Keen birdwatchers flock to the Shetland Islands during spring and autumn to glimpse migrants – a brisk southeasterly often deposits species like bluethroat, red-backed shrike and wryneck, while twitch-worthy rarities include Pallas's sandgrouse and Tennessee warbler. Some avian visitors become celebrities. Having been blown 12,000km off-course from the Southern Ocean, Albert the black-browed albatross turned up in Shetland in 1972 and spent years attempting to woo gannets at Hermaness (in the far north) and Sula Sgeir, a tiny Atlantic rock 65km from Lewis in the Outer Hebrides.

↑ **Clockwise from top left:** Razorbill, otter, orca, grey seal (Richard Winston, Giedrius Stakauskas, David Havel/S, William Gray)

Sadly for Albert (last seen in 1995), Shetland's gannets were far too busy with their own love lives to take much interest. From May to mid-August, several of the islands' sea cliffs, stacks and skerries are festooned with tens of thousands of nesting seabirds. One of the most accessible colonies – with boundary fences and walls to let you and your children view the spectacle in safety – is RSPB Sumburgh Head Reserve (♥ ZE3 9JN🖉 01950 460800 ⊘ rspb.org.uk) at the southernmost tip of Mainland Shetland.

At the height of the breeding season, every ledge is crammed with birds. Look for both the common guillemot (chocolate-brown and white, like a miniature penguin) and black guillemot (black all over, except for oval white wing patches and bright red feet). Razorbills resemble common guillemots, but have shorter, thicker bills. And what you think are cormorants are probably shags – train your binoculars on these striking birds to see their emerald green eyes, irridescent plumage and flamboyant head crests. Of course, this is all assuming you can tear your eyes away from the puffins which nest on the clifftops.

During spring, the little *Tammie Norries* (as they're known in Shetland) will be waddling through drifts of pink thrift, rubbing bills in affectionate courtship displays, and lining their burrows with grass and other vegetation. Later in the season, when there are pufflings to be fed, you'll see them with their bills stuffed with sandeels.

Don't leave Sumburgh without a long, lingering look out to sea. White-sided dolphins, harbour porpoises, orca and minke whales are often sighted offshore, while grey and harbour seals frequently haul out on rocks at the base of the cliffs. Staff at the Sumburgh Lighthouse Visitor Centre (🖉 01595 694688 ⊘ sumburghhead.com) will have all the latest sightings.

GUANO SHAMPOO AT NOSS ISLAND Looking down on a seabird cliff is only half the experience. For full sensory immersion, you also need to look up at one from sea level – and there's no better place to do this in Shetland than at Noss National Nature Reserve (🖉 01463 667600 ⊘ nature.scot). A recent survey revealed 13,764 pairs of gannets nesting on the island of Noss, located east of Lerwick and reached by boat from Shetland's capital or the neighbouring island of Bressay.

Rounding a headland, the 180m-tall cliffs turn white and the air suddenly reeks of guano. Sidling into the lee of the seabird skyscraper, you might feel a light drizzle of bird excrement raining down on your heads. The staccato clamour of 60,000 seabirds crowded above you almost drowns out the rumble of waves against the cliffs. Gannets, guillemots, fulmars, kittiwakes and shags squabble and preen on

→ Puffin (William Gray)

every inch of high-rise real estate, while a spectacular airborne contingent wheels overhead, like ash spiralling from a bonfire. Occasionally a great skua, or bonxie, scythes through the colony, looking to snatch an unwary puffin or unguarded chick. About the size of a herring gull, these pugnacious pirates will harrass birds as large as gannets, stealing their hard-won fish.

The exuberant life at Noss persists beneath the waves. We nosed into a sea cave encrusted with dead man's fingers – a type of soft coral. Elsewhere, tangled kelp forests sprouted swirling amber fronds from 20m down, and whenever we scanned the sea's surface, our gaze seemed to be met by inquisitive grey seals.

THE FURRY FAVOURITES Seabirds steal the show in Shetland, but it's also worth spending some time away from the cliffs, exploring the moors and lochs. A complete contrast to raucous Noss, the 'countryside' rarely registers anything louder than the ripple of a skylark's song or the drumming of a snipe. Whitewashed crofts stud the peatlands like chips of quartz, while meadows run riot with buttercup, ragged robin, red campion and yellow iris.

If puffins were love-at-first-sight for your children at Sumburgh or Noss, then Shetland ponies are almost guaranteed to steal their hearts. You'll see them grazing fields and moors throughout the islands, but The Shetland Pony Experience (🖥 outlooks.bitter.irritate 🔌 01595 859124 🖱 theshetlandponyexperience.com) offers a more personal, hands-on encounter. The pampered ponies can be found at the Merkisayre Stud in Burra – a 20-minute scenic drive from Lerwick. During the hour-long experience, you'll groom them and take a short, supervised ride, before leading the ponies through wild coastal fields to a secluded beach.

But even adorable ponies and puffins have a rival in Shetland when it comes to children's favourites. Follow any road in the islands and, chances are, it will eventually peter out at a deserted cove, a fishing village or a ferry jetty – all promising locations for otters. Although Shetland has Europe's highest concentration of these charismatic creatures, they're still shy and elusive. To increase your chances of a sighting, nothing beats local knowledge. Brydon Thomason of Shetland Nature (🔌 01595 760212 🖱 shetlandnature.net) lives and breathes otters. He not only knows who's who in all the local territories, but he'll show you how to read the wind direction, keep low to blend with the shoreline and find telltale signs of otter tracks, spraints and holts.

← Pole position: check fences for snipe (William Gray)

↑ Mane event: Shetland pony (William Gray)

GETTING TO THE TOP Robert Louis Stevenson visited Unst, the most northerly of the Shetland Islands, in 1869. The map he drew to illustrate *Treasure Island* bears a close resemblance to its outline. However, the 'treasure trail' you follow through Hermaness National Nature Reserve (✆ 01463 667600 ⏚ nature.scot) at the northwestern tip of Unst squelches across 1.6km of wild moorland, where belligerent bonxies fix you with haughty stares – the skuas always, it seems, on the verge of launching dive-bombing assaults if you stray too close to their nests.

Your efforts are richly rewarded: Britain reaches an abrupt and startling conclusion at Unst's magnificent sea cliffs. One moment you're striding through the strange, silent blanket bog, weaving between dark, peaty pools… the next you're standing on the brink of cliffs plummeting over 165m into a glittering sea.

Hermaness, or 'Herma's headland', is named after a mythical giant who fought with his neighbour, Saxa, over a beautiful mermaid. They hurled boulders at each other over the Burra Firth, one of which landed in the sea and became Out Stack, Britain's most northerly lump of rock. A nearby outcrop – Muckle Flugga – was once the most northerly inhabited point in the British Isles, but its lighthouse is now unmanned and remotely controlled.

Hermaness has been left to the seabirds – over 100,000 of them. The cliffs and islets are white with their guano, as if a winter squall has dusted the coastline with fresh snow. Crouching on the soft turf at the cliff's edge, we watched fulmars, gannets, kittiwakes and puffins gyrate on the ocean breeze. In some places, they filled the air like shreds of tickertape flung from a New York skyscraper – a noisy, exuberant, transfixing celebration of wildlife at the very end of Britain.

↑ The end of Britain: Hermaness (Philippe Clement/S)

ACTION PLAN

ADVENTURE ESSENTIALS NorthLink Ferries (☎ 0800 111 4422 ⊕ northlinkferries.co.uk) sail daily from Aberdeen to Lerwick, the overnight crossing lasting 12–13 hours. Hermaness NNR is 5km northwest of Haroldswick on Unst – take the ferry from Toft to Ulsta on Yell, then drive 27km north to Gutcher for the ferry to Belmont on Unst. Inter-island ferries are operated by the Shetland Islands Council (☎ 01595 745804 ⊕ www.shetland.gov.uk/ferries). For details of ferry and bus timetables, visit Shetland Travel (⊕ travel.shetland.org). Car and motorhome rental providers are listed on ⊕ shetland.org, along with suggestions for accommodation, ranging from self-catering cottages to glamping pods and campsites. As well as Sumburgh Head, Noss and Hermaness, other prime seabird-watching sites include Eshaness (for an easy coastal walk from the lighthouse) and Mousa (where special night trips are organised to view the storm petrels that nest in the famous broch). Departing from Lerwick, both Seabirds and Seals (☎ 07595 540224 ⊕ seabirds-and-seals.com) and Shetland Seabird Tours (☎ 07767 872260 ⊕ shetlandseabirdtours.com) offer cruises to the Noss cliffs. Land-based tours are available with various Shetland guides — contact Kitty Corbett at Kittywake Tours (☎ 07876 443828 ⊕ kittywaketours.com) and Laurie Goodlad at Shetland with Laurie (☎ 07525 772957 ⊕ shetlandwithlaurie.com).

In areas where you might encounter dive-bombing great skuas, hold your arm or a stick above your head to ward them off, although they rarely make contact. Do not wear waterproof over-trousers near clifftops – a slip could result in you sliding over the edge.

MORE ADVENTURE NorthLink Ferries (see above) also sail from Aberdeen and Scrabster to the Orkney Islands, where archaeological and wildlife highlights include the Neolithic village of Skara Brae and the seabird cliffs at Noup Head on Westray.

CONSERVATION HEROES Hillswick Wildlife Sanctuary (♥ ZE2 9RW ☎ 01806 503348 ⊕ hillswickwildlifesanctuary.org) cares for sick, injured and abandoned seals and otters, rehabilitating and releasing them back into the wild, as well as coordinating the rescue of stranded cetaceans around Shetland's 2,700km coast.

ALSO CONSIDER Isles of Scilly See *Island-Hopping Adventure*, page 20; **Pembrokeshire** See *On the Trail of the Puffin*, page 170; **Moidart** See *On the Trail of the Otter*, page 256.

→ Great skua: pirate of the airways (Giedrius Stakauskas/S)

FURTHER INFORMATION

TRAVEL For public transport, ⊘ traveline.info offers a comprehensive journey planner. Sustrans (⊘ sustrans.org.uk) has information on the National Cycle Network, while Ramblers (⊘ ramblers.org.uk) has a directory of walking routes. For camping, ⊘ ukcampsite.co.uk has reviews of campsites throughout Britain, while ⊘ campingandcaravanningclub.co.uk is a good place to look for a pitch.

WEATHER, TIDES AND MAPS Keep an eye on the weather at ⊘ xcweather. co.uk and visit ⊘ rnli.org.uk for lifeguarded beaches and advice on keeping safe at the coast. Tide forecasts can be found at ⊘ tidetimes.org.uk. For accurate maps, you're in good hands with ⊘ ordnancesurvey.co.uk. For navigation to precise locations, What3Words (⊘ what3words.com) divides the world into 3m squares and gives each one a unique combination of three words.

NATIONAL PARKS AND NATIONAL NATURE RESERVES For an overview of Britain's national parks, visit ⊘ nationalparks.uk; for nature reserves, rights of way and other general information on enjoying the outdoors, visit ⊘ naturalengland. org.uk, ⊘ naturalresources.wales and ⊘ nature.scot.

CONSERVATION ORGANISATIONS

Numerous NGOs work to protect Britain's biodiversity – and many of the following have junior membership schemes, or projects to inspire families and children:

Badger Trust ⊘ badgertrust.org.uk
Bat Conservation Trust ⊘ bats.org.uk
Bumblebee Conservation Trust ⊘ bumblebeeconservation.org
Butterfly Conservation ⊘ butterfly-conservation.org
Froglife ⊘ froglife.org
The Mammal Society ⊘ mammal.org.uk
Marine Conservation Sociey ⊘ mcsuk.org
National Trust ⊘ nationaltrust.org.uk
Plantlife ⊘ plantlife.org.uk

The Royal Society for the Protection of Birds (RSPB) ⊘ rspb.co.uk
Sea Shepherd ⊘ seashepherd.org.uk
Whale and Dolphin Conservation ⊘ uk.whales.org
Wildfowl & Wetlands Trust ⊘ wwt.org.uk
The Wildlife Trusts ⊘ wildlifetrusts.org
Woodland Trust ⊘ woodlandtrust.org.uk
World Wildlife Fund ⊘ wwf.org.uk

INDEX

Page numbers in plain type usually refer to the first, or main, mention in a chapter only. Listings of species under 'Wildlife Wishlist' at the start of each chapter are not always included in the Index. Entries in **bold** refer to photographs.

↑ Let the adventures begin... (William Gray)

First edition published October 2021
Bradt Guides Ltd
31a High Street, Chesham, Buckinghamshire, HP5 1BW, England
⊘ bradtguides.com
Print edition published in the USA by The Globe Pequot Press Inc,
PO Box 480, Guilford, Connecticut 06437-0480

Text copyright © 2021 William Gray
Maps copyright © 2021 Bradt Guides Ltd; includes map data © OpenStreetMap contributors
Photographs copyright © 2021 Individual photographers (see below)
Project Manager: Anna Moores
Book design: William Gray

ISBN: 9781784778422

British Library Cataloguing in Publication Data
A catalogue record for this book is available from the British Library

Photographs
All photographs © individual photographers credited beside images and also those from
picture libraries, credited as follows: Shutterstock.com (S); Superstock (SS).
Front cover **Top image:** Red squirrel, Yorkshire Dales (William Gray)
Bottom image: Sea kayaking in Arisaig (William Gray)
Back cover Puffin (William Gray)
Title page Red deer (William Gray)

Map William Gray

Typeset by William Gray and Ian Spick, Bradt Guides
Production managed by Zenith; printed in the UK
Digital conversion by ⊘ dataworks.co.in